Literature and the
French Resistance

To the memory of my father

Margaret Atack

Literature and the French Resistance

Cultural politics and
narrative forms, 1940–1950

Manchester University Press
Manchester and New York
Distributed exclusively in the USA and Canada by St. Martin's Press

Published by Manchester University Press
Oxford Road, Manchester M13 9PL, UK
and Room 400, 175 Fifth Avenue,
New York, NY 10010, USA

Distributed exclusively in the USA and Canada
by St. Martin's Press, Inc.,
175 Fifth Avenue, New York, NY 10010, USA

British Library cataloguing in publication data
Atack, Margaret
    Literature and the French resistance: cultural politics and narrative forms
    1940–1950.
    1. French literature, 1900– – Critical studies
    I. Title
    840.9′00912

Library of Congress cataloging in publication data
Atack, Margaret
    Literature and the French Resistance.
    Bibliography: p. 237.
        Includes index.
        1. French literature—20th century—History and
    criticism. 2. World War, 1939–1945—Literature and
    the war. 3. World War, 1939–1945—Underground
    movements—France. 4. Underground movements in
    literature. 5. Politics and literature—France—
    History—20th century. 6. Narration (Rhetoric)
    I. Title

    PQ307.W4A85   1989   840′.9′358   88–8351

ISBN 0 7190 2640 7 *hardback*

Photoset in Linotron Baskerville
by Northern Phototypesetting Co., Bolton
Printed in Great Britain
by Anchor Press Ltd., Tiptree, Essex

Contents

Acknowledgements

Parts of 'The concept of *témoignage*' and 'The figure of the enemy' chapters were the basis for the paper 'Political Perspectives in Resistance Fiction' given at the annual conference of The Association for the Study of Modern and Contemporary France in 1982, and published in Stuart Williams (ed.), *Socialism in France: From Jaurès to Mitterrand*, Frances Pinter (Publishers), London, 1983.

I have been greatly helped by discussions of the various arguments of this book with colleagues and others working in this field at research seminars and conferences, and with the students at Leeds who have chosen the Occupation literature course and shared my enthusiasm. Some deserve special mention.

I am particularly happy to be able to acknowledge my debt to Professor Annette Lavers, of University College London, who supervised the thesis upon which this book is based. The quality of her criticism, her care, patience and generosity, are legendary among her students; both personally and intellectually, I owe her much.

It is also a pleasure to thank colleagues at Leeds: in the French Department, Professor Philip Thody has given me constant encouragement and support, and helpful criticism on the early drafts of several chapters; Dr Howard Evans also commented very usefully on the *témoignage* chapter. Dr David Roe brought invaluable material back from France for me, and Julie Thornton produced a magnificent typescript for the original thesis. Susan Dolamore of the Modern Languages Library saved me from many a bibliographical error, and Roger Davis of the Brotherton Library has provided much practical help. I am also very grateful to Professor Malcolm Bowie and Professor Philip Ousten for their advice and encouragement. Finally, very special thanks are due to David Macey, for countless discussions of the issues, for his encyclopaedic knowledge of France in the 1930s, and for constant practical support.

Needless to say, responsibility for the finished product, with all its flaws and any errors, is entirely my own.

M.A.

Introduction

In September 1939 Great Britain and France declare war on Germany after its invasion of Poland. In May 1940 Germany invades Belgium and France. Maréchal Pétain tells the French on 17 June 1940 that he is seeking an armistice, de Gaulle makes his first speech from London on 18 June, and the *Assemblée nationale* votes full powers to Pétain on 10 July. After the months of military inactivity since the declaration of the state of war, which in English and in French are granted the status of a title – 'the phoney war' and *la drôle de guerre* – historical events and dates tumble over one another. France's defeat has the suddenness of a total collapse, and arguments rumble on as to who or what was responsible. To this military *débâcle* corresponds the collapse of the Third Republic, replaced by the *Etat français* with Pétain as Head of State, installed at Vichy in what has become the southern, non-occupied zone. Nothing encapsulates more neatly the political shift this entailed than the fact that the Republic's motto of *Liberté, Egalité, Fraternité* was replaced by the new motto of *Famille, Travail, Patrie*. The German Occupation of France was to last four years. It started in the chaos of the millions of refugees on the roads, and of routed armies to disperse or evacuate from Dunkirk; it ended in triumph for the Allies, the internal Resistance and *la France libre*, the Free French based in London. The defeated were the Germans, and those who had publicly espoused their cause, or at the very least accepted their victory, namely the collaborators and Vichy.[1] Many French men and women brought their assent, active or passive, to one or other of these 'camps', and even, in personal allegiance to de Gaulle or Pétain, very often to more than one.

Interest in all aspects of the German Occupation of France from 1940–44 has increased beyond all measure in the last ten or fifteen years, with a constant stream of scholarly investigations, films, novels and memoirs. *Le Chagrin et la pitié* ('The Sorrow and the Pity'), directed_by Marcel Ophuls, a four-hour-long film centred on Clermont-Ferrand, made for television in 1969 and shown in French cinemas in 1971 (and finally on French television in 1981), can be considered as the signal for this return to the past. It sought to present those years to a generation who, born after the war, had little idea of their complexity;[2] and by interviewing Vichy supporters, an anti-Republican Resister, a French volunteer for the German Army, by detailing the way many French people, Resisters or Jews for example, had suffered at the hands of the French themselves, by using contemporary newsreels showing, for instance, the massive support for Pétain, it gave the lie to what has come to be called the Gaullist myth – that, apart from the few committed to collaboration, the French nation was, in word or deed, solidly behind de Gaulle[3] – and as such provoked a storm of controversy. It found its academic counterpart in Robert Paxton's important work *Vichy France: Old Guard and New Order* which was quickly translated into the Seuil paperback 'Points Histoire' series.[4] Examining the variety of ideological and political positions to be found at Vichy, its objectives, legislation and effects on France, it not only demonstrated the inadequacies of the *bouclier* (shield) theory – that Vichy had served to protect France from an even worse fate – but also situated Vichy in relation to the past and to post-Liberation France. Vichy could no longer be seen as a parenthesis (temporary expediency or aberration) in French history.

This rekindling of interest in the Occupation since the late 1960s, now known as *la mode rétro* (the 'retro' fashion), has been, as its name indicates, a very public phenomenon;[5] but although it has also undeniably stimulated a great deal of academic interest in the period, one has only to consult Henri Michel's *Bibliographie critique de la Résistance*,[6] or the 'Bibliographie sélective' of *Vichy année 40* by the same author,[7] to realise the extensive body of research, memoirs and essays which had appeared since the end of the war.[8] From 1945 onwards there was particularly a veritable deluge of novels and autobiographical accounts devoted to the experiences of the French during the war, either in France, with the Free French forces in London or in prisoner of war and concentration camps. And it is an intriguing cultural paradox that many of the 'new' themes of *la mode rétro* – that France was divided, that the Resistance was divided, that commitment to a cause could be more a result of chance factors than of political conviction,[9] that Vichy embodied a particular ideological tradition of anti-Republicanism, xenophobia and anti-semitism which commanded widespread support,[10] that collaboration could be an attractive transgression,[11] – were frequently emphasised in the literature which coexisted with the rise of the Gaullist and Communist myths (and indeed were not entirely absent from Resistance literature either).

The literary production of the Occupation and post-war periods has received its share of attention. Articles and books in 1944–45 surveyed the clandestine literature, explaining the motivations of the intellectual Resistance and the conditions it worked under.[12] Since then, the poetry of the Resistance has been studied much more than the fiction, perhaps because at first, together with Vercors's *Le Silence de la mer*, it functioned as a paradigm of the French (national) Resistance so enthusiastically espoused after the Liberation. In recent years, however, there have appeared books and articles devoted either specifically to the fiction or to a critical evaluation of the intellectual Resistance where the fiction played an important part. Nevertheless it would still be true to say that critical analysis of the literary aspects of the Occupation has lagged far behind that accorded to the political, social and military aspects, and appears slight indeed (quantitatively, not qualititatively speaking) when compared to the work on the literature of the First World War.

The defeat of France in June 1940 left France divided both geographically[13] and politically. All sides placed great importance on winning the battle for public opinion, and, with newspapers, books, radio, cinema and mass meetings, the Occupation was (and remained) a war of words and images long before armed conflict restarted. Early Resistance activity involved producing tracts and newspapers, particularly in the Occupied zone where German censorship was much stricter than in the south, and was controlled by the military Propaganda-Abteilung and the German Embassy,[14] the famous *liste Otto* of books to be banned being

named after the Ambassador Otto Abetz. Vichy also had its
propaganda section, and as the number of contemporary newsreels, posters, illustrations and cartoons, as well as public appear-
ances by Pétain and his ministers demonstrate, it made full use of
visual[15] and spoken[16] as well as written means of communication
to implement its 'Révolution nationale'. In Paris many newspapers and magazines were committed to what they saw as the
Nazi revolution and the new order. Lucien Rebatet, Robert
Brasillach, Alain Laubreaux, Pierre-Antoine Cousteau wrote for
Je Suis Partout, Alphonse de Châteaubriant and Abel Bonnard
for *La Gerbe*; Jean Luchaire was the director of *Les Nouveaux
Temps*, Georges Suarez of *Aujourd'hui*. Pierre Drieu la Rochelle
took over *La Nouvelle Revue française* (henceforth NRF) and kept
it going until June 1943 with contributions from Jacques
Chardonne, Alfred Fabre-Luce, Armand Petitjean, Lucien
Combelle, Ramon Fernandez. Montherlant, Giono, Marcel
Aymé, Céline were also frequent targets in the Resistance press,
for contributing to these newspapers and for their own publications. The leaders of the various right-wing or proto-fascist
movements were themselves very public figures – Jacques Doriot
of the *Parti populaire français*, Marcel Déat of the *Rassemblement
national populaire*, Eugène Deloncle of the *Mouvement social
révolutionnaire*, Joseph Darnand of the *Service d'ordre légionnaire*
and later the *milice*.

The Occupation is, then, a period traversed by conflicting
political discourses, and the ideological battle is inescapable, for it
permeates all aspects of life – the home, the schools, the streets. It
is in this context that the Resistance writings[17] should be read. To
assess the contribution of the Resistance to the war effort in
primarily military terms entails a fundamental misrecognition of
the value to be accorded to the ideological and the discursive at
this time;[18] it is difficult to see how, without public expression,
there could have been a Resistance.

As far as the literary production is concerned, *Les Editions de
minuit*, founded by Vercors and Pierre de Lescure in 1941, was the
largest clandestine publishing house, producing some twenty
titles comprising fiction,[19] poetry and essays. Aragon, Seghers
and Eluard founded *La Bibliothèque française* in Saint-Flour,
publishing poetry and fiction.[20] In 1942 the *Comité National des
Ecrivains* was established; in the occupied zone its journal was *Les*

Lettres françaises, in the south *Les Etoiles*. Other Resistance news-papers (for example *Résistance, Cahiers de la Libération*) also carried reviews of literary publications. So although only 1,000 copies were usually printed of the *Editions de minuit* texts, they were short enough to be copied, they reached England (where they were mentioned in radio broadcasts to France and in de Gaulle's speeches)[21] and America, and were able to reach a much wider audience than the small print run suggests. They also fulfilled what was for Vercors one of their major aims, to make the voice of 'French spiritual and intellectual life' heard outside France.[22] The *poésie de contrebande*, drawing on the resources of poetic language to trick the censors and publish pro-Resistance works legally, also constitutes a considerable body of literature through individual publications and the journals *Poésie, Confluences* and *Fontaine*.[23]

In addition to the fiction and poetry, there is a considerable amount of writing on literature, evaluating both its specific role in the Resistance and its general nature. In wider terms, even a cursory reading of the literary and non-literary press would demonstrate that throughout the Resistance, ideological and political opposition to Vichy and the German Army of Occupa-tion is inseparable from a cultural reflection on the ideas and beliefs which it argues they are determined to destroy; this means that writers are proclaimed to be active *combattants* in the war, and literature an important weapon in the Resistance fight. And clearly, in a war where the Royal Air Force drops thousands of leaflets of Eluard's famous poem *Liberté* over Occupied France, the place and function of literature at this time cannot be ade-quately explained as merely reflecting the event.

In many analyses of the literature of the war, however, it would be fair to say that historical rather than literary considerations dominate. To a great extent the very category 'war literature' predetermines this, and for obvious reasons. As Stuart Hughes says, 'the Resistance ranked along with the Dreyfus case and the First World War as the third great spiritual revolution which the French had traversed in a half century'.[24] Although the omission of the Popular Front (and 'spiritually' one might say the Spanish Civil War also) is perhaps surprising here, the profound impor-tance, politically, culturally and historically of the experience of the Occupation is not in dispute. What would bear further analysis, however, is the assumption, frequently to be found in literary criticism on this period, of the transparent nature of the relations between the literature and the event or the individual experience of the author; this presents the language of fiction as a screen through which we can interrogate the world which is radically outside it. In this body of critical literature at least, the veracity of the vision is rarely questioned, but this is hardly the point. What needs to be examined is the unspoken presupposition of the identity between the literary and the historical events. This takes many forms, but basic to them all is the ultimate dominance of the historical in the evaluation of the place and value of this writing, and the concomitant subordination of its specific operation and function as literature.

Claude Duchet usefully questions the *a priori* assumptions which can underlie critical attitudes to 'society and the novel': 'To what extent does postulating at the outset the autonomy or the dependence of the literary work lead, by different paths, either to making one of the two terms disappear, or, which comes to the same thing, to giving adversarial value to the copula *and*, thus privileging now the pole 'novel', now the pole "society"?'[25] An extreme example in relation to the Occupation would be Frederick Harris's *Encounters with Darkness*: it is a literary study organised on the basis of 'areas of historical and human experience'[26] which are illustrated by scenes from a large number of novels (from the 1940s to the 1970s) which, whatever the author's intention, function as empirical data revealing what it was like to experience the war. He does raise general questions of the relations between literature and history, but apparently subscribes at one and the same time to the autonomous, dependent and adversarial views of the status of literature highlighted by Duchet. He asserts a difference between 'literary and historical truth'[27] and that literature 'can be a faithful mirror of historical reality or a distorting one'.[28] Yet, stressing that 'literary truth has necessarily been my primary concern',[29] he also says that books which 'have greater value as historical documents than as literature' have been included 'for the historical relevance of the scenes they describe'.[30] It is very difficult to see what methodological framework might emerge from this, but the corpus of the study itself draws on all manner of novels, with no concern for intrinsic narrative logic or chronology, as though the event can be 'read off' from the

fiction. I would argue with Claude Duchet that, far from unproblematically reflecting the event, the novel is on the contrary 'a
purposeful, active, transformative reading of society. From the
point of view of the novel, society is an ever-moving, mysterious,
polyphonic text, of which the novel is itself a part and which it
never stops interpreting.'[31] There can have been few periods of
history when this vision of narrative as dynamic reading of the
social can have been more apt than during and immediately after
the Occupation.

The object of the present study is the fiction published between
1940 and 1950 which takes as its subject the war in France under
the Occupation. Given the large numbers of novels written about
this period, I define the war novel very strictly, as being one where
the war is essential to the generation and resolution of the major
conflicts and oppositions of the narrative, and thus exclude
novels such as *Journal d'un salaud* by Henri Queffélec,[32] where
the Occupation constitutes only the historical setting to the narrative. Such a definition is also necessary to the aim of the study, the
elucidation of the narrative structures of this fiction and the
evaluation of the manner in which they change; the diverse
nature of the fiction where the Occupation is incidental rather
than central would not permit such an aim to be realised.[33] It is
for these reasons that the narrative structures of *L'Armée des
ombres* by Joseph Kessel[34] are not treated in detail. While the
Resistance experience is thematically central, a close analysis
reveals that it does not rely on the structure of unity, its major
narrative dynamic being constituted by the opposition between
'survival' and 'failure to survive'. Published abroad, there are
many signs in the text that its implied reader[35] is the foreign
audience it is seeking to inform. It is therefore marginal to the
structures being discussed here. That I do not include novels
published after 1950 is again in part a restriction imposed by the
wealth of material, but only in part. If Simone de Beauvoir could
write of 1952: 'The postwar period had finally finished ending',[36]
it is 1950 which is often recognised in literary history as something of a watershed, marking the turning away from the notion
of committed literature which dominated the postwar period. As
the *nouveau roman* rises more and more to the fore after that date,
rather traditional novels about the Occupation are not only fewer

in number, they are necessarily less representative. Furthermore, given the changing socio-political climate within France, and the ever greater distance in time from the events of the war, a structural homogeneity which allows similarities and differences to be isolated would be extremely difficult to establish.

The novels of the period 1940–50 which take the Occupation as their subject present a wide variety of themes, situations and styles, but structurally fall into two distinct groups, which, with some notable exceptions, can be related to the differences between the fiction written during the Occupation and that produced after the end of the war in France. Nonetheless, while the significance of this chronological distinction must be recognised (to the extent that I frequently, for the sake of convenience, refer to the distinction as operating between Resistance and postwar fiction), the date of publication of any individual novel is not in itself a sufficient guide as to which group that novel belongs, since the pertinent features marking the differences are located at the level of narrative structure. It should also be stressed that the formal analysis undertaken here is not seeking to emulate the kind of codification associated with Jakobson and Lévi-Strauss's famous analysis of Baudelaire's 'Les Chats', but, by emphasising some of the distinctive features of narrative – notably oppositional structures, tendency towards closure, different levels of narration – to demonstrate how its material is always already *structured*. Given the ideological nature and cultural codes of that material, it can also be considered to be to a certain extent *structuring*.

The fictional production of the Resistance is analysed in order to show that it relies on what is called a structure of unity,[37] where the various narrative dilemmas and oppositions are governed by the primary opposition between the Resistance and the enemy. These novels of unity are grouped in Part II under four headings – 'The figure of the enemy', 'Cultural perspectives', 'The figure of the individual: responsibility, action and choice', 'Unity' – which designate the factor which forms the major narrative dilemma. To understand the substance of these narratives and the function of literature as it was perceived at the time, it is necessary to start with the discourses and ideological configurations inherent in a pro-Resistance interpretation of the Occupation, which is the subject of Part I. Analysis of *Les Lettres françaises* and other clandestine publications reveals the importance of anti-fascism and the nationalist opposition to Germany in this respect, and the notions of France, Man and Culture emerge as key values in Resistance discourses. The political and cultural configurations of nationalism and anti-fascism form a complex grid of references which allow the Resistance to 'make sense' of the Occupation, and on the basis of which opposition to the Germans can be articulated. The intellectual Resistance takes this fight on to the terrain of fiction and poetry, using the resources of imaginative literature to encourage resistance, and, having identified an ideological as well as a military enemy, to reassert, by its very existence, the value of French, humanist[38] culture.

The aim of Part III, devoted to the novels of ambiguity, is to demonstrate that, in thematic development and narrative structure, the postwar novel constitutes a very different 'reading' of the Occupation to that of the Resistance. Thematic differences between the two groups are not difficult to establish. The positive image of Resistance activity which dominates the former is now qualified, as there emerges a picture of a Resistance torn by internal dissensions, out of touch with the majority of the French, and where few tread the paths of righteousness. The Occupation is portrayed as a time of social and moral confusion, with most people more or less muddling through, while some seized the opportunities offered at various times by the black market, collaboration or Resistance, for their own personal advantage. These novels generally present a pessimistic appraisal of the Occupation,[39] and the ambiguity of moral and political choices and behaviour is a major theme. On the other hand there are also points of similarity between the themes of the two groups, particularly in expressions of disaffection with the German presence and the themes of responsibility, action and choice. Such convergence and difference is a further reason why thematic considerations alone are not enough to differentiate these two groups, as the same theme can serve very different functions depending on the context and structure. The most obvious difference involving a major structural change is that after the Liberation, not only is the Occupation over, but quite simply it is known that the Resistance and the Allies won. This is a knowledge which cannot be present in Resistance fiction which is part of a war still being waged. This is stating the obvious, but it needs to be stated as it has major implications for the figure of the narrator: a historical gap has been opened up between the *énoncé* and the *énonciation*[40] of the narrative. It will be seen that the second major change lies in the replacement of the structure of unity by a structure of ambiguity which orders the material of the novel in such a way as to highlight constantly the impossibility of establishing a clear differentiation, either morally, politically or psychologically, between the warring groups.

What emerge therefore are two major modes of narrative discourse, two distinct ways by which the social and political realities of the Occupation are both apprehended and at the same time constituted in fiction, and which, in aesthetic and metaphysical assumptions, are quite distinct. Further work is of course needed before one could decide whether these modes are pertinent to the analysis of socio-political narrative forms in general, or whether the features and strategies described here are specific to the historical configurations of the Occupation and its reinscription in postwar discourses.[41]

Many of the novels and short stories in this study are not well known, and have received little detailed critical attention. A major concern has been to establish the literary and ideological discourses, the cultural and political configurations, which combine to form an extremely complex grid within which the narratives are inscribed. This also enables the better-known novels, such as Beauvoir's *Le Sang des autres*, or Camus's *La Peste*, to be re-situated within this specific historical context. The substantial body of criticism devoted to each has tended to read them diachronically in relation to the overall development of the author's *oeuvre*. Reading them synchronically in relation to the other novels on the Occupation allows new light to be shed on the structures of these narratives. I have therefore pursued a multiple aim in writing this work: to contribute to the ideological and cultural knowledge of the period, to establish, through a formalist approach, some general theoretical principles in relation to this body of fiction, and also to renovate the view of some well-known authors.

A final note on the translations. To help the English-reading student of France, the quotations in the body of the text have been translated, although some have been left in the notes. All translations are my own, as the demands of readability at the level of a whole text affect the nature of the translation, whereas illustrative quotations making sense of a discussion which has been based on the original French place a very different set of demands on the translation. Page references are to the French editions given in the notes. Some words posed particular problems. *Esprit* covers a wide range of meanings, 'spirit' as in 'group spirit', and 'spirit' as in 'spiritual', 'mind', 'intellect'. For the sake of continuity I have tried to use 'spirit' wherever possible. The terms 'homeland' and 'fatherland' seemed singularly inappropriate, though for different reasons, as translations for *patrie*, and I have fallen back on variations of 'France', 'country', 'own country', 'land' and the use of the adjective 'patriotic'. The difficulties which arise with *Homme*/Man are cultural and political. It is because I subscribe to the feminist critique of this term, that it indicates only a bogus universalism which in fact excludes women, that I have left it as such. It is the central term and value of the discourse of humanism which I am analysing, and it is in my opinion anachronistic to make it say what it is not saying. Far from endorsing the cultural and political implications of this kind of vocabulary, I am merely trying not to fudge the issue. For Man, read man, throughout.

Notes

1   It is axiomatic to the very establishment of Vichy and its internal logic that the war is over (see Yves Durand, *Vichy 1940–1944*, Paris, 1972, p. 23) and the collaborators too are more interested in analysing the place of a defeated France in 'la nouvelle Europe', although collaboration certainly had its militaristic side which became increasingly important as time went on, directed both against the 'terrorists' of the Resistance and against the Soviet Union in the anti-Bolshevik crusade.

2   There is internal evidence for this pedagogic intention. An early scene, from which the film's title comes, shows M. Verdier explaining to his children what life was like then, and answering their questions.

3   Though it would be just as accurate to refer to the Communist Party myth – that the nation was solidly behind the working class.

4   London, 1972; Paris, 1973.

5   It has been argued that it was no accident that these critiques of Gaullism appeared in the Pompidou/Giscard era. For a general discussion, see Pascal Ory, *Les Collaborateurs*, preface, Paris, 1980.

6 Paris, 1964.

7 Paris, 1966.

8 'La mode rétro' has, however, suscitated major interest in all aspects of collaboration.

9 Cf. *Lacombe Lucien*, directed by Louis Malle, 1975.

10 Cf. Patrick Modiano, *La Place de l'étoile*, Paris, 1968.

11 Cf. *ibid.*, and Modiano, *La Ronde de nuit*, Paris, 1969.

12 Cf. Mauriac, in a speech on the Resistance poets read out to a 'soirée de gala' in October 1944: 'Ils écrivirent des ballades que tous les petits Français recopieront un jour dans leurs cahiers d'écoliers', *Poésie 44*, no. 21, novembre–décembre 1944, pp. 5–6.

13 In addition to the division between occupied and unoccupied zones, there were five other zones, including Alsace–Lorraine which was annexed. See map, J.-P.Rioux, *De Munich à la Libération*, Paris, 1979, p. 159.

14 See Pierre-Marie Dioudonnat, *L'Argent nazi à la conquête de la presse française (1940–1944)*, Paris, 1981, pp. 19–22.

15 See Gérard Miller, *Les Pousse-au-jouir du Maréchal Pétain*, Paris, 1975, on the iconography of Pétain.

16 The importance of the radio in both Paris and Vichy can be gauged by the notoriety of Philippe Henriot of Radio-Vichy and Jean Hérold-Paquis of Radio Paris. See Ory, *Les Collaborateurs*, pp. 81–3.

17 By 'Resistance writing(s)', I refer to all the written output of the Resistance, including tracts and journalism. 'Resistance literature' refers to the fiction, poetry and essays.

18 See particularly M.R.D. Foot, *Resistance*, London, 1976, Chap.8, 'Real Impact', and 'What good did Resistance do', in Stephen Hawes and Ralph White (eds.), London, 1975. Its value for him lies in a rather disembodied morality, and the clear consciences of the participants.

19 Vercors, *Le Silence de la mer* (1942); Laurent Daniel (Elsa Triolet), *Les Amants d'Avignon*, (1943); (Edith Thomas), *Contes d'Auxois* (1943); Vercors, *La Marche à l'étoile* (1943); Santerre (Vercors), 'Désespoir est mort', in *Chroniques interdites* (1943); John Steinbeck, *Nuits noires* (*The Moon is Down*, trans. Yvonne Desvignes) (1944); Mortagne (Claude Morgan), *La Marque de l'homme* (1944); Hainaut (George Adam), *A l'Appel de la liberté* (1944), Minervois (Claude Aveline), *Le Temps mort* (1944); Lauter, (André Chamson), 'Le Puits des miracles' in *Nouvelles Chroniques* (1944).

20 Arnaud de Saint-Roman (Aragon), *Les Bons Voisins*; Jean le Guern (Edith Thomas), *L'Arrestation*.

21 *Les Cahiers du silence* were also established in London to bring the clandestine production to the English public. They published eight titles.

22 Vercors, *La Bataille du silence*, Paris, 1979, pp. 207–8.

23 Pierre Seghers founded *Poètes casqués* in 1939, and it became *Poésie* in 1940. René Tavernier founded *Confluences* in 1941. Max-Pol Fouchet ran *Fontaine* in Algiers.

24 *The Obstructed Path*, New York, 1969, p. 153.

25 'Réflexions sur les rapports du roman et la société', in *Roman et société*, Paris, 1973, p. 63. He also discusses similar problems with reference to the critical reception of Malraux's *L'Espoir*, 'The Object-Event of the Ram's Charge: An Ideological Reading of An Image', in 'Rethinking History', *Yale French Studies*, no. 59, 1980, pp. 155–7.

26 *Encounters with Darkness*, New York, Oxford, 1983, p. x.

27 P. xi.

28 *Ibid.*

29 P. xii.

30 P. xi.

31 Duchet, *Roman et société*, p. 65.

32 Paris, 1944.

33 I also exclude novels devoted to the period of the phoney war and the fighting of May–June 1940, since the historical situation and the concomitant difficulties and dilemmas are so different.

34 Algiers, 1943. (The themes and some narrative devices will be discussed in the chapter 'Unity'.)

35 Those unfamiliar with terms such as implied reader, and diegesis, extra-diegetic, which occur later, will find Shlomith Rimmon-Kenan, *Narrative Fiction: Contemporary Poetics*, London, 1983, and Seymour Chatman, *Story and Discourse: Narrative Structure in Fiction and Film*, Ithaca and London, 1978, very helpful.

36 'L'après-guerre avait fini de finir', *La Force des choses*, I, Paris, 1969, p. 364.

37 There are parallels here with the features Susan Suleiman isolates in *Authoritarian Fictions: The Novel as Ideological Genre*, New York, 1983, an extremely interesting work devoted to the *roman à thèse* which she defines as fiction which is seeking to affirm as valid a particular thesis. She also therefore discusses techniques of persuasion, exemplary narratives, and the structures of knowledge which she calls the structure of apprenticeship. She has in my view a rather narrow definition of didacticism in narrative, insisting on the way it presents its 'truth' as unproblematic and suggesting that by a variety of procedures, meaning can be set and unambiguously transmitted. She opposes this to narratives where the play of writing exceeds and defeats any didactic intent. This seems to me to be rather a tendentious opposition, and underplays the structurally important feature of 'persuasive' fiction which is to *problematise* its 'message'; otherwise there would be no difference between a didactic novel and a didactic tract. But this does inscribe the possibility of other readings, by the very nature of the oppositional structure, at the heart of any novel. A further reservation regarding Suleiman's definition is that the use of different features in the service of a socio-political thesis, such as I discuss in relation to the 'novel of ambiguity', is not treated. In fact she contrasts the *roman à thèse* and Lukács's notion of the problematic quest for authenticity in the modern world, whereas the 'novel of ambiguity' would suggest they are not at all irreconcilable.

38 In *La Crise de l'humanisme*, II, Paris, 1967, Micheline Tison-Braun neatly encapsulates, in the course of a long definition of humanism, its central value: 'Man, says the humanist, is the measure of all things' (p. 7). She stresses the importance of the mind, the will and the intelligence over the 'the destructive forces of the passions, the weakening forces of laziness and dreams' (*ibid.*), and the values of 'liberty, reason, sympathy. They are to be extended to all men and defended against any remnants of barbarism' (p. 8). Humanist discourse of the Resistance belongs to the same tradition.

39   In spite of this, however, a recurrent expression in several of these novels is that the multiple dramas of life during the Occupation had the virtue of adding a little spice to life ('On s'ennuierait après la guerre', *Mon Village à l'heure allemande*, Paris, 1972, p. 327). This is again diametrically opposed to the stress placed in Resistance fiction on the tragedies of death and torture which the Resistance is fighting to end.

40   I follow Pierre Guiraud's distinction here, between the *énonciation* or process of narration, and the *énoncé* or that which is narrated (*Essai de stylistique*, Paris, 1969, p. 151). To avoid confusion with the standard translations of these terms in linguistics, I shall use the French terms throughout.

41   Suleiman's work in *Authoritarian Fictions* does at least suggest there may be general applications.

Part One
Literature of persuasion

Chapter One

The concept of *témoignage*

Resistance literature must be among the most famous and least read periods of contemporary literature. After the Liberation, facsimile editions of *Les Lettres françaises*, and, in both Paris and Brussels, of *Les Editions de minuit* were produced, but since then, apart from Vercors, few of the clandestine short stories have been published in paperback. This literature has its place in all the textbooks of twentieth-century literature, and Resistance poetry certainly has its champions, but generally it is considered to be of minor literary value, presenting above all a documentary interest as *littérature de témoignage*, that is to say, literature which seeks to bear witness to its time. It is the purpose of this chapter, after discussing the term *témoignage* in general terms, to examine precisely what it meant under the Occupation.

In order to establish some of the major terms of the debate it is instructive to look at *Du Témoignage* by Jean Norton Cru,[1] a most detailed exposition of the nature and value of documentary literature, which examines the literature of the First World War in order to establish the criteria by which its veracity may be gauged. Two factors dominate his analysis: the importance of subjective experience and the direct transcription of that experience. His assumption that experience can constitute a kind of *tabula rasa* upon which the event is imprinted, and that writing can unproblematically record this imprint, tends not to be accepted by other critics today; Léon Riegel writes of his wish to demythologise the 'semiology of authenticity celebrated by Norton Cru',[2] and Holger Klein addresses the problems of articulating categories of 'truth' and 'subjectivity' in a discussion of Norton Cru on Barbusse.[3] True art, for Norton Cru, is the faithful record of what has been seen; ornament, embellishment, artificiality and exaggeration are the domain of 'literature' in the most negative sense : artifice rather than art. Praising immediacy, he condemns mediation as overt bias. But it is not difficult to point out the internal contradictions here, since his own analysis is based on a pacifist project – true knowledge of the war must lead to peace – which is itself determining whether experiential accounts can be admitted as authentic or not. His rather simplistic attitudes to subjectivity and writing do not however detract from the interest of his work. It is obvious that for him *témoignage* is as much *active* as reactive, and aimed at transmitting the moral lesson which the soldiers' experience, and especially the 'baptism of fire' has taught them. Later critics share his criteria of subjectivity, immediacy and presence, as well as his unproblematic reading of literature reflecting the event,[4] but, as shall be seen, for them *témoignage* tends to be passive, a reaction to an event or a crisis, and nothing more. In Resistance writings we shall again meet *témoignage* in an active sense, but the nature of that activity is very different from Norton Cru's vision.

As well as the difficulties of defining the 'literary document', another problem which immediately appears when we start to examine seriously the concept of *témoignage* is the question of the dual nature of the very term 'literature'. Resistance writings throw into stark relief the ambiguity at the heart of the term, which is not a semantic but an institutional or ideological ambiguity. The term 'literature' is at once a description of a cultural phenomenon (imaginative writing) and a value judgement (X's novels are not 'literature'), defined in relation to that which fails to meet its criteria, and it has in the past been one of the functions of criticism to elaborate what these are. In the context of the Occupation, we find that the relation with the event is variously seen as both a strength and the major weakness of Resistance literature. If considerations of historical accuracy are uppermost, the old framework of the falsity and perhaps frivolity of literature, already met in Norton Cru, reappears, as in a clandestine review of *Contes d'Auxois*: 'These are just simple stories, the kind that one meets every day, which the author has transcribed from reality without any literary effects. A moving chronicle of France under oppression, of France at war.'[5] Terms such as 'transcribed' or 'translated from reality' are frequently

met with, but to post-war critics, this is precisely the charge, not
the defence. They consider that the Resistance produced works
of circumstance (*oeuvres de circonstance*) whose literary value had
disappeared with the historical situation which had given birth to
them.[6] Maurice Nadeau, in a chapter significantly entitled
'L'Evénement suscite les oeuvres', (The event brings forth the
works) discusses the post-war fiction devoted to the war and the
eagerness of the novelists to bear witness to what they have just
gone through. 'Among the newcomers to literature, many of
these reports (*témoignages*), on the war, the concentration camps,
the Resistance, do not accede to a literary existence. They are
valuable, and often very moving, as documents. Literary works
need to step back, to "disengage" themselves from the event.'[7]

So the war literature is admitted to exist at the same time as it is
denied any literary value. Both literary and non-literary at the
same time, the central pivot is that of *témoignage*. Implying as it
does a relation of immediacy with particular circumstances, it is
judged to be weak in the name of an art viewed as a process of
mediation and critical distance. When Sartre, in conclusion to a
rather different argument in *Qu'est-ce que la littérature?* (What is
Literature?), asserts that Resistance literature produced little that
was good,[8] he is in fact voicing the general consensus of literary
criticism.

However, if we forget the literature of the Occupation for a
moment, and turn to the notion of *littérature de témoignage* in more
general terms, it can quickly be seen that the lack of standing of
the Resistance literature in the name of documentary *témoignage*
does not apply to the period 1930–50 which is hailed for all the
qualities which have damned the war literature considered alone,
namely immediacy, response to a crisis in the world outside and
engagement.

In the early 1930s, a serious, political, moral literature succeeds
the dazzling literary brilliance of the period which immediately
followed the First World War.[9] R.M. Albérès gives a succinct
account of the changing nature of the relation to the world, which
he dates from 1933 when the economic depression reached
Europe, locating the impetus to change in the event, and more
particularly in the perception of an unstable situation.[10] Brom-
bert, in *The Intellectual Hero*, takes up similar points: 'The nine-
teen-thirties are indeed a point of cleavage and a time of crisis.

Unemployment, the growth of fascism , the Spanish Civil War, the concentration camps – all serve to explain the political orientation of literature following a period of introspection and poetical escapism.'[11] It is worth remembering that a similar list is used in Nadeau's negative appraisal of documentary literature, but here the radical development that it is the political, moral and intellectual *duty* of the writer to introduce this changing world into fiction is not accompanied by any suggestion that this might entail some corresponding literary devaluation.

It is within this same framework, highlighting the productive dominance of the event and moral and philosophical importance of the historically extraordinary, that Sartre, from the point of view of the committed writer, discusses the changing forms of literature in the works of some of his contemporaries in *What is Literature?*:

What are Camus, Malraux, Koestler, Rousset etc. writing, if not a literature of extreme situations? Their characters are at the summits of power or in dungeons, on the eve of their deaths, or of being tortured, or of killing; war, coups d'Etat, revolutions, bombings, and massacres – this is the stuff of everyday life for them. On every page, on every line, it is always man in his totality who is being called into question.[12]

He also stresses the impossibility in his view of writing as before when things are no longer as before, and here it is the Second World War, not the thirties, which is the catalyst. Discussing the traditional technique of fiction, 'specifically perfected to relate events from an individual viewpoint in a stable society', he considers it enabled the presentation and explanation of a localised disruption within a peaceful world, 'whereas, from 1940 onwards, we were in the middle of a cyclone'.[13] The logical consequence of a world in crisis is, for Sartre, a 'relativisation' of the narrator in the text, as fictional technique had to move from 'Newtonian mechanics to a generalised relativity', and novels were populated with 'consciousnesses which were partly lucid and partly unenlightened (...), and of which none would have a privileged viewpoint, either on the event or on itself'.[14] The omniscient narrator, friend and mentor to the reader, is redundant. The reader is no longer presented with a ready digested world, but is placed in the position of having to make sense of it. Raising the concept of commitment in relation to the content of the novel and the writer as witness to the 'tortured era'[15] has *overtly* raised the question of the reading of the world which that narrative will produce in its reader. It is by the bias of this question that the literature of the Occupation, dismissed in far too facile a fashion under the label *témoignage*, can be more fruitfully approached.

An important element in the writings of the thirties which sought to engage with the issues of action in the world was the notion of crisis. The order of the world is no longer taken for granted, and its very disturbance has meant it now occupies the front of the cultural stage: 'The thirties brutally thrust the writer into the nightmare of History.'[16] The old signposts have disappeared and new ones need to be created. The literature of the twenties valorising style and psychological analysis is judged to be impossibly complacent and ignorant in its unspoken acceptance of a settled social order, and the central tenets of humanism can no longer be relied on, as the very notion of man and his relation to the world is threatened. The new literature, of Malraux, Saint-Exupéry, of the 'non-conformistes', finds its main stimulus in the extra-literary. The same can be said, even more forcefully, of the literature of the Resistance. It cannot be judged in isolation from the conditions of its existence; it has a mission, a purpose not grounded in literary values alone. The notion of committed literature had its theoretical apogee after the war with *Qu'est-ce que la littérature?*, but the refusal of purely literary values, the awareness of the political context of the struggle against the Army of Occupation, the ideology of Nazism, of Vichy, awareness also of the political use of culture, is inherent in all Resistance writing, to the extent that a post-war volume of poems, short stories and extracts from a wide range of writings on the war is described in its blurb as 'the first textbook of committed literature'.[17] Cultivation of the purely aesthetic is, from this perspective, at best irresponsible, at worst the hallmark of the compliance and complicity of collaboration.

This is a time when the material conditions of the production of literature and the nature of what is produced are seen to be explicitly linked : 'Only those who sing the praises of the enemy are allowed to write and speak.'[18] Approved by the Germans and Vichy, public speech is profoundly suspect, as Mounier comments with reference to bringing out *Esprit* in the unoccupied zone: 'We are told: publication alone is enough to compromise you.'[19] Many writers refused to publish in the press. Discussing the Prix Goncourt in 1943, for which *L'Invitée* (She came to stay) was considered, Simone de Beauvoir writes: 'Sartre told me the CNE had no objections to me accepting if I gave neither article nor interview to the press.'[20] Others refused to publish at all. In his preface to *Journal des années noires* (Diary of the Years of Darkness), Guéhenno writes of 'this terrible silence which was imposed on us all'.[21] Speaking of himself in the third person as 'the witness', he stresses he was lucky enough not to depend on writing in order to make a living, and says that he had renounced public pronouncements as it was forbidden to mention the one thing he wanted to write about. 'Since we were in prison, we had to live like prisoners.'[22] For Guéhenno, this meant that all one could hope to do was maintain a sense of personal freedom, since he considered, along with many others, that publication would give an impression of approval, or at least normality, to an unacceptable situation, and 'play into the hands of the jailor', as he puts it.[23]

To write and speak within officially approved limits is necessarily to be quiet about a range of issues and events whose suppression is essential to the maintenance of official discourse. 'Legal literature is a literature of betrayal', asserts, somewhat polemically, the clandestine paper *La Pensée libre*.[24] And so that which cannot be said officially has to be said unofficially. The first and most obvious thing to remember about most of the literary production of the Resistance is that it is clandestine. No literature of the period can avoid being placed across the great public/clandestine divide; at no time can arguments for the neutrality and autonomy of the literary sphere have been weaker. This is not to say that a simplistic equation between public speech and collaboration can be established, though this is a confusion fostered by many a post-war polemicist. Sartre, for example, is often accused of at best indifference to the Resistance, at worst objective collaboration, for writing and producing *Les Mouches* (The Flies) in Paris in 1943,[25] but many reviews in *Les Lettres françaises*, including that of *Les Mouches*, are devoted to detailed consideration of the substance of what has been officially published or performed, rather than a blanket and automatic rejection. And of course many writers contributing to clandestine publications are also writing 'contraband' works to get the Resistance message across, a phenomenon not limited to literature alone. Actors and playwrights are also encouraged in the clandestine press to do this since, in their choice of subjects, their use of intonation and gestures, they are said to have subtle ways, which will escape the enemy, of celebrating 'noble feelings and national aspirations'.[26] What it is necessary to stress here is that the awareness of a political context determining what can or cannot be said is a crucial element in the Resistance discussion of the place, function and nature of literature. The championing of the values of 'pure literature' is derided as a transparent means, on the part of the collaborators, of silencing uncomfortable references to the real situation, and, towards the end of the Occupation, as part of the tactics of fear. Kleber Haedens is warned that he is 'placing himself in a camp where he is in grave danger of meeting a Brasillach who is also convinced, but rather too late, that the practice of "literature" can be an alibi.'[27] Ironic references are made to shifts in allegiances:

The Hitlerian writers of France, the Brasillachs, the Drieus and their accomplices from Thérive to Fernandez, have for the most part abandoned militant politics and found refuge in pure literature. They are outdoing each other in enthusiasm for Balzac, Racine or Giraudoux. Literature is their maquis. Not a maquis to fight in, like the other one. A maquis to hide oneself in.[28]

Many of these attacks are couched in terms which recall the rejection of the 'dazzling' literature of the twenties by the younger generation of the thirties. A letter written to her husband by a young Communist prisoner is quoted and produces the following comments: 'Beside such courage, such faith and such joyous self-sacrifice, the psychological conflicts in so much contemporary literature are in our view petty and artificial.'[29] From the perspective of the Resistance, the realities of the situation are such as to call into question even poetic appreciation, and, with strong irony, to underline the function of poetry in collaborationist writing:

Well, Chardonne cannot say everything. While he does not mention *Mein Kampf*, he does tell us about a glass of brandy which a man in Champagne offers and which a German officer drinks in a particularly distinguished manner, about Renan, about the voracious intelligence of Drieu la Rochelle, about the exquisite colour which (...) cabbages under the skies of the Ile de France region take on. It is enough to calm our fears.[30]

Clandestine literature, on the other hand, is part of the Resistance *activity*. To read the fiction, or indeed the tracts and newspapers, as documents reacting to or reflecting the events is to pose the question in false terms and really to miss the point. These words are not reflecting the struggle, they are deliberately and overtly part of it. The second issue of *Les Lettres françaises* publishes an 'Appeal to French writers': 'Become involved in active resistance by publishing works which celebrate patriotic love and freedom, which pay homage to the Francs-Tireurs and Partisans who are fighting courageously to kick the Nazi hordes and their Kollaborator valets out of France.'[31] Resistance writing is 'the repressed and censored voice of France',[32] the proliferating refutation of the official silence on the war and the oppression. To speak officially is to present partial truths, to distort the truth or to lie,[33] so it is because language is seen as a weapon of the Germans that writing is so clearly not a neutral, but a political, national and cultural activity,[34] and, inevitably, great importance is given to the evaluation of *what* is said, to the meaning of a book, play or film. This has several consequences. A literature committed to transmitting the truth of a particular situation highlights, within its own appraisal of itself as literature, certain key notions : the direct relation to the world, truth and reality. In other words, the referential function of the text is valorised, and this is accompanied by a devaluing of stylistic considerations, for the duty of the writer and the text is to voice the unspoken background of the official discourse. This is introducing what I propose to call 'the historical real' (that which the text validates as historically true) as the most important factor in the text, which serves as the yardstick by which all is judged. In the fiction of the Resistance, this coincides with 'the narrative real' (the purely fictional reality presented nonetheless as realistic and true), but the same is not true of texts, considered to be pro-Resistance, which are produced publicly. 'What is the point of putting the Greeks on stage', said Sartre after the Occupation, 'if not to disguise one's thought under a fascist régime'.[35] Divorcing the reality constructed through the narrative from the historical reality to which it refers was successful in the case of *Les Mouches* in getting past the censor and presenting publicly a pro-Resistance refusal of Vichy ideology and the Occupation, although not without some debate.[36]

The insistence on the part of the Resistance on the literary contribution to the fight against the Germans means that it is not surprising to find many references to literature being by its very nature opposed to oppression. However much he is anticipating the well known arguments of *Qu'est-ce que la littérature?*, Sartre is merely expressing a typical Resistance view when he writes in a clandestine (and anonymous) article:'Literature is not a song of innocence and facility which can adjust to any kind of regime. By its nature it poses the question of politics: to write is to demand freedom for all men.'[37] Therefore the function of literature is to be a weapon in the struggle, a vehicle of the truth of that struggle, but this truth can only be spoken from within and under cover of silence. The two elements are inextricably linked – the clandestinity of the writing is essential, for obvious practical reasons, *and* the essential guarantee of its own veracity. The thematics of silence, both assumed and imposed, run thoughout the writings, and were not unnoticed at the time. Jacques Debû-Bridel praised the author of *Le Silence de la mer* for 'having chosen silence as the essential theme of his admirable tale, for having known how to express that silent, persistent rejection by the French people of the advances made by the enemy'.[38] The advice at the top of a newspaper or tract, for example, 'Be careful, do not read this paper in public. Only pass it on to friends you can trust',[39] is *also* entering into the signifying circuit of the text, producing a reader who accepts the opposition to the official order. The significance of clandestinity lies in its didactic function in the text, and cannot be separated from the literary project taken as a whole, which is to refuse neutrality. The place of literature is clandestinity, its nature is opposition, its function to wage war; *littérature de témoignage* and *littérature de combat* are virtually interchangeable terms at this time.[40]

The first issue of *L'Ecran français* in 1943 defines its role as being one of combat (*journal de combat*), its aim to convince and persuade.[41] 'Convince and persuade' could be the banner of all Resistance writing, and clandestine fiction is aiming specifically at producing narratives which will end on a pro-French, pro-Resistance position. It is this active assumption of its positive effect which I feel is not happily served by the term of *témoignage* in its usual sense; 'literature of persuasion' is more appropriate, for by its nature literature will change attitudes: 'Let us hope that all

those who, through some inexplicable weakness, are still tempted
to excuse the senile Bazaine of the Hôtel du Parc, will read this
poem, for it analyses and dissects him, taking apart piece by piece
the whole operation of the ambitious old traitor.'[42] This is of
course a literary statement rather than a report on any practical
effect, which is notoriously difficult to determine. In *Resistance in
Vichy France*, H.R. Kedward states that a high percentage of
journalists might be assumed to be 'sceptical of the capacity of
marginal tracts to correct majority opinion. Among individuals
who started tracts and newsheets in 1940 was a balancing idealism
which believed that the facts of the situation, clearly stated, would
carry a conviction of their own.'[43] He also gives evidence from M.
Pavoux, a railway worker in the Communist Party : 'He could not
exaggerate, he said, the importance of tracts and publications in
convincing fellow workers of the reality and origins of the
repression',[44] but still points out that 'the clandestine press in the
winter of 1941–42 provides plenty of evidence of the difficulty
experienced by the various movements in convincing the public
that action was necessary'.[45] However, as an *attitude*, persuasion is
essential to any attempt to answer the question 'what is literature?'
at this time. What one might call 'the stylistics of persuasion' are
constantly present in phrases such as 'Everyone must know/
understand that...'.[46] If propaganda, as a term, were not inevitably tied to notions of falsehood and distortion, it would be the
ideal word to encapsulate the notion of the production of knowledge about the situation. It is in this sense that André Labarthe
uses it: 'It is essential that we stop the Germans deceiving their
victims. We must make all the oppressed nations understand
what the new order means in reality. In this sense, propaganda
must become, in the service of the Allies, a weapon of the first
importance.'[47]

The political and cultural structures of Resistance writing,
informing the reader about the reality of oppression under the
Occupation – the executions, the hostages, the camps – as well as
pointing out the half-truths and false statements of German and
collaborationist writing, are clear enough. But *témoignage* cannot
be reduced to the realm of the purely factual; orientated to the
present, it is however articulated across time, seeking to place a
specific historical moment on the platform of History, and to
affirm a continuity with the values it speaks. It is this particular

articulation of these two categories, the moment and duration in time (*durée*),[48] which is invariably present in any contemporary discussion of the *value* of this literature:

We expect literature to be *exemplary*. And naturally by this we do not mean the fatuous moralising of a Montherlant, nor the drivelling sermons of a Pétain. (...) But that a book appears which challenges everything about us, despairingly, until, from the depths of negation and tragedy, the secret which can found a reason for living shines forth at last, we recognise suddenly the great voice which, across the centuries, ensures our action and our duration.[49]

The adjective 'exemplary' could not be better chosen. It encapsulates perfectly the idealism of the vision of literature where any literary artefact is always standing for something else which it can neither contain nor exhaust, as well as the didactic implications of the mode of writing which is thus privileged. And the usual term for this exemplary literature is *témoignage*. Jean Lescure, in his preface to *Domaine français*, a special number of *Messages* published in Switzerland and devoted to writing in France, writes that what is important, in this publication, is to 'reassert, however crudely, the obscure passion which links us to the duration (*durée*) of a civilisation. And therefore we have attempted here to produce nothing more than a historical work of witness (*témoignage*).'[50]

As well as designating the committed nature of Resistance writing, *témoignage* is also therefore the key term articulating the works of literature with the values which the Resistance represents.

Notes

1 Paris, 1967.
2 Léon Riegel, *Guerre et littérature*, Paris, 1978, p. 8.
3 Holger Klein (ed.), *The First World War in Fiction*, London, 1976, pp. 4–5.
4 For example, David Schalk, *Roger Martin du Gard, The Novelist and History*, Ithaca, 1967, p. 16, defines *témoignage* as 'the direct consequence of the overwhelming effect of contemporary events on the life of the individual writer', and considers the problem it raises as being 'whether or not it is more than a glorified form of journalism – a *reportage* sustained by emotional force and a certain degree of literary talent' (p. 14). He also raises the question of the religious meaning of *témoignage*, bearing witness for Christ, which he sees as a parallel to the modern usage. There are certainly echoes of this under the Occupation (Aragon writes on the

executed hostages of Chateaubriant as 'Le Témoin des martyrs'), but I would argue that this is again more active a sense than Schalk's definition of modern usage above.

The distinction he establishes between a religious *témoignage* and engagement in *The Spectrum of Political Engagement*, Princeton, 1979, in relation to Mounier, is not pertinent to Resistance writing.

5   *Les Lettres françaises*, no. 17, juin 1944, p.8. (All the articles in *Les Lettres françaises* were unsigned.)

6   See Bersani et al., *La Littérature en France depuis 1945*, Paris, 1970, p. 13.

7   Maurice Nadeau, *Le Roman français depuis la guerre*, Paris, Idées, 1970, p. 36.

8   Jean-Paul Sartre, *Situations II*, Paris, 1948, p. 257.

9   See Jean-Louis Loubet del Bayle, *Les Non-conformistes des années trente*, Paris, 1969, Introduction.

10   R.M. Albérès, *L'Aventure intellectuelle du XXe siècle*, Paris, 1969, pp. 30–1.

11   *The Intellectual Hero*, Philadelphia and New York, 1960, 1961, p. 137.

12   *Qu'est-ce que la littérature?*, p. 237.

13   *Ibid.*, p. 252.

14   *Ibid.*, pp. 252–3.

15   *Ibid.*, p. 19.

16   *Ibid.*, p. 137.

17   Jean Paulhan and Dominique Aury (eds.), *La Patrie se fait tous les jours*, Paris, 1947.

18   'Le Manifeste du Comité National des Ecrivains', *Les Lettres françaises*, no. 1, septembre 1942, p. 1.

19   *Mounier et sa génération*, Paris, 1956, pp. 268–9 (dated 10 novembre 1940).

20   *La Force de l'âge*, Paris, 1970, p. 644.

21   Paris, 1960, p. 5.

22   *Ibid.*

23   P.6. See also for similar discussion J.H. King, 'Language and Silence: Some Aspects of French Writing and the French Resistance', *European Studies Review*, 2, no. 3, 1972, pp. 228–9. Cf. 'Résister, c'est déjà garder son coeur et son cerveau. Mais c'est surtout agir' (*Résistance*, no 1, 15 décembre 1940). And Guéhenno was of course involved in clandestine publications.

24   N. 1, février 1941, p. 4.

25   This is surprising, given the wealth of documentation concerning Sartre's clandestine articles and membership of the *Comité National des Ecrivains* from 1943. And one wonders why *Les Lettres françaises*, *Combat* and *La France libre* were publishing his articles in the immediate post-Liberation period if he had been so indifferent. Equally surprisingly, Michel Contat suggested in *Le Monde* that *Les Mouches* could not have been 'contraband' writing as no such thing existed at that time. Which no doubt would have come as something of a shock to the contributors to

Poésie, for example. It is worth quoting Claude Roy, writing publicly before the Liberation, in relation to a phrase in one of his articles which had been considered ambiguous : 'Qu'on discute avec M. Sartre, comme avec M. Camus, tel ou tel point de doctrine ou d'esthétique, c'est possible. Mais chacun sait qu'il est d'autres querelles, aujourd'hui, et que l'un et l'autre écrivain ont donné depuis des années l'exemple du caractère et de la rectitude quand trop d'écrivains (et même de valeur) n'ont pas toujours été dignes de notre estime et de notre amitié. M. Sartre et M. Camus n'ont certes besoin ni de certificats de talent, ni d'attestation de bonne conduite. Je tenais pourtant à écrire ceci, et à le signer.' *Poésie 44*, no 19, mai–juin 1944, p.68. For a discussion of the hostile reaction to *Les Mouches* from the collaborationist press, see Patrick Marsh, 'Le Théâtre à Paris sous l'Occupation allemande', *Revue d'histoire du théâtre*, vol. 33, 1981, pp.262–4. For a discussion of the Contat article and reactions to it, see Howard Davies, *Sartre and 'Les Temps Modernes'*, Cambridge, 1987, pp. 2–3.

26   *Les Lettres françaises*, no. 14, mars 1944, p. 5, 'Echec à la propagande "culturelle" '.

27   'M. Haedens n'est pas content', *LF*, no. 12, décembre 1943, p. 2.

28   'Domaine interdit', *LF*, no. 14, mars 1944, p. 7.

29   'Lettres de la prison', *LF*, no. 4, décembre 1942, p. 4.

30   'Jacques Chardonne et "Mein Kampf" ', *LF*, no. 11, novembre 1943, p. 2. For discussion of the short story referred to here, see the chapter 'The figure of the enemy'.

31   October 1942, p. 2.

32   'Du Silence de la mer aux Chroniques interdites', *LF*, no. 7, juin 1943, p. 6.

33   The importance of being aware of distortions of meaning is a constant preoccupation : 'On sait que, dans l'étrange terminologie pronazie, *traître* signifie *patriote*, comme *libérateur* signifie *oppresseur* et *Allemagne, Europe* ('Dans le bourbier', *LF*, no 17, mai 1944, p. 8).

34   King argues in 'Language and Silence' that this is because 'the French have always attributed an excessive importance to literature and language. In all French intellectuals there is a subconscious belief that French culture is synonymous with universal culture'(p.257). My argument is that it makes more sense to read this in relation to the ideological divisions and discursive configurations under the Occupation.

35   'Pour un théâtre de l'engagement – je ferai une pièce cette année et deux films', interview par Jacques Baratier, *Carrefour*, no. 3, 9 septembre 1944, quoted in Contat et Rybalka, *Les Ecrits de Sartre*, Paris, 1970, p. 90.

36   See Simone de Beauvoir, *La Force de l'âge*, p.621, and Gerhard Heller, *Un Allemand à Paris 1940–1944*, Paris, 1981, p. 160.

37   'La littérature cette liberté', *LF*, no 15, avril 1944, p. 8.

38   'Du Silence de la mer aux Chroniques interdites', *LF*, no. 7, juin 1943, p. 5.

39   *La France libre*, no. 4, août 1941, reproduced in *La France libre* (London), III, no. 17, March 1942, p. 414.

40   Majault et al., *Littérature de notre temps*, Paris, 1966, does use both terms, but soon distinguishes between them (only poetry is 'de combat') and then goes on 'Littérature de combat ou de témoignage, la littérature est devenue reflet du monde', perpetuating the traditional view, pp. 227–32.

41   Quoted in Olivier Barrot, *L'Ecran français 1943–1953*, Paris, 1979, p. 31.

42   Review of *Le Musée Grévin*, *LF*, no. 12, décembre 1943, p. 4. Bazaine was, like Pétain, a *Maréchal de France*. He surrendered Metz in 1870, was tried, condemned to death and pardoned.

43   *Resistance in Vichy France*, Oxford, 1978, p. 72.

44   *Ibid.*, p. 60.

45   *Ibid.*, p. 150.

46   'Il faut que chacun sache...' or 'Il faut faire comprendre...'.

47   'L'Exploitation économique des régions occupées', *La France libre* (London), I, no. 2, 16 December 1940, p. 112.

48   In *Les Chiens de paille* (Straw Dogs), Drieu la Rochelle, while wishing to criticise as decadence a metaphysical view of France, in fact demonstrates this articulation perfectly: 'La France était devenue (...) une éternité. (...) C'était un seul moment indestructible qui vivait dans l'esprit en dehors des contingences', p. 127.

49   Review of *Les Noyers de l'Altenburg* published in Switzerland as the first part of *La Lutte avec l'ange* (Lausanne, Yverdon, 1943), *LF*, no. 10, octobre 1943, p. 1.

50   *Domaine français*, Genève, 1943, pp. 13–14. For a general discussion of this issue and its contents see Seghers, *La Résistance et ses poètes*, pp. 298–300; Lottmann, *Albert Camus*, London, 1979, pp. 286–7; *Les Ecrits de Sartre*, p. 92.

Chapter Two

Les Lettres françaises

Les Lettres françaises, the journal of the Comité National des Ecrivains in the occupied zone, published poems, short stories, literary articles, and reviews, as well as general political and cultural articles. Many of the writers who contributed to Les Editions de minuit also wrote for it. Its history is well known.[1] In 1941, after the creation by the French Communist Party of the Front National pour la Libération et l'Indépendance de la France (National Front for the Liberation and Independance of France), Jacques Decour, who was then one of the Communist organisers responsible for students and intellectuals (the others were Georges Politzer and Jacques Solomon), gets in touch with Jean Paulhan, through Aragon, and, with the help of Jacques Debû-Bridel, founds the Comité National des Ecrivains (The National Committee of Writers. henceforth CNE) which has seven members.[2] Decour gathers texts for the first number of Les Lettres françaises, the CNE's journal, obtaining contributions from Georges Limbour, Jean Blanzat, François Mauriac, Jean Paulhan, Jean Vaudal, Pierre de Lescure and Debû-Bridel. However, before the number could appear, Decour, Solomon and Politzer were arrested along with many others in the vast swoop on PCF members which began in November 1941.[3] They were shot in May 1942. The texts of that first issue were destroyed. So Les Lettres françaises finally appeared in September 1942, the work of Claude Morgan who had been in contact with Decour but did not know which printers were going to produce the journal. He takes three months to find them. Nor did he know either Paulhan or Debû-Bridel, and it was the novelist Edith Thomas who put them in contact with each other so that the CNE could be reformed. By February 1943 there were ten members : Paulhan, Eluard, Debû-Bridel, Vildrac, Guéhenno, Sartre, Thomas, Blanzat, Vaudal and Morgan. Early efforts to produce a printed journal were unsuccessful, and *Les Lettres françaises* appeared as six pages of roneotyped sheets until October 1943 when the participation of George Adam finally enabled them to produce a printed journal of four pages. At this time the CNE was meeting regularly at Edith Thomas's flat, usually with about twelve or fifteen members, though a famous meeting of twenty-two is often recalled. It was expanded to eight pages in March 1944, with the addition of *L'Ecran français* (The French Screen), the journal of the *Front National du Cinéma*, and *La Scène française* (The French Stage) the journal of the *Front National du Théâtre*, and 12,000 copies were printed. This compares with about 150,000 for *Combat*,[4] 400,000 for *Défense de la France*.[5] *Les Lettres françaises* appeared monthly from September 1942 until August 1944, with the exception of January, March, May and August 1943 because of production difficulties. There were in all nineteen clandestine issues, with a special number dated 1er août 1944 on the massacre at Oradour-sur-Glane. The final issue was sold openly in Paris during the fighting, and on the news-stands after the Liberation, 30,000 copies being printed.

Le Front National

The first issue of September 1942 carried on its front page the CNE's Manifesto written by Jacques Decour. It is explained that the founding group of the 'Committee' comprises writers 'very diverse in background, tendencies and beliefs, but united by their love of their country'. Edith Thomas endorses this description of their different allegiances, explaining that this was due to the *Front National*'s wish to be a truly national movement: 'There were Catholics like Mauriac or the Révérend Père Maydieu, agnostics like Paulhan, atheist existentialists like Sartre, Christian existentialists like Gabriel Marcel, socialists like Jean Guéhenno, communists like Eluard, Morgan and myself.'[6] Nevertheless, in inspiration, direction and politics, *Les Lettres françaises* is still a Communist Party publication, born of the *Front National de l'Indépendance de la France* which was first launched in May 1941 (that is to say before the German invasion of the Soviet Union) and whose objectives were set out in a tract entitled 'Building a National Front For the Independence of France. The French Communist Party addresses all those who think French and wish to take action as Frenchmen'.[7] Courtois explains how the change in position of the Communist International produces the development of a *Front National* in France at this time, with the accent being firmly placed on the anti-fascist struggle, patriotism, and unity for national liberation under the leadership of the Communist Party.[8] The overall strategic aim remained the socialist revolution. After the German invasion of the Soviet Union in June 1941, the Party shifts from its position that this is an imperialist war, and the defence of the country of socialism becomes the first priority, displacing the struggle for socialism, and putting the need for immediate military action in the occupied countries at the centre of the analysis. The PCF therefore continues to promote the union of all the French in the *Front National* and also to promote direct action against the Germans through the military organisations such as *L'Organisation spéciale* and the *Francs-Tireurs et Partisans*.[9] The politics of the *Front National* undergoes many changes from its inception in May 1941, including a period during which it is not even mentioned in the Communist press. The policy of building an alliance with the PCF at the head of the internal Resistance goes off course after de Gaulle's much quoted rejection of terrorist armed action,[10] one of the essential planks of PCF policy, and his insistence on the military operations being organised and run from London, thus placing the Party in an unacceptably subordinate position.[11] It is only in May 1942 that *L'Humanité* again mentions the word 'gaulliste' or indeed the *Front National* itself.[12] This cannot, however, mean that it disappeared completely from the Party's strategy, as Decour's Manifesto was drawn up for the first issue of *Les Lettres françaises* before his arrest in February 1942. Certain similarities of expression suggest the May 1941 tract had been used, for in the tract we read: 'WE MUST BRING ABOUT THE UNITY OF THE WHOLE NATION, EXCEPT FOR THE TRAITORS AND CAPITULATORS WHO ARE DOING THE INVADER'S DIRTY WORK FOR HIM. WE MUST BUILD A GREAT NATIONAL FRONT OF STRUGGLE FOR THE INDEPENDENCE OF FRANCE.'[13] Decour wrote: 'The mighty movement of resistance against the German oppressors and their French agents has found expression in the NATIONAL FRONT OF STRUGGLE FOR THE LIBERTY AND INDEPENDENCE OF FRANCE. The National Front brings together all the people of France, except for the traitors and the capitulators who are doing the enemy's dirty work for him.'[14] For the most part, however, Decour's Manifesto is clearly determined by the extended notion of the *Front national* which dates from after the invasion of the Soviet Union. The phrase 'with the Communist Party at its head'[15] does not appear nor are there any references to de Gaulle's movement being 'reactionary and colonialist in inspiration, in the image of British imperialism' as there were earlier.[16] On the contrary, the union of different groups is stressed, both nationally – 'Gaullists, Communists, Democrats, Catholics, Protestants'[17] – and internationally, as admiration is expressed for the 'struggle being waged against barbarism by the peoples of Great Britain, the Soviet Union, the United States and China'.[18]

This manifesto is therefore as much a political statement as a literary one; throughout its existence, *Les Lettres françaises* continues to give space to the non-literary, and it is here that it can clearly be seen that it is informed specifically by the politics of the PCF. The first three issues carry communiqués from *France d'abord* about FTP activities (acts of sabotage, derailment of trains).[19] All the editorials bar one[20] are concerned with non-literary matters. To give just a few examples : No. 1, 'La victoire en 42' (Victory in 42);[21] No. 2, 'D'un front à l'autre' (From one front to the other); No. 3, 'Onze novembre' (11 November). All bar two were written by Claude Morgan, and those were by Pierre Villon, an important Party organiser who represented the *Front National* at meetings with Gaullists to discuss PCF participation in the *Conseil National de la Résistance*, and was later the *Front National* representative at the CNR.[22] So it is not surprising that in these editorials the *Front National* themes of patriotism, unity, armed struggle and mass insurrection dominate:

There is now but one united France whose every effort must be for victory. She has her African Army and her combat troops, her workers resisting deportation and sabotaging production, her peasants resisting requisitioning, her intellectuals fighting in the shadows.[23]

Facing the bursts from the firing squads, Communists and Catholics, Monarchists and Republicans are dying facing the same bullets, while singing the same song.[24]

The fidelity to the position elaborated in the article in *L'Humanité* of February 1943, 'S'unir, s'armer, se battre' (Unite, arm ourselves, fight),[25] a text 'which will be a point of reference for Communist policy until the Liberation '[26] is maintained throughout, with strong emphasis on the importance of the FTP and the maquis, and, in 1944, on calls to join or form *milices patriotiques*.[27] And just as de Gaulle will turn to the *Résistance intérieure* to strengthen his hand against the Americans, so the PCF stresses the importance of mass action and resistance to avoid being subsumed under the Allies and especially de Gaulle.

Les Lettres françaises and anti-fascism

To trace a convergence between *Les Lettres françaises* and the political line of the PCF, to stress that it is above all a Communist literary journal, is not to reduce it in its entirety to being the simple direct expression of the PCF, but rather to establish the context which enabled it to develop in the way it did. What tends to set it apart from many other clandestine publications is the insistence on the opposition to fascism rather than to the German nation. Henri Michel writes : 'Unlike the Communists, the Resistance movements do not think, or do not say, that the German people is also struggling against its oppressors, or that it has hidden stores of goodness', arguing that because the Resisters were waging armed warfare, you could hardly expect them to qualify their opposition to the enemy – it could be dangerous for them to do so.[28] No doubt this is true, yet it underestimates the extent to which hostility can be directed to a political rather than a national enemy. The PCF certainly did establish a clear distinction between the two: 'Today it is the victim of an odious national oppression, but the people of France will not proffer words of hatred against the German nation, for it does not confuse the latter with its current masters',[29] and one has only to recall the famous cry of A. Timbaud before being shot at Châteaubriant in October 1941, 'Long live the German Communist Party',[30] to realise the strength of the personal commitment to a political fight.

Three elements can be singled out as contributing to this position in *Les Lettres françaises*: the importance of the internal Resistance to the PCF, the commitment to the ideological struggle

against fascism, and the history of opposition to fascism shared by
Communist and non-Communist contributors. As has been seen,
the internal Resistance is important to the PCF for its own position of strength both within France and *vis-à-vis* de Gaulle and the
Allies, but it is also an integral part of its analysis which stresses
both national liberation and anti-fascism. This emphasis on
popular action which can overthrow oppressive regimes allows
links to be established politically between the French and German
peoples. Following the surrender of Italy and the fall of Musso-
lini, the September 1943 issue carries an editorial which underlines the lesson to be drawn from these events, that dictators are
vulnerable and can be brought down by popular action. It also
describes Nazi Germany yet again as the oppressor of its own
people as well as of other nations.[31]

The second factor, the importance given to the ideological
struggle, is inseparable from the recognition given to the specific
nature of fascism which is seen as wishing the destruction of all
culture, all art; in short, to be a political system which 'threatens to
stifle the genius of man'.[32] That such emphasis be laid on the
necessity for a ideological as well as a military struggle to combat
the German dominance of information and cultural institutions is
not surprising in a committed literary journal; indeed, this was
precisely its role according to Villon. Interviewed by Jacques
Debû-Bridel, he suggests that the Resistance would never have
had the impact it did have if it had been a purely military
phenomenon, that is to say without the emphasis placed on the
national struggle against enemy propaganda, against Hitler's
'New Order'.[33] Yet this is another instance where national oppositions as such are not primarily and necessarily at play, given the
definition of Nazism as being anti-humanist, monstrous and
barbarous, as committed to the destruction of German culture as
it is to that of the French. That is to say that the defence of culture,
and specifically French culture, is *de facto* ideological opposition to
Nazism, and this is the basis on which German culture can also be
defended. An anthology of German poetry produced by the
Editions Stock in 1943 presents such famous figures as Goethe
and Schiller and Rilke only to close with modern poets, a 'batall-
ion of S.A. lute carriers' involved in the Nazi movement according
to a *Lettres françaises* article.[34] In July 1944 appears the review of a
clandestine volume of the 'banned German poets', a direct reply

to the Stock anthology : 'There is no mistake here when we mention German poets. Everything is a weapon in the battle we are waging for Man.'[35] That Jacques Decour was a specialist of German language and literature was often recalled. 'He knew and loved the real German culture, of Lessing, Schiller, Goethe, Heine and Thomas Mann. Because he loved it, he could not bear to see his own land subjected to Hitlerian terror and oppression.'[36] The fourth issue prints a poem by Erich Kaëstner written in 1931, 'If we had won the war.'[37]

Finally, anti-fascism was the basis for the unity between Communist and non-Communist intellectuals, and not just from 1942. Of the forty-three contributors identified in the facsimile edition,[38] many were already active in the anti-fascist circles of the thirties. Guéhenno was a typical example, having belonged in the thirties to the *Comité des intellectuels anti-fascistes*: 'We all met up again in 1940 – we'd never really lost touch – and it was natural I felt an affinity with those who had been on the left in 36-38-39. We were in the same situation and we shared the same views.'[39] Edith Thomas, who joined the Communist Party in 1942,[40] also recalls her participation in the anti-fascist movements in the thirties.[41] Axiomatic to those in the anti-fascist organisations was solidarity with the victims of fascism everywhere, be it in Spain, Italy or Germany, as many of the speeches at the meeting organised by the *Association des Ecrivains et Artistes Révolutionnaires* on 21 March 1933 show.[42] In his opening address, Gide stressed that what had brought them together was the 'extremely serious fact that a significant section of the German people, precisely those with whom we would and should wish to share an understanding, has been gagged',[43] and nearly all the contributions affirm the theme of their solidarity with the German comrades.[44] The same is true of Daniel Guérin's *La Peste brune* (The Brown Plague).[45] However, the fact that, in the preface to the post-war edition, he needs to recall and explain the arguments for making a distinction between the German people and Nazism, is eloquent proof of the growing strength of the purely national opposition under the Occupation.

The accent on unity, the appeals for concerted action by the whole nation and the concomitant valorisation of patriotism, do not suddenly appear in 1942 either. They were insistently present in Communist and non-Communist pronouncements in the thirties. The importance of France, therefore, is a constant, and, more significantly in the context of mapping the contours of the political discourse in *Les Lettres françaises*, is inseparable from anti-fascism. Historians of the period agree that what really united the Popular Front was the rise of fascism, especially in France.[46] The external threat of fascism was hardly ignored, but it was the danger represented by internal forces, especially after 6 February 1934, which was perceived as a threat to the Republic itself. The demonstrations in Paris on 14 July 1935 and 1936, and before *Le Mur des Fédérés* on 25 May 1936, are a massive affirmation of the Republican tradition.[47] But this is also a national tradition. Of the demonstration on 14 July 1935 (the idea for which came from the anti-fascist *Comité Amsterdam-Pleyel*), Dubief writes : 'The themes developed in the speeches are above all patriotic. The left is laying claim to the heritage of Joan of Arc, of the military glory of the great Revolution, and of Verdun, which is linked to socialism and the October Revolution. Those present swear to "remain united to defend democracy" '.[48] The PCF strategy of unity, promoting political and class alliance against the 'enemies of the people', places it firmly within the same configuration. In his famous 'main tendue' (outstretched hand) speech, Thorez addresses himself to 'all the French people' to tell them that the Communists have reconciled the 'tricolour flag of our fathers and the red flag of our hopes'.[49] Their political assessment of the dangers of fascism leads them to set the boundaries of unity as wide as possible, culminating in the idea of a 'Front of the French' against fascism. This position informs Vaillant-Couturier's report 'Au Service de l'esprit', a celebration of French virtues and traditions which affirms their homogeneity with Communism: the argument is that because the highest value of Communism is man, by this humanism Communists show themselves to be true and faithful inheritors of French cultural traditions.[50] It is because France is defined *qualitatively*, in opposition to fascism, that patriotism is so important.

In the May 1941 tract launching the *Front National* (which maintains the anti-imperialist fight and the demands for peace), the stress on national liberation from fascism goes hand in hand with patriotism. The vocabulary of the thirties is still present: 'We hold out the hand of fraternal friendship to all French people of good will.'[51] 'The Party will devote all its energies to UNITING

THE FRENCH in the common struggle for national liberation'.[52]
The very fact that fascism has produced a foreign invader inevitably increases the emphasis on France and the French; after the
invasion of the Soviet Union which brings the question of national
liberation firmly to the fore, this tendency can only be accentuated. The imperative now is to be united, to be armed and to
fight. 'The French cause will be lost if salvation depends on
outside help. We must save ourselves by our fight, and tomorrow
we will be able to make our voice heard and claim, with all the
authority of a people which has fought hard, the right of this
France of ours to liberty, independence and greatness.'[53]
(Neither for the first or the last time, there is a definitely Gaullist
ring about PCF pronouncements, and vica versa, of course.)
Henri Michel argues that the Communists are slipping into
nationalist clothes here,[54] but I would suggest that the logic of this
opposition is different from the nationalist one; in the former,
patriotism is one element in the opposition to the fascist invader,
whereas the latter remains within the boundaries of nationality. It
is this patriotism which runs through *Les Lettres françaises*. An
excellent example is to be found in the first issue, in the article
'Adieu à Jacques Decour'; having recalled his history of opposition to Hitlerism and his love of German culture, and given an
account of his arrest and death by firing squad with Georges
Politzer and Jacques Solomon, it continues: 'All three were Communist. They died as revolutionaries, faithful to their ideal, and
as patriots, faithful to France which they had enriched with their
work and their writings.'[55]

The appeals to history in *Les Lettres françaises* are an equally
clear example of the vision which founds the Resistance as both
political and patriotic action. The article 'Notre Paris'[56] ends with
the 'haunting vision' of the *Mont Valérien*, and recalls both its
importance during the Commune and 'the 98 hostages STULP-
NAGEL had ordered to be shot, with the connivance of the Vichy
government'. It was indeed an emotive site for such executions,
yet this recall of history is but one of a series of references. Michel
finds that the Revolution, especially Valmy, the Commune and
the actions of the Francs-Tireurs of 1870, and the First World
War are common references to be found throughout the Communist clandestine press.[57] *Les Lettres françaises* is no exception,
but then neither is the non-Communist press, if one recalls some

of the titles from the Resistance movements: *Franc-Tireur, La Marseillaise, Le Père Duchesne, Valmy*.[58] Nor is it surprising that they meet on the terrain of history, for these are the privileged moments of Republicanism, which the Communists have also claimed as their own. In each case, what is recalled is armed resistance to a foreign, German or Prussian, invader within the context of the Revolutionary and Republican traditions of the French people. To this must be added Munich and the Spanish Civil War, elements in the specific history of anti-fascism. *Les Lettres françaises* also establishes itself, via frequent mentions of the execution of Jacques Decour[59] and the Resistance itself, as part of the same tradition. To take two very typical examples:

Like the soldiers of Valmy, like the heroes of the Marne, of Verdun, of Dunkirk, of Bir Akem, like the hostages executed by firing squad and the sailors of Toulon, our Francs-Tireurs et Partisans will enter history.[60]

Not long ago we used to wake up in the night thinking: Madrid or Guernica. Then it was the turn of our own people. Facing the same guns.[61]

As during the Popular Front, the appeal to history realises the unity of the combatants across time, from the Revolution onwards, and across space, both within and outside France.

Les Lettres françaises and nationalism

The insistence on the political nature of the German Occupation is an essential part of *Les Lettres françaises*, but it is impossible to reduce it to a statement of political opposition alone. This is partly due to the diverse allegiances of the contributors, but more importantly to the fact that this defence of French land, French culture, tradition and history is so close to the purely national defence of France from the German as to merge with it at times. Longer expositions especially tend to slide into a patriotic fervour where the unique quality of Frenchness is indistinguishable, on its own, from the qualitative definition proper to nationalism. In the October 1942 issue, Maupassant's writings are celebrated for presenting 'at their purest, the gentleness of the landscapes of France, the reflections of its waters, the lights of its skies'.[62] Patriotic opposition to the Nazis is therefore using many of the same elements as the nationalist opposition: and inevitably the

logic of such an insistent celebration of patriotism produces an
account of an invader who is as foreign as he is oppressive, firmly
anchored in the tradition of national opposition to Germany,
especially in denotations of militarism, uniformity and barbarity.
'Notre Paris', in the same issue and already referred to for its use
of history, bemoans the transformation of Paris with its German
street names.[63] It ironically describes German soldiers singing
their songs of war and love, while their military instructor
screams at them to sing more sweetly. Both these articles demonstrate how far defence of the French territory is also a defence of
an essential Frenchness, here embodied in the evocation of the
Parisian landmarks.[64] This qualitative definition of France,
stressing its moral or spiritual nature in which all true Frenchmen
necessarily partake, means that those who are collaborating with
the enemy can no longer be truly French: their betrayal can be
traced also in a loss of an essential Frenchness which serves to
exclude them from the homogeneous national group. A discussion of Jacques Chardonne in 'Jacques Chardonne et "Mein
Kampf" ' in November 1943 is clearly drawing on these oppositions, though it will be seen that the stress on his earlier 'illogicality' both opens the possibility of his later career and yet also
denies it, precisely by the power of that 'Frenchness':

Before 1940, (...) at least no one excluded him from that special feeling
which the French reserve only for things from home – the delicate
acceptance an animal has for its own smell and none other. An attitude
which was not without its paradoxes, since to tell the truth the author of
Claire displayed none of those qualities which we have come to expect of
our writers since the age of classicism.
　But that is just the point, one has to be very French to be able to discard
with some grace the very things that make one French. Illogical, vague
and confused as he was, Chardonne seemed vaccinated by ten centuries
of French literature against the dangers of confusion, vagueness and
illogicality. Of course, a conversation with *Eva* or *Claire*, a meandering
walk in Barbézieux would leave us only the memory of an evasive,
restrained murmuring. But we did not forget the accent. (...) An accent
which cannot betray us without betraying itself.
　Well, we were wrong, Chardonne no longer finds it difficult to choose
between yours and ours, he looks to himself alone. He has chosen,
gleefully, elsewhere.[65]

The judgement on Michel Simon is much less complex: 'His
talent made M. Michel Simon a naturalised Frenchman; his
baseness now strips him of that moral nationality.'[66] This is the

final sentence of an article criticising Simon for returning to the Paris stage, not to support a young French author, but to take a role in a play by M. Eugen Gerber, 'the German ex-spy in France'. Now, this is not a simple confrontation of French and German in purely national terms, but rather relies on an analysis of the Nazi use of culture, imposing German culture on the French as part of the process of subordination, a German culture which the Nazis have no compunction in distorting to serve their own ends. 'Echec à la propagande culturelle'[67] denounces their control of the media, theatre and cinema, the transformation of the Opéra de Paris into a 'subsidiary of Berlin', the Comédie Française into a 'German company'; rejection of public performance of German culture is therefore necessary at this time as part of the struggle against the Nazis: 'No more celebrations of Germany, of German jubilees. No more commemorations of German masterpieces stolen by the Nazis! Long live the genius of the French!' The theme occurs regularly. The review of *La Marche à l'étoile* in *LF*, no. 13, refers to *Le Silence de la mer* in the same terms: 'Vercors's first book had made us painfully aware of the necessity for and the justice of our hatred , aware that Nazism had rendered love between Germany and us quite impossible.'[68]

In 1944 the *Editions de minuit* publish three texts by Jacques Decour which are reviewed in the March issue of that year. In the second, an article originally published in *Commune* in 1939, the analysis of Nazism as anti-humanist and therefore destructive of German culture, and of France as coterminous with humanism, is articulated with a statement of the specifically German character of national–socialism. The support of millions of Germans for the national–socialist regime, Decour argues, relies on ancient and persistent Germanic values to which Hitlerism has given new life, but which have a long history, having already been used 'to enslave Germany from Arminius to Rosenberg, through 18th century Prussianism, Bismarck and Pangermanism'. Essentially, this coincides with the attitude of the Resistance as a whole which Michel sums up as: 'Nazism and Germany are the same thing.'[69] The reviewer of the Decour volume responds to his final quotation: 'To Pangermanism aimed at the intellect (esprit) we oppose the humanism of France' with the words 'Not a single word of this rigorous analysis needs altering today.' Nazism breaks with the universalist German culture only to renew with a specifically nationalist German culture: the analysis has closed on a purely nationalist opposition. In July 1944 *Les Lettres françaises* publish their most distinct portrayal of the German within the purely nationalist opposition, in 'Les Voyageurs fantastiques' (The fantastic travellers),[70] a story by Elsa Triolet in which three Russians, having escaped from a camp, talk of their experiences, describing German soldiers at length as robots built to destroy, totally closed to any human sentiments because obedience is the basis of the German character.

It is perhaps not surprising that by 1944 the oppressor had a German rather than a fascist face, as Guérin pointed out. But Decour's article was first published in 1939; it is difficult to avoid the judgement that the project to ally the analysis of Nazism to such peculiarly national configurations was a profoundly ambiguous one. On the other hand, careful distinctions were still being drawn in February 1944, in an article entitled 'La Poésie conscience de la France', and the review of the banned German poets appeared in the same issue as 'Les Voyageurs fantastiques'. Two points should be made about this. There are definite overlaps in the national and political discourses – for example both, from their different perspectives, single out the barbarous nature of the enemy (the logic of which in each case will be discussed in more detail later). Together with the defence of the nation inherent in the *Front National* politics, this means that the frequent use of the adjectives 'German' or 'barbarian' in *Les Lettres françaises* in fact partakes of both discourses and serves to blur the distinctions between the two. But the most important point, in view of the analysis of the fiction of the Resistance in the next section, is the fact that these two discourses can coexist in the journal in this way. The particular nature of the Front National politics determines this on one level, as does the fact that individual articles are fairly autonomous in narrative terms, but what is more interesting is that it is *formally* possible for *Les Lettres françaises* to be written across two heterogeneous types of opposition. In the fiction of the Resistance, the demands of narrative logic make this formally impossible.

Denunciations of collaboration

The main target of *Les Lettres françaises* is the literary and cultural expression of the edifice of collaboration, from the Resistance perspective that 'co-operation', as it is officially called, in fact means oppression and exploitation; it thus aims to show that the collaborationist writers are objectively and usually deliberately serving the enemy:

> It is not a case of condemning en masse all the decent French men and women who might have been temporarily deceived by Pétain and the lies of Vichy. But it is a case of punishing the crime of dealing with the enemy.[71]

> MM. Delamain and Boutelleau should remember that in the other war, bad Frenchmen who had done no more than they were arrested and condemned for dealing with the enemy.[72]

The first quotation comes from the editorial saluting Pucheu's execution,[73] the second from the article attacking the publishers of the anthology of German poetry.[74] The similarity of expression clearly indicates that literary collaboration was not treated as incidental or peripheral to the military or economic aspects of the Occupation, but as central.[75] There is no such thing as partial co-operation. French culture, the French intelligentsia are to be integrated into the structures of collaboration, providing an air of normality and acceptance, or promoting the new Europe, to forge a new order united in the anti-Bolshevik crusade. So in a journal which considers that the defence of culture and the commitment of the writers to the Resistance is as important as direct action, it is not surprising to find a sustained attack on collaboration at three levels: institutions, individuals, literature and culture.

It examines the activities and members of literary institutions such as prize juries, especially the Académie Goncourt,[76] and frequently focuses on the collaboration of publishers.[77] *La Scène française* examines the machinations to get Alain Laubreaux (theatre critic of *Je Suis Partout*) appointed manager of the Comédie Française,[78] or the way the *Service du Travail Obligatoire*[79] is operating at the level of the theatres with registration of personnel.[80] *L'Ecran français* often deals with the financing of films and the operations of film companies such as the Continentale or Nova-Film, and discusses the COIC (the *Comité d'Organisation de l'Industrie Cinématographique*)[81] at length.

Over one hundred names appear, denounced either for activities amounting to treason and betrayal, or for foolishly

44 Literature of persuasion

compromising themselves – about seventy appear only once, and
the attacks are concentrated on a small number.[82] There are
fairly lengthy discussions of books promoting the 'new order'[83]
and many articles which can be grouped under a general heading
of 'explanation of the collaborator', concentrating on present
motivation and past history. Drieu la Rochelle is a particular
focus for this, from the veritable chronicle in numbers 4 and 5
under the heading 'La Solitude de Drieu', through 'Drieu la
Rochelle ou la haine de soi' in number 6, to 'Les Faux Calculs de
Drieu' in number 19, but the same is true of Montherlant, Giono,
Rebatet, Laubreaux, and Guitry. There are several constants in
these deliberately polemical analyses: cowardice, generally
applied to Giono and Montherlant, but also to those retreating
from collaboration by 1943/44;[84] the opportunism of the medio-
cre talent, profiting from the more honourable silence of his
betters (Laubreaux and Fernandez are particular targets here);
homosexual fascination with the virile young German victors,
involving a whole rhetoric of 'la femelle' (which, denoting as it
does the female animal of a species, is derogatory if applied to
women, even more so when applied to men).[85] These articles are
backed up by the 'Echos', little anecdotes. In October 1943 for
example, we learn that Brasillach has fallen out with *Je Suis
Partout*, Paul Morand is off to Bucharest to represent the Vichy
government, Ramon Fernandez has resigned from the PPF and
will no longer be seen in his fine uniform.[86]

Finally, battle is engaged in the literary and cultural domain.

Speaking the unspoken

The use of history

Jacques Decour has been killed. This is what we will never forgive the
traitors who intended or allowed this murder to happen, and who are
now, like Brasillach or Drieu, making a great show of their fidelity to
French cultural traditions.[87]

The essential function of the 'historical real' in Resistance
writing is to recall events which are not present in the official
discourse, which are properly unspeakable for they are
necessarily excluded by the insistence on Franco-German co-
operation which orders it. These events serve as indicators of a
reality which is in direct contradiction with the notion of

harmonious co-operation which underpins the collaborationist
position and therefore functions as the truth which reveals not
only the falsity of that position, but also its ideologically
orientated use of culture. Much of the attack on the anthology of
German poetry in 'Au Service de l'ennemi' (In the service of the
enemy) uses this mechanism. Having quoted from the preface's
vision of peace and understanding between the two nations, it
continues with heavy irony: 'So there you are. Goethe and Schiller
will finally manage to make the French understand what the
Gestapo, the firing squads, the tortures, famine and mass deportation have not yet got into their heads.'[88]

There are also examples of what could be called a properly
journalistic use of the 'historical real', using the possibilities of
layout to juxtapose contradictory statements, and thereby
denounce the collaborationist enterprise by revealing its
unspoken basis. The fourth page of the ninth issue in September
1943 is divided into two columns. On the left, under the heading
'L'Etendard sanglant est levé!' (The bloody banner is raised), is an
account of the deportation of one hundred women to Auschwitz.
It mentions several names, among them Mae Politzer, Hélène
Solomon, Yvonne Blech, Marie-Claude Vaillant-Couturier
'whose crime was to be the widow of Paul Vaillant-Couturier' and
Danièle Casanova 'whose error was to have been, for 20,000
French girls, a friend, an example and source of hope'. The rest
of the article describes the filthy conditions, lack of food, harsh
treatment, and high mortality rate in Auschwitz. It ends: 'Of the
one hundred women who were deported from Romainville last
January, ten at least have died because they loved France and
freedom.' The right-hand column is an extract from an article on
Parisian society. There is no heading. At the bottom is the
reference: Jacques de Ricaumont, *Panorama* du 22.7.43.

Thanks to a group of society ladies (*maîtresses de maison*) who bear the
names (among others) of the Marquise de Polignac, the Viscountess
Curial, Mme Crisso Veloni, the Duchess de Clermont Tonnerre, and
Mlle Le Chevrel, the French proved that they did not consider the defeat
excused them from practising, with the same care and brilliance as in the
past, the virtues of society life, which are the most personal and therefore
the most precious of the national values which they like to think they
were fighting to defend, and which they defended so badly.

It goes on to discuss the political orientation of these salons, and especially that of the marquise de Polignac, whose husband displayed the generosity typical of eminent patriots, 'in promptly bringing the prestige of his name to the policy of reconciliation'. Every Sunday there gathered the principal architects of Franco-German understanding, politicians, industrialists and scientists of the two countries. It ends with the judgement it says the 'social historian' would pronounce: 'Parisian society, which is so quick, through coquetterie, masochism or simple humility, to denigrate itself, can be confident that he will pay homage to the dignity and the elegance with which it wore the mourning of France.'

Richness and privilege is thus opposed to the squalor of Auschwitz, and the destinies of the women in the Resistance or suspect to the Germans contrasted to the life of women prepared to collaborate; the structure which underpins the elegant salons is shown to be one of violence and oppression; the story of the defenders of French values who are facing death shows the defenders of national values in the salons to be perpetuating French subservience, and places that article in a context which makes it inevitably appear as part of an ideological apparatus which talks of France and French values the better to conceal the dominance and brutality of Hitler's Germany. The 'historical real', the textual function which founds an appeal to what is really happening, is the pivot around which the true/false distinction can be introduced.

Contextualisation
The other major element in the literary and cultural criticism in *Les Lettres françaises* is 'contextualisation', by which I mean the process of inserting a work into a different, non-literary context, that of the major opposition between the Resistance and the enemy, leading to an interrogation of its values or literary vision in relation to Nazi and collaborationist ideology. This process operates on the basis of the refusal of the autonomy or neutrality of literature.

Many articles set out to save an author from collaborationist interpretations. 'Haro sur Maupassant'[89] attacks Morand's *Vie de Maupassant*. 'Psichari par Daniel-Rops'[90] combats what it sees as Daniel-Rops's unjustified extrapolation from Psichari's work. It quotes him as saying that, although the stage of great conflicts is passed, Psichari's qualities are still useful in these times of 'anxious peace'. *Les Lettres françaises* attacks this as a quite cynical admission that the greatness of France can only be discussed in the past tense : 'Forget the firing squads and the looting. Forget our national humiliations. We must no longer talk about them. Abandon the fight.' André Salmon is attacked for trying to turn Apollinaire's 'esprit nouveau' and cosmopolitanism into 'the spirit of Europe 1943'.[91]

A convergence is established between the favourable attitude towards collaboration of certain writers and their literary vision which stresses various permutations of anarchism, decadence, pessimism and absurdity. To place the accent on despair and a scorn for man is shown not only to dovetail neatly with the anti-humanist stance of the Nazis, but also to carry the political message that resistance is futile. Montherlant, Giono, Anouilh and Aymé are the specific targets of this analysis. The themes of ennui and decadence occur frequently in the articles on Drieu la Rochelle. In contrast, Elsa Triolet's novel, *Le Cheval blanc*,[92] whose main character Michel dies bravely during the fighting of summer 1940, is praised, in terms which deliberately recall Drieu's works, for taking a hero from 'an almost cruel indifference', from 'a total lack of awareness of a reality he is incapable of discovering', and from the kind of attitudes which lead to suicide, to a cause worth dying for.[93]

Other favourable reviews of published works such as *Les Mouches* or *Pilote de guerre*, like the reviews of the clandestine publications, stress the notions that resistance to tyranny is possible, that freedom is all important. The review of Marcel Aymé's *Vogue la galère* is notable for the distinction it draws between Aymé on the one hand, and Brasillach and Châteaubriant on the other, arguing that the first has been foolish, but that the other two are criminals. The pessimism of the play is singled out for comment after a brief summary of the plot: slaves revolt and free themselves, but indulge in such excesses that they need to be brought back to order and discipline by being enslaved once more. Here is at first sight a fascist play, but, it continues, that it is not the point. The point is that the play has been saluted in the press as the first to be inspired by the principles of National–Socialism and that they have the same basis: 'scorn for Man'. This is contrasted with the difficult conditions, the personal tragedies faced by those in the Resistance, and the optimism of its writing where the accent is on courage, solidarity, freedom and confidence in man.[94]

It can be seen that the two types of writing, official and unofficial, are opposed at every level (content, values, tradition). The lesson from this process of 'contextualisation' is clear. In the words of *La Scène française* which summarise the position perfectly: 'Neither the author, nor the director nor the actor has the right to place his art in the enemy's service.'[95] As well as clearly stating the terms of the opposition (for or against the enemy: 'au service de l'ennemi' is a phrase which runs throughout the journal), this quotation is also symptomatic of the correlation, already noted in the discussion of Montherlant, Giono and the rest, between the artist and his art, his political sympathies and the values in the work. It would be misleading to see this as nothing more than the naive identification known as the intentional fallacy. That is certainly there, but is rather an inevitable corollary than the basis of the analysis. *Les Lettres françaises* is not seeking to found a theory of literature or of political culture,[96] but to engage in the Resistance and spread the Resistance message. This is why the author or the director is always directly referred to in these articles: the writers of the Resistance and the collaborators have this much in common in the pages of *Les Lettres françaises*; they are *responsible* for their work, and necessarily so. At the heart of a rhetoric of persuasion must be the possibility of choice.

The defence of culture

So this is polemical writing which places the Resistance struggle at the centre of its literary analysis and practice, using mechanisms such as the invocation of history which brings the war as *event* into play, and 'contextualisation', which interrogates literature in relation to the wider struggle between the Resistance and the enemy. No cultural manifestation discussed in its pages can avoid being placed in that opposition, for, as we have seen, appeals to purely literary values are denounced as collaborationist attempts to provide a false air of normality or to cover the tracks of the fainthearted as Germany's power wanes. The choice of subject and the values promoted are therefore all important in determining the judgement of any individual work; the criteria of that judgement, the factors which mediate the opposition between the Resistance and the enemy in the cultural sphere, can be grouped under two main terms, France and man.

The film criticism in *L'Ecran français* tends to concentrate upon 'the defence of France'. A negative image of France will promote 'Hitler's view of France as a worn-out country, a republic of bandits',[97] and several films are criticised for doing just this. A major article, 'Le "Corbeau" est déplumé'(The 'crow' is plucked)[98] opposes Clouzot's *Le Corbeau*, full of characters who are 'mutilated', 'amoral', 'corrupt', and Grémillon's *Le Ciel est à vous* (The sky is yours), with 'characters full of French vigour, of authentic courage and moral well-being'. The reasons for denouncing a negative view of the French are serious ones, but the precise manner in which the two films are contrasted tends to make one wish the critics (identified as George Adam and Pierre Blanchar) could have tempered their enthusiasm for *Le Ciel est à vous*, especially in the light of another article in the same issue describing Vichy's 'propaganda of virtue' producing unpopular films full of a sickly moralism.[99] They damn Clouzot for his morally and physically deformed characters, praise Grémillon for his portrait of a young mother of France who is 'modest and strong'. 'For the anonymous letters and their hideous effects in *Le Corbeau*, *Le Ciel est à vous* substitutes airplanes performing arabesques of glory in the sky; for the stench of Freudianism it substitutes simple hearts full of burning enthusiasm; it replaces Clouzot's manure with the azure.'[100] This rather exaggerated language shows us how unequivocally the presence of France functions as edification, as we meet once more the qualititative definition of the true France: 'true Frenchmen, who in France greatly outnumber the Huns true or false, recognise in this film their blood and their truth, and applaud with their tears'.

On one side of the opposition lie *France, we Frenchmen, truth, courage* and *dignity*; on the other *the enemy* and *Vichy*. The literary articles, it will be remembered, group the notions of courage, solidarity and freedom around the 'defence of man'. To place France and man, the twin pillars of the defence of culture, at the centre of its polemic, produces a clear-cut moral opposition which reproduces exactly the political oppositions. I would argue that the central position of the defence of culture to *Les Lettres françaises* is the essential factor in a structure which articulates the opposition of the Resistance and a heterogeneous enemy.

As has been seen, the enemy has several faces here: fascist, collaborationist and German. But there is no similar fragmentation, at any level, of the Resistance, no hint of the internal difficulties and quarrels which can surface in other clandestine publications.[101] The Resistance is the unequivocally positive pole of the polemic whose political, moral and literary values concord absolutely, precisely because they are all subsumed under the major terms common to them all. The inseparable nature of patriotism and anti-fascism, both historically and in the politics of the *Front national*, allies the defence of France from the fascist invader to the defence of France, embodiment of humanism, from the fascist assaults on man. Therefore this writing can permit a multiple enemy precisely because the fascist, the collaborator and the German *also* concord in their opposition to France and to man. The nature of this overall structure is such as to allow many variations at the level of individual articles – for example the alliance of German and French culture under the umbrella of universalism and humanism in opposition to fascist barbarity. But as a body of writing, like the fiction of the Resistance, *Les Lettres françaises* relies on a structure of unity which clearly differentiates between the terms of its oppositions, between the Resistance and the enemy.

Notes

1 See especially Claude Morgan, *La Vie cachée des Lettres françaises*, *LF*, nos. 21–3, 16.9.44, p. 8, 23.9.44, p. 8, 30.9.44, p. 8. A brief résumé of its history is given in front of some of the numbers of the post-war facsimile edition.

2 Decour, Paulhan, Debû-Bridel, Vildrac, Guéhenno, Blanzat, le R.P. Maydieu.

3 See Stéphane Courtois, *Le PCF dans la guerre*, Paris, 1980, pp. 240–1.

4 Azéma, *De Munich à la Libération*, p. 261.

5 H. Michel et B. Mirkine-Guetzévitch, *Les Idées politiques et sociales de la Résistance*, Paris, 1954, p. 8. As the authors point out (p. 10), such figures are a very unreliable guide to readership, given the difficulties of production and distribution, and the number that were passed from hand to hand.

6 Jacques Debû-Bridel, *La Résistance intellectuelle*, Paris, 1970, p. 59.

7 Reproduced in Courtois, *Le PCF dans la guerre*, pp. 554–65.

8 Courtois, pp. 185–202.

9 From April 1942 *L'Humanité* carries communiqués of their activities under the heading 'L'Action des patriotes', or 'L'Action contre les Boches', Courtois, p. 252.

10 'Discours prononcé à la radio de Londres', 23 octobre 1941 in *Discours et messages pendant la guerre juin 1940–janvier 1946*, Paris, 1970, pp. 122–3.

11 Courtois, pp. 233–4; after the spring of 1942, when several Resistance leaders were starting to visit London, de Gaulle changed his mind on this matter. To have the support of a strong internal Resistance movement also strengthened his position *vis-à-vis* the Allies, especially the Americans. See Touchard, *Le Gaullisme 1940–1969*, Paris, 1978, pp. 60–2 for a brief résumé of the evolution of de Gaulle's attitude to the *Résistance intérieure*, and H. Michel, *Les Courants de pensée de la Résistance*, Paris, 1962, p. 61.

12 Courtois, p. 237.

13 'Pour la formation d'un Front National', Courtois, p. 558.

14 'Manifeste du CNE', *LF*, no. 1, septembre 1942, p. 1.

15 'Pour la formation d'un Front National', Courtois, p. 558.

16 *Ibid.*, p. 564.

17 'Manifeste du CNE'. However, as Courtois points out, these appeals are to individuals, not to movements or parties.

18 'Manifeste du CNE'.

19 These tend to disappear in favour of anecdotes about literary collaborators, the *NRF*, Goncourt panel and prizes, and can probably be attributed as much as anything to the early difficulties of getting into its stride as a literary and cultural journal.

20 'Défense de l'intelligence', no. 13, février 1944; and even here it is aiming at producing a call to join the armed struggle, form *milices*.

21 Which was the PCF slogan in 1942. See Courtois, *op.cit.*, pp. 249–51.

22 Courtois, p. 334, 375. After the war, Jacques Debû-Bridel refers to him as 'une sorte de Lazare Carnot de la Résistance'. For Mauriac, he was ' "mon" communiste', Jacques Debû-Bridel, *La Résistance intellectuelle*, p. 99.

23 'L'Union pour la victoire', *LF*, no. 5, janvier–février 1943.

24 'Discipline de la Résistance', *LF*, no. 10, octobre 1943, p. 13.

25 Reproduced Courtois, *op.cit.*, pp. 568–9.

26 *Ibid.*, p. 323.

27 'La structure essentielle de cette levée en masse, ce sont les milices patriotiques.' For a discussion of the formation of these groups, see Courtois, pp. 434–5.

28 *Les Courants de pensée de la Résistance*, p. 210.

29 'Pour la formation du Front National', Courtois, p. 557.

30 André Tollet, *La Classe ouvrière dans la Résistance*, Paris, 1969, p. 126. See also Gaucheron, *La Poésie, la Résistance*, Paris, 1979, p. 185.

31 *LF*, no. 9, septembre 1943, p. 1.

32 'La Poésie conscience de la France', *LF*, no. 13, février 1944, p. 3.

33 Jacques Debû-Bridel, *La Résistance intellectuelle*, pp. 260–1.

34 'Au Service de l'ennemi', *LF*, no. 13, février 1944, pp. 1–2.

35 'Réponse à un défi', *LF*, no. 19, juillet 1944, p. 7. Review of *Les Bannis*, Editions de minuit, 1944. Préface by Mauges (pseudonym of

Claude Bellanger), trans. by Armor (pseudonym of René Cannac). See Seghers, *La Résistance et ses poètes*, pp. 343–4.
36 'Adieu à Jacques Decour', *LF*, no. 1, septembre 1942, p. 3.
37 *LF*, no. 4, décembre 1942, p. 5. Reproduced in Seghers, *La Résistance et ses poètes*, Paris, 1974, pp. 342–3.
38 And incomplete, as Guéhenno is not identified, probably because it was joint work.
39 Jacques Debû-Bridel, *La Résistance intellectuelle*, p. 29.
40 *Ibid.*, p. 59.
41 *Ibid.*, p. 65.
42 Printed in the pamphlet, *Ceux qui ont choisi*, brochure éditée par l'AEAR, 1934.
43 André Gide, opening address, *Ceux qui ont choisi*, p. 7.
44 Francis Jourdain, *ibid.*, p. 13. See especially the contributions of A.P. Antoine, pp. 9–10; Docteur Jean Dalsace, pp. 11–12; Ozenfant, pp. 15–16; Wallon, pp. 16–17; 'un écrivain allemand', pp. 18–19. See also Vaillant-Couturier, 'Au Service de l'esprit (rapport présenté au Comité central du Parti Communiste Français le 16 octobre 1935 et approuvé à l'unanimité)' in *Vers les lendemains qui chantent*, Paris, 1962, where the twin themes of 'unité humaine' and internationalism explicitly embrace the German people in the name of peace. Especially pp. 256–7, 260.
45 Paris, 1965. This edition comprises articles written in the 1950s, an account of his first journey to Germany, 'Avant la catastrophe', based on articles published at the time, the preface to the 1945 edition and the articles published in 1933, gathered under the title 'Après la catastrophe'.
46 Azéma et Winock, *La Troisième République*, Paris, 1978, p. 274, and Dubief, *Le Déclin de la troisième République*, Paris, 1976.
47 Léon Blum, 'Ils sont morts pour la République', *Le Populaire*, 24 mai 1936. Quoted in Bodin et Touchard, *Le Front populaire*, Paris, 1961, pp. 102–4.
48 Dubief, p.169.
49 Given on Radio Paris, 17 April 1936. Quoted in Bodin et Touchard, pp. 52–3.
50 'Au Service de l'esprit', p. 274.
51 'Pour la formation d'un Front National', Courtois, *Le PCF dans la guerre*, p. 562. Cf. 'Nous allons, la main tendue, à tous les hommes de bonne volonté', 'Au Service de l'esprit', p. 276.
52 'Pour la formation d'un Front National', Courtois, p. 562.
53 'S'unir, s'armer, se battre', Courtois, p. 569.
54 *Les Courants de pensée de la Résistance*, p. 600.
55 *LF*, no. 1, septembre 1942, p. 3.
56 *LF*, no. 2, october 1942, pp. 5–6.
57 *Les Courants de pensée de la Résistance*, pp. 601–3.
58 *Ibid.*, pp. 796–7.
59 Many issues carry at the top of the front page: Fondateur Jacques Decour. Fusillé par les Allemands le samedi 30 mai 1942.
60 'Une Seule France', *LF*, no. 11, novembre 1943, p. 1.

61 'C'est vous qui êtes la loi', *LF*, no. 14, mars 1944, p. 1.

62 'Haro sur Maupassant', *LF*, no. 2, octobre 1942, p. 3.

63 'Notre Paris', *LF*, no. 2, octobre 1942, p. 5.

64 In virtually every issue of *La France libre* is a full-page photograph of either a well known monument or a village scene, which fulfils the same function for the exiles in London.

65 'Jacques Chardonne et "Mein Kampf" ', *LF*, no. 11, novembre 1943, p. 2.

66 'A la solde des Nazis' (In the pay of the Nazis), *LF*, no. 17, mai 1944, p. 5 (Simon was Swiss).

67 *LF*, no. 14, mars 1944, p. 5.

68 'La Marche à l'étoile', *LF*, no. 13, février 1944, p. 4.

69 *Les Courants de pensée de la Résistance*, p. 209.

70 *LF*, no. 18, juillet 1944, pp. 1, 4.

71 'Justice de la France', *LF*, no. 15, avril 1944, p. 2.

72 'Au Service de l'ennemi', *LF*, no. 13, février 1944, p. 2.

73 Vichy's Minister of the Interior who defected to Algiers. There were many appeals for his execution from the Resistance, for having chosen hostages to be shot, for allegedly being present at the torturing of Decour.

74 Published in 1942. The work of René Lasne and Georg Rabuse, preface by Karl Epting, director of the Institut Allemand. Discussed in Ory, *La France allemande*, Paris, 1977, pp. 92–3.

75 The Germans shared the same view and placed great importance on the control of the media and the attempt to foster an atmosphere of cultural normality favourable to the new European order and to Germany. See Ory, *Les collaborateurs*; Dioudonnat, *L'Argent nazi à la conquête de la presse française 1940–1944*; Gérard Loiseaux, *Littérature de la défaite et la collaboration*, Paris, 1984.

76 'L'Académic Goncourt et les agents de l'ennemi', *LF*, no. 5, janvier–février 1943, p. 3; 'Quelques-uns des Goncourt', *LF*, no. 12, décembre 1943, p. 2.

77 'Avertissement aux éditeurs', official statement from the CNE to the CNR, *LF*, no. 11, novembre 1943, p. 3; 'Les Ecrivains et les éditeurs', *LF*, no. 16, mai 1944, p. 2, reproduced from *Les Etoiles*, as was the preamble, from the French publishers, to the *liste Otto*.

78 'La Comédie Française à l'honneur', *LF*, no. 16, mai 1944, p. 3.

79 In June 1942, Laval launched *La Relève*, the system whereby for every three skilled workers leaving for Germany, one prisoner of war would return. Unsuccessful in recruiting the numbers necessary, it was replaced by the *Service du Travail Obligatoire* (STO).

80 'Gare à la déportation', *LF*, no. 14, mars 1944, p. 6.

81 Bertin-Maghit, *Le Cinéma français sous Vichy*, Paris, 1980, gives a useful résumé of German and French institutions of control of cinema, pp. 16–18, 139–41.

82 Bonnard, Brasillach, Céline, Chardonne, Châteaubriant, Drieu la Rochelle, Fernandez, Giono, Laubreaux, Montherlant, Rebatet, Salmon, Thérive.

83   Cf. 'Jacques Chardonne et "Mein Kampf" ', *LF*, no. 11, novembre 1943, p. 2.

84   This is in part a response to the splitting in the collaborationist ranks discussed by Ory in *Les Collaborateurs*, pp. 124–7. 'La Grande Colère de M. Cousteau', *LF*, no. 14, mars 1944, p. 2, signals the differences between Brasillach and Cousteau, deals with Cousteau's insistence on 'les durs', those not changing their beliefs with the reverse in the German Army's fortunes.

85   'Jacques Chardonne et "Mein Kampf" ', *LF*, no. 11, novembre 1943, p. 2.

86   *LF*, no. 10, octobre 1943, p. 3.

87   'Pages choisies de Jacques Decour', *LF*, no. 14, mars 1944, p. 8.

88   'Au Service de l'ennemi', *LF*, no. 13, février 1944, p. 2.

89   *LF*, no. 2, octobre 1942, p. 3.

90   *LF*, no. 3, novembre 1942, p. 5.

91   'Apollinaire citoyen de Paris', *LF*, no. 6, avril 1943, p. 6.

92   Elsa Triolet, *Le Cheval blanc*, Paris, 1943.

93   *LF*, no. 11, novembre 1943, p. 4.

94   'L'Espoir fait homme', *LF*, no. 18, juillet 1944, p. 2.

95   'Echec à la propagande culturelle', *LF*, no. 14, mars 1944, p. 5.

96   Even Sartre's articles, which are discussing questions of the nature and conditions of literature ('La littérature cette liberté', 'Drieu la Rochelle ou la haine de soi', 'L'Espoir fait homme') or film ('Un film pour l'après-guerre') are predominantly polemical rather than analytical in this context.

97   'Die Französische Jugend', *LF*, no. 14, mars 1944, p. 4.

98   *LF*, no. 14, mars 1944, pp. 3–4. Clouzot is vigorously defended after the war by François Truffaut in his preface to André Bazin, *Le Cinéma de l'Occupation et de la Résistance*, Paris, 10/18, 1975.

99   'Petits films', *LF*, no. 14, mars 1944, p. 3.

100   'Le "Corbeau" est déplumé', *LF*, no. 14, mars 1944, p. 3.

101   Cf 'Etre forts', in Indomitus (pseudonym of Philippe Viannay), *Nous sommes les rebelles*, Paris, 1945, pp. 31–2.

Part Two
Novels of unity

Introduction

It has been essential to establish the key role played by the discourses of anti-fascism and nationalism in articulating the defence of France and culture, in order to situate Resistance fiction in terms of *témoignage*, that is to say, to elucidate the knowledge which it seeks to present as truth. But however close ideologically it may be to the positions and analyses expressed in *Les Lettres françaises* and other Resistance journals, concentrating on thematic considerations alone means that the specific devices and structures whereby a fictional representation of reality is created tend to be neglected. Furthermore, abstracting themes and key statements from narratives without paying attention both to the oppositions which sustain them and to the overall development in which they are inscribed can lead to the *value* of a particular theme in the narrative economy being overlooked. This is of course equally true of non-fictional discourse; while the Resistance is attacking the collaborationist theme of decadence, the collaborators themselves, for very different reasons and to very different ends, are also attacking the same thing, and in the case of Drieu la Rochelle, the Resistance as its supreme expression. Similarly the themes of betrayal, cowardice and weakness, to be found across the political spectrum in relation to the defeat of France, are serving very different functions in, say, Ilya Ehrenbourg's *The Fall of Paris* and Montherlant's *Solstice de juin*.

Much of the following analysis is therefore devoted to detailed consideration of individual narratives in order to establish the structure of unity governing Resistance fiction, and the pertinent features which distinguish it from both the non-fictional Resistance writing and the post-war fiction.

Chapter one

The figure of the enemy

In *L'Allemagne vue par les écrivains de la Résistance*, Konrad Bieber writes: 'The figure of the German soldier, while never forgotten, is not a constant presence in these tales.'[1] This is perfectly true and can be attributed quite simply to the fact that the enemy is rarely the subject of the text but is usually serving a particular *function*, which changes according to the narrative order in which it is inscribed. In the chapter on the figure of the individual, we shall see that the function is to clarify the conflicts of the narrative, often in a moment of identification and recognition, so that they can be concentrated on the opposition between the Resistance and the enemy. This chapter will concentrate specifically on those narratives whose subject is the *process* of identification of the enemy, and demonstrate that the figure of the enemy has a structural position as the negative 'other' opposed to the Resistance.

To talk about the figure of the enemy is to talk about very complex structures. Relations between the French and the Germans were not born with the Second World War, but partake of a long history. Secondly, those relations cannot be discussed effectively without reference to questions of narrative order. And thirdly, the figure of the enemy is not necessarily German – the presence of the foreign invader is a constant, but can be subsumed under the internal enemy represented by Vichy. These three questions form the basis of the present chapter.

From Mme de Staël's *De l'Allemagne* to the Franco–Prussian war of 1870, French views of Germany could be said to be positive in the cultural and political fields, and rather mixed towards German

psychology. These were the times of the admiration of German
Romanticism, science and music which were accompanied by a
view of the German people as rather ponderous and submissive,
lacking individuality and initiative on the negative side, and
passionate, idealistic and naive on the positive side.[2] Prussian
nationalism had provoked some anxiety in the 1840s,[3] but it was
1870, the Franco–Prussian war, which was the major historical
turning point, with the introduction of the notion of *les deux
Allemagnes* (the two Germanys), that is to say, Goethe and culture
contrasted to Bismarck and Prussian militarism. In spite of the
contacts between individual soldiers during the First World War
and the strength of pacifist ideas which followed it, the First
World War did not effect any major reappraisal.

Until the advent of Nazi Germany, therefore, there are two
major strands to the image of Germany in French literature.
Firstly, Germany is a barbaric monster created by the Germanic
hordes of the past, the irrational, demonic soul as exemplified by
Romanticism and especially Wagner, and the brutal military
machine which subjugates all to it. This is the dangerous neighbour, *l'ennemi héréditaire* (hereditary enemy), *l'Allemagne éternelle*.
But the tradition of the 'two Germanys' creates a distinction
whereby the true Germany of culture is crushed by Prussian
militarism. It is rare to find a precise distinction between the two –
partly because both rely on a belief in national identity and
psychology, and therefore cultural distinctions within Germany
go hand in hand with the recognition of a specifically German
psychology, and partly because the other term of the opposition,
France, tends to be culturally and psychologically homogeneous.

Gide's 'Réflexions sur l'Allemagne', published in 1919, is a
good example of this: 'The best of German thought is rising up
against Prussia which is leading Germany into battle.'[4] He is
arguing against the attitude which rejects all things German just
because they are German since, in his opinion, Goethe, Nietzsche
and Wagner are culturally on the side of France and therefore
against the militarism of Prussia; to dismiss all things German is in
fact for Gide to reinforce its unity. He seeks rather to break
Germany down into units so that it can defend itself against its
Prussian element which he describes as a 'poisonous virus'.[5]
When he talks of the German character, however, there is no such
distinction made; the impossibility for 'an individual of their race'

to detach himself from the mass, to 'individualise himself', is an unqualified judgement.[6] The same is true of Romain Rolland's novel *Jean-Christophe* whose hero is a musician who leaves Germany, exasperated both with its militarism and the sentimentality of its music. He turns to France, 'ever a refuge for Germany when it loses its bearings',[7] but even so remains psychologically marked by the German character, which is a source of frequent misunderstandings between him and his French friend Olivier. Olivier is at one point described as a mixture of faith, liberty, passion, irony and universal doubt, a mixture which bemuses Christophe who in turn makes Olivier smile because his lively intellect is also clumsy, ponderous and unsubtle. Other qualities singled out for comment include his lack of psychology, his sentimentality and cult of force, 'that German faith in the moral excellence of the fist'.[8]

As can already be seen from the above, these portraits of the German do not exist in isolation. J.-M. Carré writes that 'our intellectuals and writers have rarely judged Germany in itself, but nearly always in relation to ideas being argued here. They have judged it through the prism of their own beliefs.'[9] For him this is a defect; it is also the statement of inescapable fact, that the 'German' is inscribed within an oppositional structure where the 'French' is the other term. To take just twentieth-century fiction – the major examples of novels examining the German character are set either in France or Germany or both, bringing a German character to France or a French character to Germany.[10] The structures of the Occupation novel, opposing French and German within France, are not renewing formally what is essentially the primary narrative mechanism of this opposition. Nor do they renew the terms which mark the differences and mediate the opposition. These fall broadly into two main categories, establishing either an irremediable antagonism or a complementary union. All these novels are dominated by metaphors of love between the countries (an alliance of France's grace and Germany's strength) and are often asking the question 'can France and Germany be friends instead of enemies?' That is to say, they are constructed on the basis of a tension between the two options which gives the narrative its impetus, especially as it is frequently split across two sets of narrative figures: the nations and the characters.[11] In the fiction of the Occupation also, individual

narrative figures mediate the attraction and hostility which structure the opposition.

The rise of fascism in Germany continues the distinction
between a cultural and a military Germany. On the one hand it is
the latest example of *l'Allemagne éternelle*, on the other hand it is
specifically Hitler's Germany, an anti-cultural force, a return of
the barbarian monster. Romain Rolland writes to the *Kölnische
Zeitung*: 'How can you fail to see that this "national-fascist Germany" is the worst enemy of the true Germany, that it denies it?'[12]
This political opposition can also see Nazism as accentuating
features of the German character. André Chamson's novel *L'Année des vaincus* (The year of the defeated), published in 1934,
presents Nazism as primarily a nationalist force. This is a story of
a group of French and German workers – the Germans have
come to work in France – three of whom, Carrière, Karl and
Ludwig, travel to Germany to collect some machine parts. It is
1933, and Carrière's first encounter with the vast demonstrations
of support for Hitler. As someone who has fought in the First
World War he is torn between the hostile dismissal of 'they are still
the same', and the realisation that this is something new: 'Even at
the front I had never seen them like that. Then at least we shared
something – our misery. Now they're singing like savages.
They're happy to be lined up in rows, marching, dressed alike.
Everything I loathe... And I thought they were like me.'[13] Karl
accepts this new force, believing it will lead to a 'Republic of work',
but nonetheless explains it to Carrière in national terms: 'Listen,
there are some things you can't understand... (...) because you
aren't German.'[14] Ludwig disappears, presumably arrested since
he has a history of opposition to Nazism. For Carrière, the specifically nationalist aspects of Nazism are destroying the basis, both
humanist and political, of internationalism. There are no more
workers in your country, he tells Karl, there are only Germans.
All true men must be with Ludwig.[15] And the destructive nature
of the Nazi movement is denying all value to men as individuals.[16]

In spite of the insistence in this novel that the Nazi movement is
something new, and its serious attempt to refuse explanations
which rely on statements such as 'they are still the same', there is
no possibility of avoiding the specifically national element in
Nazism when the terms of the debate are those of the opposition
essential to humanism between the particular and the general.

Humanism posits a common universal humanity in which each unique individual partakes, and respect for the individual is a recognition of the value of this human quality. To criticise Nazism in humanist terms is therefore to present it as a negative image which rejects the notions of the individual in the name of the collective outside which the individual has no worth, and rejects the universal in the name of the national. As we have seen, these are also elements in the traditional images of Germany. The humanist denunciation, an integral part of political opposition to fascism from the thirties on, tends therefore to continue the dichotomy of 'the two Germanys' even when it is insisting on a specifically dated rather than the general national opposition.[17]

Nazism does however introduce a new distinction within the military tradition. Nazi soldiers can be presented as brutal monsters in contradistinction to soldiers of the old Prussian, and often aristocratic school, who have a sense of military honour and codes of behaviour. The German commander von Rauffenstein in Renoir's *La Grande Illusion* of 1936 is a classic example.

Under the Occupation, the Resistance writings about the German continue the complex articulation of the Prussian, the Hitlerian and the Germanic. The combination of the inhuman nature of Nazism and the reign of terror in France tends to produce two kinds of responses. Either the notion of inhumanity and evil predominates, in which case the distinction between the German culture and Nazism, between the German people and Nazism can be maintained. But it should be noted that the German soldiers, by perpetuating this evil, are marked by it; they are no longer human, but symptoms of an inhuman force which must be eliminated, as in the derailment and ambush which concludes *F.T.P.*: 'Then, quite calmly, the six men opened fire. With no more hatred than a surgeon would feel.'[18] Alternatively, the twin strands of evil and nationality can become completely confused, as is the case with 'Propos sur la haine' (Thoughts on hatred), which appeared under the pseudonym of La Valentine in the clandestine *Nouvelles Chroniques*,[19] where Audisio argues that there is no difference at all between the Nazi (leadership) and the German (people), that they must all suffer in their turn the sufferings that have been inflicted in their names and with their connivance. In the appendix to that chapter reprinted in *Feuilles de Fresnes*, dated 23 septembre 1944, he quotes in French a passage from *The Second Faust*, in order to comment that it reads like a report to the Gestapo or the SS, and quotes from the German in order to draw attention to the 'Germanic brutality of its rhythm' and its rhymes 'marching in step two by two with a little sound of boots',[20] concluding that if Goethe, who epitomises the German genius, understands violence so well, that says something about the unchanging nature of the German people. It is this interchangeability of Nazism and Germany in all its aspects which is the mark of the modern version of *l'Allemagne éternelle*.

References to the traditional attributes of the German character are commonplace throughout Resistance writing, and often take the form of short ironic comments such as praising M. Epting for handling euphemism with 'a truly Teutonic lightness of touch'.[21]

The military confrontation between the French and the Germans is not the only factor in understanding the context of Resistance writing; the other vital element is the collaborationist writing on peace and reconciliation, for collaborators are obliged to write *against* the weighty tradition of the German as enemy as much as the Resistance writes against collaboration, and they do so by presenting it as a *possibility* in the discourse in order to actively eliminate it.

Les Décombres by Lucien Rebatet is as much a hymn to Germany as a burial service for the old France. Germany has proved herself to be 'Europe's backbone, the sole healthy and resistant nation in a sick continent'.[22] France's destiny therefore lies in the greatest possible understanding with Germany, calming down the long quarrel between the two nations.[23] This can be achieved after Germany's victory in what is virtually a crusade. Rebatet insists on the necessity for France of collaborating with Germany in the just war she is waging: 'I have had perhaps my most profound feelings of patriotic joy (...) on realising after the armistice that this road was being opened to us. I hope for Germany's victory because the war she is waging is *my* war, *our* war.'[24] However, the strength of the discourse constituting Germany as the traditional enemy of France means that differences must be marked and suspicions of servile subservience or naivety explicitly set aside. Rebatet notes the foreignness of some German attitudes, their faults such as a rigid compartmentalisation, and states that his admiration makes him neither a 'Germaniser' nor a

Germanophile.[25] He also recalls his years at *Action française* where anti-German feelings went without saying, in order to be able to voice certain suspicions about Germany's intentions.[26] But all this can be overcome because the project is to build a grandiose peace, commensurate with the vision of its architect Hitler, who is a man of peace, a great warrior, a man of immense genius.[27] Therefore France's destiny is to be the *compagnon d'armes* in this adventure, equal with Germany behind Hitler, 'as long as it remains a sovereign nation'.[28] In other words, the whole rhetoric is constructed in such a way as to present any objections, and specifically anti-German sentiments, as condemning France to subservience:

Antigermanism in our country has been a product, not of the national spirit, but of a political system chosen by a troop of theoreticians, soldiers, businessmen and Government ministers. This antigermanic system has caused us to make a mess of one victory and lose two wars. Enough, it seems to me, to condemn it without remorse.

If German clearsightedness, and the French desire to put an end to an interminable quarrel, could only come together at last, it will be one of the great events in the history of this planet. Such prospects, such a possibility for us to take up our place once more among the great nations of the world, deserve better than a weary satisfaction, or a moderate, tepid response. They are destined to inspire in the French, at last able to think about their country, the enthusiasm others once used to envy.[29]

National and political perspectives: *Le Silence de la mer* and *Le Tilleul*

Le Silence de la mer[30] is probably the single most famous Resistance story, a curious destiny for a novel which Sartre considered would quickly lose its relevance. In fact Sartre was right, the precise circumstances in which it was written, the policy of collaboration, the meeting of Hitler and Pétain at Montoire, before the developments leading to increasing repression,[31] all this has been virtually forgotten, and it is read above all as a paradigm of what Resistance was.

Much of the discussion of this story has focused on questions of verisimilitude. For Arthur Koestler,[32] the silence of the old man and his niece, and the character of von Ebrennac, the German officer and composer, was 'phoney', and the refusal on the part of the two French people to speak to this anti-Nazi because he was German revealed politically reactionary attitudes or worse:

Koestler speculated that 'Vercors' might turn out to be a collaborator. Sartre discusses *Le Silence de la mer* in *Qu'est-ce que la littérature?*, in the context of the theoretical question of a readership, as an example of the shared knowledge of author and audience. He agrees with Koestler that psychologically von Ebrennac and the silence of the French is false, but disagrees with his judgement. There was no point, in Sartre's opinion, in portraying the German as a vicious brute, as the politics of collaboration at that particular time meant that such a portrait would have been meaningless: Koestler's ignorance of the realities of the Occupation prevented him from understanding the story. He represented the wrong audience, not the one Vercors was trying to reach. Sartre rejects the notion of truthfulness in favour of notions of context and efficacy: 'A work which had depicted German soldiers as ogres would have made people laugh and failed in its aims.'[33] Which only goes to show how vexed a question verisimilitude can be, since a portrait which is not ridiculous, but on the contrary believable and persuasive, cannot be 'untrue' either. Von Ebrennac is a coherently developed and psychologically credible figure because this narrative is structurally defined, and structurally generated, by the conjuncture of a certain number of elements, none of which were invented by, or even specific to Vercors. This is not to say that Vercors did not know what he was doing. In *La Bataille du silence* he gives a long account of the personal genesis of the story and the anecdotes and experiences he drew on.[34] He was writing 'for those who were still hesitating, still full of illusions, and above all for the writers', in order to instil some kind of critical awareness towards German expressions of pro-French sentiments. The catalyst here seems to have been *Jardins et routes* by Ernst Jünger, which he describes as a panegyric to the defeated France, and which he read with embarrassment and annoyance; if the book had been deemed suitable for publication, the French should be wary.[35] It is not so much what is said that matters, but who can say it and why; like *Les Lettres françaises*, Vercors is seeking to give expression to the unspoken context which he considers is masked by such publications. The opinion that the Germans are friends must be shown to be a false one.

The basic narrative enigma of *Le Silence de la mer* is similar to that of many pre-war novels about the German: is he friend or foe? This is the question the story *will have* answered by its end, and this has two consequences. Firstly, the narrative is always teleologically subordinated to the answer it is going to produce, and secondly, both options are present until the matter is resolved. Mere statement is not enough, as the subject of *Le Silence de la mer* is precisely the *process* of identification of the enemy. If there is to be a question at all, the figure of the German as friend must be plausible,[36] but if there is to be a resolution in favour of the German as enemy, then the figure of the friend must also contain the possibility of its reversal. So here, in contrast to *Les Décombres*, it is the figure of the German as *friend* which must be present as a possibility in the narrative so that it can be actively eliminated.

A second important point is that these relations of hostility and friendship between France and Germany are devolved on to individual characters, their actions and statements. The primary opposition is therefore split across a multiplicity of figures who are virtually reducible, in this very short story, to functions of that opposition. To take the elements of the German first: this is constituted by the military invader (the soldiers who approach the house, von Ebrennac who is billeted there); German culture and especially music (von Ebrennac is a composer); German brutality (von Ebrennac's fiancée tears off a mosquito's legs one by one, von Ebrennac ends the engagement); Nazi oppression (von Ebrennac's German friends in Paris who inform him they are pretending to want an alliance with France the better to destroy her). These are the terms of the pre-existing oppositional structure France/'the two Germanys' which *Le Silence de la mer* is written within and not renewing, and to which individual psychology is subordinated. France is the other homogeneous term constituted by the old man and his niece, who just *are*, and are French, with no particular qualifying attributes.

What is new, though not without precedent,[37] is the context of the Occupation. The situation of the officer billeted in a French home is admirably suited to the fictional rendering of the troubling question, friend or foe?, so much so that it could almost be called the classic schema of that question.[38] What is necessary is proximity, contact, presence, in order that the demarcation lines between 'the individual' and 'the enemy' can be blurred, as structures of personal contact enter into conflict with 'Manichaean' structures of the other. In *La Marque de l'homme*[39] this occurs in one episode and, as will be seen, is integrated into a different narrative finality, that of the passage to action. Within that, however, it serves a similar function of difficulty and doubt about the enemy. But it can also operate in the other direction, to prove the Germans are friends. Part of Jacques Chardonne's 'L'Eté à la Maurie',[40] is the account of the reaction of Eugène Briand, a veteran of Verdun, to the soldiers occupying his house. As in *Le Silence de la mer*, they arrive and ask to see the room, but what is stressed here is their impeccable behaviour, courtesy and generosity. A German officer arrives to check with Briand on his men: 'Well sir, you can see for yourself the Germans are not looting and killing anybody.' After establishing that Napoleon 'was at Jena, I am in your country, we are quits', that war is a dreadful thing, that they were both at Verdun, the exchange ends:

It must be painful for you to see us here.
– I would prefer to have invited you. But there is nothing I can do to change things. Enjoy my cognac, I am giving it to you willingly (de bon coeur).[41]

In all these stories the relations between the French and the German are being mediated by reception. Eugène Briand says: 'There is nothing I can do to change things' ('je ne peux rien changer à ce qui est'), a sentiment not expressed in the Resistance fiction. However, the requisitioning of rooms in a house is not something the individual can say no to – the only area of effective choice is in the *manner* of his or her reception. 'L'Eté à la Maurie' stresses the warmth of the welcome extended to the Germans; while silence is not the only possible counterpart to this (anger and hostility can be verbalised), it is a fact that the refusal in *Le Silence de la mer* to welcome and speak to the officer is the main focus for the question of friend or foe, individual or enemy. The silence is not taken for granted, but needs to be re-stated and renewed throughout the story, especially by the old man, the narrator who, being more conscious of their transgression of the normal rules of interpersonal behaviour, finally breaks the silence and accepts the German as individual, a gesture already prefigured in an early remark: 'I cannot without suffering offend a man, even if he is my enemy.'[42] Again it shows how judgments on the basis of a general psychological truth can distort the question of verisimilitude. To mark dignity and protest, silence is a perfectly credible option, given that the alternatives in official publications denoted welcome and acceptance. This is all the more the case here as von Ebrennac explicitly understands their silence in these terms.

Unlike *Le Silence de la mer*, *Le Tilleul*[43] is written from within an overtly political perspective. Edith Thomas herself sees them as different facets of a similar project:

Then if one returns to Resistance literature, one notices also that hatred was not *racial*, or *national* – French against Germans – but hatred born of a struggle against an ideology created for reducing man to slavery and degradation. And so *Le Silence de la mer*, which had an enormous impact at the time, presented a decent, upright German. And so, in *Les Contes d'Auxois*, I brought in anti-Nazi Germans.[44]

Narratively there are, however, definite differences between them. In *Le Silence de la mer*, defence of humanism is elided with the defence of the spiritual and cultural soul of France which is fully present in the two French people. This position is clearly illustrated by R.P. Chaillet, in the context here of Christian resistance: 'It is enough to have loved France in order not to betray her. (...) The French have only obeyed the law of their being and nothing has been able to distract them from this essential loyalty.'[45] The figure of the German in *Le Silence de la mer* is a composite one, and necessarily so in a narrative structure which uses it as the focus for the articulation of the military, the cultural and the individual. France and the French are homogeneous and inseparable: the atmosphere in the room, the dignity of the individuals constitute the tangible embodiment of the spiritual essence of France. All they have to do is to *be* in order to coincide with the values of honour and humanism, for that is their being. It is difficult not to see here the reason for the post-war popularity of *Le Silence de la mer*; all the complexities, and indeed the nastiness of the period, disappear in favour of a confrontation between two national entities, where Resistance is equated with a dignified refusal, both noble and poignant, which is innate to the French character. And I would suggest that this is partly because, after the event, it is no longer functioning as an argument, but as a statement.

The organisation of *Le Tilleul* is similar to that of *Le Silence de la mer*; from an undifferentiated group of Germans, one will

gradually be singled out for special attention. Their presence is
again unexplained and unquestioned. But there is one major
difference. In the opening sequence of *Le Silence de la mer*, the
activities are dominated by the Germans, the space is introduced
as they use it. Here, however, the Germans and French are
juxtaposed: 'From the beginning "they" had occupied the "big
house". From her lodge, she watched their comings and goings.'[46]
Their activity does not command her presence, she is not directly
subordinated to them. The group itself is undifferentiated and
impersonal: 'All day long there was a racket from their boots,
engines and songs.'[47] Her activities remain restricted to watching
them; there is no contact. The movement of pity which she feels
for one young soldier whom she sees being beaten has no sequel,
as that particular group leaves. Others arrive and make the same
racket. The individual soldiers make no difference to the way in
which they are designated. However, no one comments on these
soldiers : 'They are so polite' (*Ils sont si corrects*), which was the great
refrain of the early days of the Occupation. La Renaude decides to
clean up the château after the second group leaves and finds the
floors marked, fine chairs broken, and the books from the library
dumped on the lawn. This cultural barbarity, together with the
military brutality of the episode of the maltreatment of the young
soldier, serve as indicators of the German as 'other', which at this
point is further underlined by being contrasted with the
behaviour of the woman, who has a respect for books which she
does not read herself.

The third group to arrive is immediately differentiated from
the other two. The major difference, as always, is that one of them
speaks French, and a contact is established. The process of indivi-
dualisation of the German – it is at this point that we learn his
name, Hans – and his gradual involvement with the French
person has the same basis as *Le Silence de la mer* and other stories of
this type, namely proximity and contact. The tension is absent,
however. The woman's positive evaluation of Hans is to be confirmed as he relates his own family history of hostility to the Nazis,
and the situation in Germany. It is shown that Hitler's first victory
was over fellow Germans. We are not the victors, says Hans, we
have been defeated since 30 January 1933.[48] Those hostile to
Hitler, like Hans's father, hold meetings after dark, have to be
careful of those who were known to be Nazis. The parallel with the

Resistance is obvious; the arrests, the tortures, the trust that those caught would not give the names of the others, everything recalls the life of those opposed to the Occupation in France. The distinction is thus firmly established between the Nazis and the German people, as it is between the collaborators of Vichy and the French people like La Renaude, though the Germans are still seen as the agents of oppression in France: 'Hitler will find men among you to do those things.'[49] The defeat of the German opposition, symbolised by the capture and death of Hans's father, allows the Nazis to claim they are speaking in the name of the German nation. People are gradually forced to believe that they are free: 'There are many who, after constantly repeating what they are told to do, end up thinking they are doing it of their own free will.'[50] They have been duped, and one of the major ways in which this was achieved was by the suppression of certain books. Only by refusing this partial perspective can these things be understood.

The enemy is seen to have a political basis for his power – there is no contradiction between Hans's criticism and the reality of the Nazis for, unlike von Ebrennac, he is formed within a historical and political perspective. The importance of culture is not to uphold the superiority of France, but to understand the French defeat. The values which the Nazis suppress are those which undermine their own power.

Le Puits des miracles and the internal enemy

For the Resistance there was not only a German enemy but also a French one: the exponents of the official policy of collaboration in Paris and at Vichy. Formally the constitution of the figure of the enemy as French in the narratives is no different to that of the German, as it also relies on the identification, within an oppositional structure, of the 'other' who is shown in the course of the narrative to be an enemy, and therefore to be fought against. The distinction between the national and political configurations also pertains, for the collaborator can be denounced either as national traitor and enemy agent or as fascist oppressor.

The figure of the traitor is inherent in the national opposition where the distinctions between the two groups are mapped on to the contours of national identity. The traitor, the enemy agent who has betrayed the nation and sided with a foreign power, is transferred from one side of the opposition to the other without disturbing its nature. This is not to suggest that collaboration was not a very disturbing and ambiguous phenomenon. Historically the Occupation was a confrontation between the Resistance and the Germans, and the nationalist discourse which presents it as the French against the Germans is an ideological effect of a particular Resistance position, and of the rhetoric of persuasion which posits that the Resistance is France, France is the Resistance, and appeals to all Frenchmen and women to recognise that fact and understand the true nature of the situation. The constant references to both collaborators and Vichy as traitors is therefore also serving to reinforce this image of a national confrontation. This is the perspective to be found in de Gaulle's writings and speeches, for as Jean Touchard comments of the pre-war *Vers l'armée de métier*, he firmly believes in national characteristics and the psychology of nationality.[51] It is perhaps not surprising that the writer who can discuss Franco–German relations using the words 'Gauls' and 'Franks' will be saying during the war: 'We are well aware that the German is always the German. We doubt neither his hatred nor his ferocity. We were convinced that this unstable people would not constrain its nature for long.[52] He is equally intransigent in his condemnation of Vichy as a collaborationist regime with no claims to legitimacy, so much so that Touchard comments that de Gaulle was more aggressive, and from an earlier date, towards Pétain than most of the Resistance was for a long time, apart from the Communists.[53] The protagonists of de Gaulle's speeches are these three interlocking figures of the national opposition; the enemy, the traitors and the French nation: 'On the one side there is France who has been handed over to the Germans, looted, and gagged. On the other side the traitors, who are taking her apart, physically and morally, to feed the enemy. (...) The outcome of this terrible battle is not in doubt. France will, as always, triumph over treason. But woe betide those who did not dare to choose! France: your place is with us!' ('La France: avec nous!').[54] The 'persuasive' nature of this discourse is also revealed here: the very fact that 'France' and 'the French' do not coincide is the basis for the appeal for the latter to identify with the former, which is of course semantically overdetermined as their rightful place.

The discourse of political opposition to Vichy comes from the internal Resistance, from the PCF but also from the movements which developed in the southern zone for whom the enemy, if not at first then very quickly, was Vichy. The political divergences and meeting points between the Resistance and Vichy are extremely complex, as Vichy was as much a composite phenomenon as the Resistance was.[55] Firstly, the distinction Vichy/Resistance cuts across conventional political lines of right and left, a point Claude Roy makes in his autobiography *Moi je*, for he had friends at *Action française* who were more anti-German than some socialists who were collaborating with Vichy.[56] The nationalist anti-German Right was found on both sides of the fence, at least for a time. The strong anti-German current of feeling in some elements at Vichy (which its nationalism could be said to have 'legitimised') meant that some early Resisters were also active at Vichy, or were often protected there when that was not possible for them.[57] The strict division which Claude Bourdet presents between north and south is therefore probably not quite as sharp in the early days as he believes. He argues that in the southern zone, the enemy was Vichy until 1942, which gave a strong political and anti-fascist complexion to their activity as well as excluding from the Resistance the majority of conservative currents which had all more or less joined forces with Vichy;[58] whereas Frenay writes of the change he underwent between July 1940 and the spring of 1942, when he recalled the pro-Pétainist sentiments of his first clandestine manifesto with astonishment. But 'at that time there was no contradiction in engaging in the struggle against Nazism and placing hope in Pétain'.[59]

However, the importance of stressing the different situations between north and south is not in doubt. Bourdet sees the military national confrontation with the enemy in the north as leading to a concomitant underestimation of the importance of the propaganda war in favour of military action: 'How many times have I heard militants and leaders of the northern zone reproach representatives from the southern zone with being "too political".'[60] The presence or absence of the Germans is therefore crucial: 'And so the notion of a politico–military war, (...) which the Resistance in the southern zone reinvented without having read Lenin or Mao Tsetung, could not develop in the same way in the occupied zone, especially as that zone did not enjoy the relative peace which allowed the propaganda organisation of the southern zone to be set up.'[61] Frenay's account of the policy of collaboration being their immediate target certainly bears out this analysis of action in the south,[62] and Kedward makes it very clear that this political dimension was inseparable from the identification of the enemy: 'In the absence of Germans in the southern zone it was clear by 1942 that some of the major advances in Resistance had been made when *other* enemies had been openly identified.'[63] And he goes on to list them, including the capitalist class for the Communists and socialists, the ' "two hundred families" who had been held responsible by Popular Front propaganda for carrying France towards fascism and capitalist dictatorship', the 'evils of censorship, injustice, clericalism, and anti-semitism',[64] the collaborators, the scarcity of food. He sums up: 'None of these, except for the collaborator, was a new enemy, so that a recognition of these as acceptable objects for Resistance hostility and action was a successful enlistment of past conflicts into the current battle.'[65] Narratively this historical perspective is equally essential to the identification of a political enemy for it constitutes the Resistance as the culmination of a long struggle against fascism.

To the politics of the *Front National*, then, must be added the analysis and practice of the southern movements (which Bourdet considers eventually prevailed in the north) in the formation of a political configuration where the foreign invader is joined by the internal enemy, the agent of fascism in France.[66] In its vocabulary and tradition, the politics of the *Front National* (which it will be remembered grouped many non-Communists) was also the politics of much of the Resistance.

Le Puits des miracles, written by André Chamson and published in 1945,[67] is set in a small town which is never given a name nor located. The fact that at the end of the novel large numbers of soldiers in green uniform arrive on 11 November places the town in the unoccupied zone, and the year as 1942. None of this is ever mentioned explicitly, but it becomes obvious fairly quickly that this is a novel of the Occupation whose target is the ideology and practice of the Vichy state, and especially those elements of the population – the rich and the profiteers – whose purposes it serves and whose privileges it protects. That explicit historical references to contemporary events in the shape of names and dates are on the whole absent, that their function is filled by allusions, which in fact build up to form an efficient and complex referential system, is an early indication of one of the major themes of the novel, that Vichy's ideology serves to obscure the processes of history, and to hide the causes of the present situation.

The novel starts *in medias res*; this is 'the time of misfortune', a time of poverty, wretchedness and suffering. The first part is entitled 'The World of the Dog Killer', and the novel opens with a chapter relating the nocturnal activities of this man, who is only ever known by this title. In a courtyard overlooked by the narrator's room he is keeping stray dogs and killing them at night in accordance with an order from the mayor. But this only gradually becomes clear, for at first the descriptions stress the narrator's bewilderment at the strange, disturbing cries, the incomprehensible actions and mutterings of the man. This first episode is important, for the alternation of description and explanation serves to highlight the confusing, mysterious nature of the experience, introducing the major rhythm of the narrative where explanations only surface gradually; and the suffering and death of the victims faced with an arbitrary power they do not understand is a paradigm for the development of the first part as indicated by its title. The narrator experiences it as a world gone mad isolated from history and reason. The reaction to the fate of the dogs elucidates the fact that the town is divided into two groups, the poor who are suffering and the rich and important, who are not. The poor are indignant at the massacre, the group of the powerful is indifferent, and their indifference does not stop there: 'They never gave a thought to the immense hecatomb which at that time was covering the world in blood.'[68]

Each group is specified by a small number of characters; the Palmyre sisters who sell rabbit skins, the children the narrator watches at play, and whose fathers are prisoners, an unnamed woman and her daughter who are involved in the Resistance, as well as the workers in general, form the group who try and hide stray dogs from the dog killer; in the other group figure M. Tourinas, the richest and most powerful man in town, M. Boccard, the mayor, Delpoux the butcher who is making a fortune on the black market, Mme Paintendre, the widow of a factoryowner, grotesque figures such as 'the hydrocephalous man' and 'the

microcephalous man' who are never named – to them is added M.
Connard, the visiting 'Academy member' who comes to speak at
the town fête.

The grotesque features of the times lie not only in the suffering
and humiliations endured[69] on one side, and the opulence and
self-satisfaction on the other, but also in the kind of pronouncements of the rich which are inappropriate both to the situation of
the poor and to their own behaviour: 'It's materialism which has
brought us to this pass. People wanted to live too well. The great
act of penitence was necessary!'[70] This discourse, which is the
discourse of Vichy,[71] is both a weapon and a mask, protecting
their interests, and their real greed. Furthermore, this manoeuv-
ring on the part of Tourinas and his kind is revealed as the latest
manifestation of a particular historical *type*, servants of the aristocracy under the Ancien Régime, of the Thermidoriens, of the
Directoire, of the Emperor:

They obstinately served the bourgeoisie, under the names of Tourinas,
Delpoux, Paintendre, Martin, Durand, Dupont, and Laval, all bourgeois
or employees of the bourgeoisie, while declaring themselves the faithful
servants of the king, the Empire or the Republic, of freedom, of religion
or of the country. Never had they confessed that they were only really
serving the Tourinas. They always had their alibi, an ideal, a voice of
conscience, a devotion to some higher cause. It was the first time they
recognised they had no need to serve anything else than the Tourinas.
The times of misfortune had at least stripped them of their masks.[72]

That Vichy is a haven for the rich is something of a commonplace
for Resistance writing;[73] that it is allied in this novel with a
veritable roll call of the major events of the Republican, Revolutionary tradition places it specifically within the political perspective drawn from the Popular Front which denounces the rich
parasites living off the people. In a later chapter 'Discovery of the
Me-Me-Me',[74] Pétain is the crowning figure of this hierarchy of
wickedness: 'The old are the worst. I realised this when I had
worked up the chain of the Me-Me-Me (...) to the shifty old man
who was at that time confusing our unfortunate country and his
own person.'[75] But Vichy is not relying on ideology alone for its
power, and many other aspects are introduced – its paramilitary
forces typified in the dog killer who becomes a hunter of men,
torturing and killing in the courtyard men he has apprehended
with untranslateable puns on 'Gaullist' such as 'Ah, te voilà gaulé,

gueule de gaullard';[76] the pervasive atmosphere of fear and suspicion of a police state; the training of the young to the new values of order, discipline and leadership at the *ecole des chefs* (leaders' school), a reference to Vichy's *écoles des cadres*; the 'gigantic raid' of the summer carried out in 'the working class districts and lodging houses crammed with refugees from all over France and Europe'.[77]

Allusions to the Resistance are also present, as in the case of the mother and daughter already mentioned; the former would ask the narrator to do her a favour by dropping envelopes into letterboxes, while strongly warning him to be very careful, as 'we live in times when we have to distrust everyone and place total faith in a few',[78] advice he does not really understand. This elucidates one of the mechanisms by which these times are presented as incomprehensible – the narrator is ignorant (and is therefore the focus of the transition to knowledge). His ignorance and mystification are partly responsible for the proliferation of adjectives denoting the irrational – *strange, mysterious, hallucinating, delirious, mad, fantastic, monstrous,* – but this is also due to the general opposition of dreams and reality, also found in Triolet's *Les Amants d'Avignon* and Vercors's *Le Songe*. The narrator's dreams elide and distort images of both rich and poor, images which have nothing in common except their monstrous abnormality. And such distortions do not belong only to the night. So although the hardship of reality is presented as antithetical to dreams, for 'no one was dreaming of love any more', 'we were too much prisoners of our misery to dream',[79] it is still a monstrous nightmare. The two terms are constantly being substituted the one for the other. The dominant characteristics of the narrator, who is both extremely clearsighted and in a daze,[80] are essential to this so that he can act as both faithful recorder of events and mediator of its hallucinating quality which is beyond mere dreams, until the moment when the Germans arrive and reintroduce time and meaning into the town: 'After two years of hallucination (...) History took us once again by the arm (...) tearing the dreams that had been piled up around us and substituting the most brutal reality for their derisory spells.'[81]

The last two chapters, the account of the Germans arriving and the subsequent pointing to future action, which were also published clandestinely in *Nouvelles Chroniques*, are the crucial reintegration into a historical sequence of cause and effect. The figure of the enemy has however already been identified; the long chronicle of the differences between the monsters of the town and the townspeople culminates in a great ceremony, a celebration of 'idealism' and the end of 'materialism'. A banquet for 200 dignitaries is laid out under a monstrously large picture of Pétain, and the hierarchy of power is revealed. Connard, the 'académicien', makes his speech, and it is this speech which will be the *moment* of identification, when he says: 'But I prefer this broken France, this France crushed by misfortune, to the other one', a direct recall of the famous, or infamous phrase 'We would rather have Hitler than the Popular Front.'[82] The narrator's reaction is unequivocal, lining the speaker up in his sights, aiming at him an imaginary rifle. He recalls an incident from the war when he was really aiming at an enemy soldier. As the man ran away, he found this 'human action' made it impossible to shoot; no such recognition of humanity protected Connard, however, only the lack of the rifle.[83]

The Germans take control of the town and its previous masters. Their narrative function is that of the enemy, in the sense of the military opponent in a war. But this does not coincide with the *figure* of the enemy, the absolute other of the text, the ruling clique of the town. The function of the introduction of the military dimension to the situation is to end the lies and illusions; this is then the final moment of the process of identification to which the military enemy is subordinated. Three points will help to clarify this. Firstly, the town's masters are ultimately responsible for the power of the soldiers: 'These green men? We had already been handed over to them, but it was in the middle of the battle and the arrival of misfortune had hidden the secrets of the betrayal from us.'[84] Secondly, the historical military purpose of the German invasion – in response to the Allied landings in North Africa – is never mentioned. Its sole function here is to bolster the position of Tourinas and the rest. Tourinas is exultant at the sight of them, and 'freed from his terror'. 'They have come to calm the fears of M. Tourinas with their tanks and machine guns.'[85] Thirdly, taking up once more the distinction established during Connard's speech, the individual soldier is not reducible to his function of enemy, he is a contingent, not an innate enemy: 'One cannot destroy all human relations with the enemy', and this is extended to the Army of Occupation as the narrator looks at the green men and thinks: 'they are masons and workers, peasants and woodcutters. These exterminating demons could become men again',[86] whereas the rejection of the ruling clique is absolute:

But those traitors? By what sacrifice could they reestablish anything in common with us? It is too late! The pact is broken. It is broken by the conflict between fear and hope, between their smile and our suffering. Nothing can return them to a human order, neither their punishment nor our revenge. They are the monsters of the time of misfortune, hydrocephalous, inverts, paralysed brains crazed with pride or trickery, a tapestry of ghosts who crowd in the cold bedrooms of those with empty stomachs, figures of famine and untruth, of degradation and dishonour![87]

The final chapter is the account of the first overt act of Resistance involving the narrator, when he joins a man and his young son in the courtyard where they are hiding a gun. The fact the narrator shares the dislike and knowledge the other two have of Tourinas is the basis of their understanding, and throughout this sequence the internal enemy is the only one to be mentioned. The long process of identification has consisted in the accumulation of the negative qualities of this group. The distinction between them and the rest of the population is absolute and unambiguous, a differentiation which operates at every level: they are physically monstrous and wicked by nature. Socially they are rejected in political terms as enemies of the people, the last avatar of the anti-Republican tradition, which also turns them into traitors: their first allegiance is to money and power, not *la patrie*. There is no place in this set of oppositions for the importance of nationality and the qualities innate to being French.

The enemy as metonymic presence

These analyses have dealt with those narratives where the constitution of the enemy is the subject of the text. In most stories the enemy is the German who fulfils a particular function and is therefore present in the text through a series of references. Two main elements are the very economical markers of the enemy; uniform, especially the boots, and language, serving to summon up the German military presence in France. The primary mechanism is therefore metyonymy.

The emphasis placed upon external military attributes serves to distance the German from the civilian population. This can be seen in *Les Amants d'Avignon* as well as in the novels in this section. The boots are the audible register of the presence of the military (Army and Gestapo), and, as can be seen in *L'Arrestation* by Edith Thomas, the presence of the German will merely confirm information which has been fully conveyed by the sound of the boots, as a woman hears footsteps approaching along a hospital corridor and *knows* it is Germans in uniform coming to arrest her. As with *Le Silence de la mer* the arrival is situated within a military context by the sound which has preceded it, a sound which also serves to highlight the entering of the military into a civilian context. *L'Arrestation* deals with the French/German conflict in a particularly sinister context, where the French woman has to face the repressive power of the Germans and the possibility of torture and death. That her resolve is equal to their force is conveyed by the same image, which in fact closes the story, the sound of her heels on the floor being as hard as their boots.

These attributes are doubled by others which are not specifically military but which are characteristically German – blond hair, fondness for singing, efficiency. Language differences are used to stress the fact that the Germans are foreign to France: 'They spoke French very well, with just a very slight accent';[88] 'There was one, the small one, who spoke quite good French';[89] 'Anne Roger, asked one of the Germans with a strong accent'.[90] The military hierarchy which prepares the way for von Ebrennac is also reflected in the differing degrees of fluency of French: the first two low-ranking officers speak in 'what they seemed to think was French', the next one addressed the niece 'in reasonable French' ('un français correct'), whereas for von Ebrennac, 'the accent was slight, stressed only at the hard consonants'.[91]

All these mechanisms serve to constitute the Germans as being different from the French with whom they come into contact. The German within these novels is inseparable from the perspective in which he is placed, that of being *other than* the French. The obvious consequence of this is that the two groups are sharply delineated, and the difference between them is unambiguous. The same is true of Vichy, its representatives[92] and supporters, and the group which opposes them. The enemy is localised to one group which functions as the negative pole. The opposing group is unequivocally positive. This is, in my opinion, the clearest example of the structure of unity which I have singled out as marking these novels. In each one, the elaboration of a coherent group (French/Resistance/oppressed), opposed to the enemy, is structurally significant.

Notes

1 Genève, 1954, p. 45.

2 See Jean-Marie Carré, *Les Ecrivains français et le mirage allemand 1800–1940*, Paris, 1947, for a detailed exposition, which does not however question the basic premise of national identity and characteristics. On the contrary, the book is written to expose past misrecognition of the true nature of Germany, due to the 'mirage' of cultural fascination, and to provide knowledge of this dangerous neighbour. In spite of a more rigorous analysis of the various stages, it is thus not dissimilar to Jacques Bainville's *Histoire de deux peuples*, which it considers shows a 'terrible lucidité', p. 179. Cf. also S.B. John, 'The Ambiguous Invader: Images of the German in Some French Fiction about the Occupation of 1940–1944', *Journal of European Studies*, vol. 16, part 3, no. 63, September 1986, pp. 227–88, for a discussion of German cultural stereotypes and characterisation.

3 See Carré, deuxième partie, chap. 6, 'le cri d'alarme', pp. 62–71.

4 *NRF*, vol. 13.1, 1919, p. 36.

5 *Ibid.*, pp. 37–8.

6 P. 39.

7 'Eternel recours de l'Allemagne en désarroi'. Livre de poche, vol. II, p. 60.

8 *Ibid.*, p. 429.

9 P. x.

10 Cf. Giraudoux, *Siegfried et le Limousin*, Paris, 1922, and *Siegfried* (1928), *Théâtre complet*, vol.I, Neuchâtel, 1945; Romain Rolland, *Jean-Christophe*; André Chamson, *L'Année des vaincus*, Paris, 1934. This is continued with novels examining post-Hitlerian Germany: G. Auclair, *Un Amour allemand*, Paris, 1950; Michel Boutron, *Hans*, Paris, 1950; Jean-Louis Curtis, *Siegfried*, Paris, 1946.

11 In *Siegfried et le Limousin* this is focused on the main character of Siegfried, who thinks he is German but who is really French – can he be both French and German or must he choose? In *Colette Baudoche*, Colette finally rejects the offer of marriage from the German M. Asmus when she re-discovers the importance of nationality: 'Colette, maintenant, perçoit avec une joyeuse allégresse qu'entre elle et M. Asmus, ce n'est pas une question personnelle, mais une question française', p. 252.

12 Quoted in J.-M. Carré, pp. 193–4.

13 *L'Année des vaincus*, p. 148.

14 P. 159.

15   P. 164.

16   See pp. 194–5.

17   Cf. the discussion above of the review of Jacques Decour's article in *Les Lettres françaises*; this question of humanism and nationalism will be developed in the section on culture.

18   'F.T.P.' in *Contes d'Auxois*, p. 60.

19   Editions de minuit, 1944.

20   Gabriel Audisio, *Feuilles de Fresnes*, 1945, p. 51.

21   'Au Service de l'ennemi', LF, no. 13, février 1944, p. 2.

22   *Les Décombres*, p. 603.

23   P. 604.

24   Pp. 604–5. 'Je souhaite la victoire de l'Allemagne' was also a phrase used by Laval on a radio broadcast which for many justified his execution after the war.

25   See pp. 605–6.

26   P. 616.

27   P. 617.

28   *Ibid.*

29   Pp. 619–20. This book operates within a purely nationalist opposition. The whole basis to the distinction Nazi/German is absent. The country which does fulfil the oppositional function of national enemy is England.

30   Vercors, 1942.

31   Vercors himself discusses the transition from courtesy to repression in 'Souffrance de mon pays', *Le Sable du temps*, Paris, 1946, pp. 15–42.

32   'The French Flu', in *The Yogi and the Commissar*, London, 1945, pp. 25–7.

33   *Qu'est-ce que la littérature?*, p. 121.

34   *La Bataille du silence*, Paris, 1967. See pp. 179–81.

35   *Ibid.*, pp. 180–1.

36   Vercors himself writes: 'Il faudrait que sa tentative de séduction se montrât efficace presque au point d'aboutir. L'Allemand serait donc sympathique', *La Bataille du silence*, p. 182.

37   The fiction of this war has in fact more in common with Barrès, *Colette Baudoche*, which is to all intents and purposes an Occupation novel, than with Maupassant. Wolfgang Babilas comments that *Le Silence* is a 'réécriture' of *Colette Baudoche* (*Literatur der Résistance und Kollaboration in Frankreich*, III, p. 96).

38   With variations: in *Colette Baudoche* the German is a lodger, in *Le Tilleul* he is staying nearby and invited into the Frenchwoman's home.

39   Mortagne (pseudonym of Claude Morgan), 1943.

40   In Jacques Chardonne, *Attachements*, Paris, 1943 (but first published 1941). Extracts in Ory, *La France allemande*.

41   See pp. 192–4.

42   *Le Silence de la mer et autres récits*, Paris, 1980, p. 31. It has already been noted how general the thematics of silence as a mark of protest is in Resistance writings (and Vercors says he is writing especially for the writers); it is also found in his story *Désespoir est mort*: 'Ce mess était à l'image de ce pays, où seuls les lâches, les malins et les méchants allaient continuer de pérorer; où les autres n'auraient, pour protester, que leur silence', *ibid.*, p. 10.

43 In Edith Thomas, *Contes d'Auxois*, 1943.

44 Jacques Debû-Bridel, *La Résistance intellectuelle*, pp. 61–2.

45 Quoted in Louis Parrot, *L'Intelligence en guerre: panorama de la pensée française dans la clandestinité*, Paris, 1945, p. 90.

46 *Le Tilleul*, p. 29. 'Elle' is La Renaude, the main French figure of the story.

47 P. 29.

48 P. 33.

49 P. 35.

50 P. 36.

51 Jean Touchard, *Le Gaullisme 1940–1969*, p. 37.

52 'Discours prononcé à la radio de Londres le 23 octobre 1941' (the famous speech condemning attacks on German soldiers), *Discours et messages pendant la guerre*, p. 122.

53 Touchard, *Le Gaullisme*, p. 60. Cf. 'The Resistance Movements inside France did not immediately take up a position of total rupture vis-à-vis the *Etat français*, unlike the Free French, its rivals, or the Communists, its victims', H. Michel, *Les Courants de pensée de la Résistance*, p. 157.

54 'Discours prononcé à la radio de Londres le 3 décembre 1941', *Discours et messages*, p. 147.

55 Added to this is the further complexity of the evolution of Vichy: there was a steady disaffection with Vichy as it became more authoritarian and identified with Germany. A crucial year was 1942: in November the Germans invaded the unoccupied zone, but the arrests of large numbers of Jews during that summer had already shocked many. See especially Marrus and Paxton, *Vichy France and the Jews*, New York, 1983, chap.6, 'The Turning Point: Summer 1942', pp. 217–79.

56 Claude Roy, *Moi je*, Paris, 1969, p. 390.

57 See Henri Frenay, *La Nuit finira*, Paris, 1973, and Marie-Madeleine Fourcade, *L'Arche de Noë*, Paris, 1968.

58 'La Politique intérieure de la Résistance', *Les Temps modernes*, numéro spécial La Gauche, nos. 112–113, mai 1955, p. 1842.

59 Frenay, *op. cit.*, p. 184.

60 Bourdet, *op. cit.*, p. 1843.

61 *Ibid.*, pp. 1843–4. Cf H.R. Kedward, *Resistance in Vichy France*: 'This relative freedom allowed ideas to gain more substance and assume more ideological proportions than in the occupied zone', p. 46.

62 Frenay, *op. cit.*, pp. 170–1 (NB: Bourdet was Frenay's second in command in the movement *Combat*).

63 Kedward, *Resistance in Vichy France*, p. 230.

64 *Ibid.*

65 P. 231.

66 Kedward, *Resistance in Vichy France*, p. 230.

67 André Chamson, *Le Puits des miracles*, Paris, 1945.

68 P. 21.

69 For example, inadequate nourishment means the children are all wetting the bed at night, or that one of the Palmyre sisters is difficult to understand as her jaw is shrinking and her false teeth no longer fit properly.

70 P. 23.

71 Cf. 'The wave of materialism which has submerged France, the spirit of pleasure ('esprit de jouissance') and facility are the deep cause of our weaknesses and failures (abandons)', Général Weygand, lettre du 28 juin 1940, quoted in Gérard Miller, *Les pousse-au-jouir du maréchal Pétain*, Paris, 1975, p. 110.

72 Pp. 75–6.

73 Cf. 'The struggle against the financial powers (les puissances d'argent) has been one of the favorite themes of Pétain and his team, but money has never weighed so heavily on our people as since July 1940', *Combat*, no. 59, août 1944, quoted in H. Michel, *Les Courants de pensée de la Résistance*; 'We should be attacking Vichy's supercapitalism', 'L'Ecran français', *LF*, no. 17, juin 1944, p. 3.

74 'Découverte des Moua-Moua-Moua' i.e. 'moi, moi, moi'.

75 P. 109 – a reference to Pétain's famous armistice speech, 'Je fais don de ma personne à la France.'

76 P. 166.

77 P. 197 – referring to the arrests of Jews in 1942.

78 Pp. 38–9.

79 P. 11, p. 219.

80 'Envahi d'une extrême lucidité' and 'frappé de somnolence', p. 64.

81 P. 223.

82 The insistence on the 200 places, and the rejection of the 'other France' are also renewing the Popular Front vocabulary here. For 'Plutôt Hitler que le Front Populaire', see A. Tollet, *La Classe ouvrière dans la Résistance*, Paris, 1969, p. 86, p. 113.

83 P. 207.

84 P. 223.

85 P. 222. This is a continuation of the previous chapter 'La Grande Peur', when the increasing repression of police activity is seen as due to the growing fear of the rulers, matched by the feelings of hope of the population.

86 P. 224. This distinction is clearer in the clandestine edition. The later edition adds virulent expressions of revenge on the Germans: 'Mais que leurs villes s'effondrent d'abord sur les gestes protecteurs des mères hallucinées! Que leurs enfants pissent le sang!' (p. 225), and there are minor but significant changes: 'Ils pouvaient retrouver leur humanité dans la douleur, le désespoir et la honte de leur puissance' (*Nouvelles Chroniques*, p. 90), 'Ils ne retrouveront leur humanité que dans la douleur, le désespoir et la honte de leur puissance',(Gallimard, p. 225).

87 P. 234.

88 *Les Amants d'Avignon*, p. 72.

89 *Le Tilleul*, p. 87.
90 *L'Arrestation*, p. 45.
91 *Le Silence de la mer*, pp. 25, 26, 35.
92 And it is interesting to note that in *Aragon's Les Bons Voisins* (in *Trois Contes*, Londres, 1945), where a flat is searched by the French police, their use of slang and colloquial French indexes their lack of politeness and their arrogance.

Chapter two

Cultural perspectives

In his essay on neo-realism in the Italian cinema, Mario Cannella considers that the anti-fascist movement defined culture 'precisely in the old bourgeois[1] terms as a "kingdom of values", a sacred place: culture "naturally" became antifascist, since fascism represented "barbarity", i.e. non-culture'.[2] The French Resistance posits a similar equation, and the defence of cultural values is a most important feature of this literature.

Culture is defined essentially as Western humanism. This is a broad term indeed, but as these writings are not concerned with enquiring into the nature of humanism, rather with reaffirming its importance and validity, it tends to be used very broadly, and as it always enters into specifically oppositional structures, it is evoked, it is *stated*, in the face of what is construed as its opposite, the barbarous nature of Nazi Germany. Guéhenno provides a typical example:

Culture is a tradition and a hope. We shall remain faithful to each. A man of the West is this conscience, this individual whose moral worth Socrates defined, for whom Jesus died, to whom Descartes taught the means of his power, whose duties and rights were established by the Revolution of the 18th century: three thousand years of reason and courage have definitively set the *path of man* in a particular direction. Totalitarian propaganda, (...) the noise of tanks and planes, the *zusammen-marchieren* of the armies, the restrictions, the sufferings will not change this.[3]

Cannella gives a succinct account of the particular characteristics of the imbrication of antifascism and humanism in the Italian context:

The strong links between the inter-class politics of antifascism, antifascist culture and neo-realism, are apparent in the common framework in which they operate: the concept of 'man'. The values adopted by these movements are the struggle against 'evil', 'barbarism' and 'egoism'; universal brotherhood in the wake of catastrophe; the union of all good and honest men for justice and peace; and the pitiless 'denunciation' of social injustice, with the aim of getting it 'put right'. The war was 'irrational chaos', expressing the worst side of 'human nature'; 'evil' had forced everyone to do something they should not have; the 'survivors' had to cling onto each other, overcome the old barriers, and work together – if they were 'honest' and 'in good faith' – to create a just society, not of subjects[4] but of 'people'. Isolation and solitude were broken down, men recognise each other as companions in misfortune, sharing the same morality. The enemies – the egotists, the unjust – would soon be overwhelmed by this wave of love.[5]

In this accurate if somewhat ironic summary are many features recognisable in the (French) Resistance use of humanism, and, it could be argued, stemming from the same dynamics of an inter-class political basis to anti-fascism. Notions of civilisation and humanity, which place at the fore the idea of the individual and the spiritual attributes of the human mind – reason, tolerance, dignity – are opposed to their own negative image of Nazi Germany which, by the logic of the oppositional structure, is formed by the humanist discourse itself: for example, the devaluing of the individual in favour of a collective group identity which is inseparable from the discipline of militarism, is given special significance, and, in opposition to the predominantly analytical qualities of the mind, Nazism often bears the mark of 'non-reason'. But the analogy with Italian neo-realism cannot be taken too far. Firstly because, although drawing upon both the politics of anti-fascism and the spirit of the Resistance, it belongs to the post-war period, whereas in France a clear distinction must be made between the Resistance and the post-war period if misleading judgments in the cultural sphere are to be avoided. Secondly, in France the constituent elements of the opposition which could be summed up as that of humanity/inhumanity often coincide with those of the France/Germany opposition; together with the strength of the notion of patriotism in the discourse of anti-fascism, the fact that the national opposition is reproducing the discourse of humanism gives a particular force to the cultural meaning of France.

It is rare for French culture to be denoted as too particularised in a negative sense; this is usually the mark of the negative aspects of German culture. To be considered positive, national culture must combine particularity with universalism. 'The most authentic Germans have known how to speak a language which was thoroughly German and universal at the same time', in the words of Jacques Decour,[6] for whom Nazism renews a too narrowly nationalist culture. In other words, it is the imbrication of the particular and the universal which is important. This position is not born with the Occupation; in 'Réflexions sur l'Allemagne', Gide already argues that 'it is in nationalising itself that a literature takes its place in humanity'.[7] in the same way that 'the most individualised of writers is also the one who presents the most general human interest.'[8] Again it is the *exclusively* national which cannot be integrated. Now logically this position seems quite untenable, as the particularity of the national appears to be condemned and praised in the same breath. But in fact this illogicality is the inevitable result of the intersection of the discourses of nationality and humanism. France is humanist, Germany (or Prussia, or Nazi Germany) is not. Within this perspective, the discourse of humanism is essential to the construction of national identity, and national identity is equally essential to the placing of national frontiers around these moral forces. The specifically national attributes of a country (France) can therefore be the living embodiment of a universal essence of humanity, whereas the attributes of anti-humanism signal the *absence* of the universal and close the national back in on itself as pure negativity.

The brotherhood of man and the defence of France therefore combine to provide a composite picture, as in the review of *Le Cahier noir*[9] which salutes it as: 'The true manifesto of the French spirit which, faithful to the traditions inherited from Christianity, humanism and the ideology of 1789, refuses, even under the yoke, any idolatry of force and deceit, the foul religion of success based on scorn for and enslavement of man'.[10] In fact the notions of 'l'esprit' and 'l'esprit français' are virtually interchangeable at this time, in the same way that Germany or Nazism, depending on the perspective, are synonymous with barbarism. Discussing the *Musée de l'Homme* Resistance group, Roland Penrose wrote: 'With the entry of the Germans into Paris this museum at once became a centre of resistance; a symbol of something that the Germans could never conquer because it was something that they could never understand.'[11] It is the very nature of the opposition, situated within the overall framework of humanism, and accentuating the unique value and intellectual tradition of France, which produces such clear-cut distinctions between what are formally interdependent terms.

It is also worth noting that the idea of the 'non-cultural' enemy manipulating 'universal' values to his own ends can entail a reaffirmation of *national* values: 'To be "universal", to have no "country", in reality that implies, for our art, the existence of one single country, one single universe: Germany.'[12] The defence of French culture in opposition to the Nazi imposition of a (distorted) German culture has already been noted. A further variant is to be found in the phrases: 'Music might know no country, but musicians have one';[13] 'Art knows no country... But artists have one'.[14] Another major element in both German and collaborationist pronouncements was that the Germans in their crusade against Bolshevism were the defenders of Western civilisation. To emphasise French culture is therefore also to refuse its integration into that ideology, and much energy goes into denouncing the 'unspiritual' behaviour of the 'civilising force': 'A large contingent of the defenders of Western civilisation kicked in the doors of the houses.'[15] 'The defenders of our continent, as Pétain would say, of Western civilisation, as Brasillach and Salmon would say, of the true Christian order, according to Châteaubriant, have massacred, with the connivance of their agents at Vichy, the best representatives of the French intelligentsia.'[16]

Many of the statements on culture quoted so far are also emphasising a *continuity*, either of an intellectual tradition or of the nature of national identity (the Germans *never* understand culture). To the universality of the values France incarnates corresponds its unchanging nature through time. Henri Frenay judges this to be a result of the complex uncertainties of the situation: 'Where was France? In London, as in front of the Hôtel du Parc in Vichy, troops dressed in the same uniform were paying the same honours to the same flag, to the sound of the same *Marseillaise*. Where was my country?'[17] There is justification for this view. The political divisions are indeed responsible for the invocations in various discourses of an essential France under whose sign the discourse places itself as patriotic, a mechanism to be found as much in the pronouncements of *La France libre* and de Gaulle, of Vichy and Pétain (for example the famous poster:

'Etes-vous plus français que lui?' (Are you more French than he is?) under a close up of Pétain's face) as in those of the Resistance. But the frequency of the occurrence of such statements in Resistance writing suggests there is a deeper necessity operating here, a necessity inherent in the articulation of a particular culture with humanism and eternal values, in which framework its function is to be the embodiment of an essence which transcends it. The appeal to the past is therefore as essential as the notion of universality in the construction of 'France' as a value in the discourse. Not surprisingly, this identity in time is often spoken through the temporal structures of *témoignage* which subordinate the individual moment to the continuity (*durée*) which it is expressing. 'France' can occupy either position in this structure; as the tangible embodiment in the present of the universal and eternal ideals of humanism, and, elliptically, as the transcendant entity which confers value on what is done in its name.

In Vercors's second clandestine story published by Les Editions de minuit, *La Marche à l'étoile*, the notion of an ideal France is essential, both to the construction of the main character, Thomas Muritz, and to the manner in which the behaviour of certain groups of Frenchmen under the Occupation is discussed, for its degradation under the Occupation is the central theme. The passion for France is the mainstay of Thomas's character. In fact, apart from this passion, his character, in conventional psychological terms, is remarkably undeveloped. One could see his love for France as being the driving force in his psychology (which is how the narrative presents it), but it is equally possible to reverse the terms; Thomas is created to present, and is reducible to, a certain image of France. Nearly all Thomas's attributes (for example, his love of justice and freedom) reproduce, on a personal level, values which are characteristic of this image of France, which itself is not reducible to its geographical reality, but is rather a cultural and moral entity, a spiritual force. Apart from his love for France, Thomas does not exist; all that remains is a passionate being. The energy, content and psychology of that passion are furnished by France.

The Occupation will bring about the destruction of Thomas's love and faith in France. The major question posed in the opening sentences and which, it could be argued, is the primary narrative enigma, is one of responsibility: who is guilty? The development of the realisation of Thomas's project maintains the possibility, the narrative option, that Thomas himself is responsible, firstly by constantly stressing the singularity of his behaviour and motivation and asking whether it is so strange as to be unreasonable. It is a function of the narrator, by presenting this interpretation and then disagreeing with it, to voice this enigma. The other element reinforcing the singularity of his behaviour is the incomprehension it is met with, narratively linked to laughter and surprise. His family and friends, however, generally reach an understanding and a respect for his ideals. The one group who does not is that of the industrial and business world who the narrator expects will find Thomas's devotion laughable. This kind of opposition between the generosity of an ideal France and the pettiness and calculating attitudes dictated by money is hardly new. In a more elaborate form it is one of the constants of the work of Bernanos, for example. In this text, the Occupation is presented as the apotheosis of this group. The opposition between the narrative figures of Thomas and the industrial group partakes of the wider opposition between the ideal values and their degradation, and this is the main reason why the narrative enigma of guilt will be so difficult to resolve. 'Thomas' is constituted by a passion for France, and thus enters into two structures; as an individual trait, this passion is ambiguous, but as the expression of a force articulated through time, it functions textually as the embodiment of an unambiguous ideal. It is the convergence of these two structures at the specific time of the Occupation which means his death will be impossible to explain in purely individual terms.

The problem of the attribution of guilt is never solved: various solutions are presented, but the interrogative mode predominates. Finally, the narrator transposes the guilt to a level of generality which transcends any particular nation or individual, in asking God why Thomas had, at the end, to see 'that horrible face – the face we all, nations or men, carry within us – of desperation which has always belonged to Mammon. What have you punished him for? What have you punished me for?'[18] However, the insistence on punishment allows this revelation of a less edifying side of humanity to be articulated with a continuing belief in an ideal France. Thomas might be considered to have been punished for various reasons: for being blinded by passion

to the true realities of the Occupation, or even for having believed
his passion could enable him to escape his family destiny. But the
narrator's punishment, that he cannot forget Thomas, nor the
final moment of his despair, serves to maintain the ideal France
through the mechanism of the narrator's emotional distress. The
clandestine reviewer of *La Marche à l'étoile* makes the same point:
'Whoever reads *La Marche à l'étoile* without feeling oppressed by
an indescribable anguish, without feeling forever stained in
himself and in humanity by an indelible stain, whoever is able to
look on Vichy France without a feeling of revulsion thereby
appoints himself the enemy of France and the shame of humanity.'[19] The review continues that it is precisely in the recognition
of this 'terrible abjection where the defeat has plunged us' and the
refusal of the attitude which says 'these crimes are not our fault'
which is the lesson of this story. In this way the French can pass
through the necessary purge and purification which is their only
way forward. The ideal France has been degraded by the French
themselves who have not been able to rise above the situation they
find themselves in; in other words, 'France' is not the source of the
degradation and remains a transcendent value. One sees the
importance of the double structure of moment and duration in
order to separate them. But that the awareness of this degradation is a positive factor, that the reviewer's description, 'an
exemplary short story', which renders well its 'persuasive' structure,
is fully justified, is demonstrated in the final paragraph as the
narrator comments on the self-satisfied reaction of those 'who
weigh a nation's greatness by the size of its profits', who could well
consider his distress as a sign of weakness and give him lectures in
patriotism. 'What shall I reply? they are stronger than I am, they
will stop me speaking.'[20] But they are not the strongest, as the
very existence of the story is meant to show.

While *La Marche à l'étoile* is forged within a nationalist perspective, *Les Moules et le Professeur* (The Mussels and the Teacher), one
of the *Contes d'Auxois* by Edith Thomas, starts with a rather
specific definition of culture, and moves through a series of shifts
in the narrative to culminate in a strong reaffirmation of the
humanist vision. The narrative relies on the Life/Art, action/
thought dichotomy which codes individual creation as apart from
other action, as a retreat from the world. However, a further
distinction within this perspective needs to be made. 'Life' in this

story means life under the Occupation, constituted chiefly by the material difficulties of food, housing, heating and lack of money, which intrude upon and interrupt the seclusion essential to artistic pursuits. 'Art' is here the world of scholarship and learning, and therefore specifically the written word, embodied in the figure of M. Poncelet, a retired teacher who is writing a book on the *Aeneid*.

The very title of the story indicates the two orders of the material and the cultural whose juxtaposition generates the narrative. It could also be said to signal, by the grammatical structure of co-ordination, the narrative solution to the opposition, which will substitute relations of complementarity for the relations of dominance and exclusion which initially prevail between them. This will be seen most clearly in the repetition of the key words which mediate the two orders, 'in spite of', and 'although', where the one, and this will apply especially to Art, can only be affirmed *in spite of* the other. The story opens with the physical intrusion of the one upon the other, as Mme Poncelet enters her husband's study to remind him he has to do the shopping, and apologises for disturbing him; wrapped up in his work, he hardly sees her; to see her *properly*, he has to leave the world of the *Aeneid*. Significantly, 'properly' means that she is surrounded by the marks of poverty and age as well as of love. The material difficulties to be faced under the Occupation are constituted by precise references (to the prisoners of war, rationing, the two zones, for example) and particularly by lack of money. The teacher does the shopping because of his wife's heart condition. That he can do nothing more is directly attributable to the Occupation; he cannot compete with the prices the Germans pay for domestic help in Paris, nor can he afford the inflated prices in the south. Such details introduce an economic dimension[21] in sharp distinction to *La Marche à l'étoile* where the accent is laid rather on the suffering of the poor and the selfishness of the 'bourgeois' which tend therefore to be assimilated to moral than social categories. But in *Les Moules et le professeur* also, economic divisions have an import beyond the purely social: 'And then in Paris you felt you were resisting. You were resisting. And the old man, on his way to the fishmonger's (...) was close to thinking that he was carrying out an act of resistance, and was a minute but necessary link in the rigorous chain (enchainement) of history.[22] The importance given to Paris and its inhabitants is informed, then, by a 'populist' ideology, as will be seen more clearly later.

The relations of exclusion between the two orders are translated into the psychology of the character of M. Poncelet in his ambivalence towards his life's work, first indicated as he leaves his room with a backward glance of 'sadness, regret and irony perhaps'.[23] The same relations govern his comments on reaching the long queue outside the fishmonger's, as the difficulties of 'Life' overwhelm the value of 'Art' to the extent of denying any *quality* to life itself as well as to intellectual pursuits: 'We are no more than ants whose anthill has been kicked in by someone's boot. We have been reduced to the level of animals. Man comes later. He gave a thought to his great work on *The Origins of the Aeneid* which was the purpose and justification of his life, and shrugged his shoulders.'[24] His long wait in the queue forms the structure to the story, and it is during this wait that the shifts which will produce the optimistic ending occur. Through the wildly exaggerated stories and news, he comes into contact with a different kind of cultural life to that of scholarship, one that is compared to the oral tradition of Homer and the *Chanson de Roland*. This reference to the *Chanson de Roland* no doubt inevitably evokes the fighting French and therefore the Resistance. It is certainly used in this way in *F.T.P.*, another story in the same collection. It also introduces a cultural activity which is not governed by a retreat from the world, and whose value is underlined by being placed within a recognised cultural tradition, in a direct relation to illustrious antecedents such as Homer. While continuing therefore the value of a *popular* culture – it is described as 'the epic poem ('la geste') of a whole people' – it also constitutes a first break from the exclusively 'written' nature of culture. A concomitant change in 'Life', no longer negatively denoted solely as hardship, is present in his next comment: 'Life was a strange thing.'[25]

A German soldier who passes by, announced as usual by the sound of his boots, provokes derogatory comments from the women in the queue. Experience of the harsh conditions of the Occupation is now presented as a source of knowledge in opposition to the written word which in this case (the 'German newspapers written in French'[26])is intended to deceive, thus constituting a further shift from the original terms of the opposition as well as clarifying the ideological importance of the people which is the basis for the shift: 'The people had understood, much more quickly and more accurately than the bourgeois, acknowledged M. Poncelet, that collaboration was the name of deception (imposture), covering a whole continent being reduced to slavery. (...) Real collaboration can only come later, when man had been restored, M. Poncelet said to himself. And it is not the masters who will create it, but the peoples themselves when they have had enough of suffering.'[27]

The final necessary stage is for this to be integrated into the principal figure of the narrative, as M. Poncelet recognises that 'human beings were worth more than he thought, when he stayed at home with his nose in a book'.[28] The change in perspective leaves the cultural code intact, does not disturb the equivalence between creation and a retreat from the world. But the inclusion of popular experience, and the value placed on it, has displaced the absolute hierarchical dominance which initially prevailed. The scholar has been replaced by the humanist and the two formerly opposing elements of material difficulty and his life's work are now aligned and subordinated to the central notion of man. It is the contact with the people of Paris which has accomplished the transformation. The barrier which separated creation and action is no longer operative, for both have been subsumed under 'Life': 'Yes, life was a marvellous adventure',[29] is the final comment from the retired teacher at his desk.

The figure of the artist

'What the barbarian cannot do is create.'[30]

Within the context of a 'spiritual war' where writing is a privileged weapon, the nature of creation and creativity is an important theme; important in itself, certainly, but also for the metaphoric structure of fecundity as opposed to sterility which conveys the irremediable difference between creativity and barbarity. This distinction is informed by the definition of the external threat, variously German or Nazi, as inhuman and non-cultural, bent on the destruction of man and the value of the individual, but it cannot be reduced to those terms alone. The creations of culture are in the vanguard of civilisation; they are therefore *particularly* under threat. They must also be seen to be an unambiguous refutation of the negative values of the enemy. In other words, creation and creativity constitute a very important frontier demarcating the two orders; the conflict between good and evil, between the forces of moral strength and the forces of destruction – which is ultimately the conflict between the humanist and the barbarian – is focused especially, in the pages of *Poésie* and of *Les Lettres françaises*, on the relation to and the status of Art. In the fiction, however, which depends on the complexities and ambiguities of narrative problems and dilemmas, the figure of the artist (poet, painter or musician) fulfils a special function, either enabling a real difference between the two orders to be established, or, towards the end of the Occupation and in the post-war period, of being the focus for the doubts, the hesitancies which are beginning to undermine the optimistic belief in this clear-cut distinction.

Throughout *Poésie*, poetry and art are denoted as life-giving forces,[31] sentiments which can even take on the strongly religious overtones of a spiritual bread of life.[32] Aragon's 'L'Année du chèvrefeuille' (The Year of The Honeysuckle)[33] is shot through with an insistence on birth and renewal. In part overdetermined by the very word creation, the key term in this metaphoric structure is fecundity. Claude Jacquier quotes Mauriac writing in *Tunis-Soir*: 'It appears that everywhere the earthquake has unleashed the springs of poetry. They gush forth especially in the unoccupied zone', and comments, 'This poetic outpouring characterises these arid, burning years.'[34] Oasis in the desert, irrepressible springs overpowering heat and aridity, this 'fertile renewal'[35] is always that of poetry, but in the veiled language of *Poésie*, also a metonym for the nation itself. 'La Terre brûlée' (The Burnt Earth) by Armand Guibert uses the image of the land burnt off after the harvest. Both are undergoing the rigours of winter and 'the slowing down of life that imposes'. But this is the time of the 'inner gestation' – 'no period of recollection has ever been sterile'.[36] The fecundity of rebirth is already revealed with the 'resurgence of Africa':[37] 'With the vitality of forces which have been dammed up for a long time, it raises to the sky its branches heavy with buds, intertwined with the forest of the new French poetry.'[38] Guibert concludes: 'Those who survive will have earned the grandeur which is here being announced, this festival of germination and sap below the burnt earth, the surging of the springs through all veins.'[39]

As 'contraband' writing, *Poésie* cannot examine clearly and explicitly the nature of the enemy to be combated – no such restrictions apply to *Les Lettres françaises*; using material that also appears in his novel *La Marque de l'homme*, Claude Morgan assesses the relation of the 'barbarian' and Art as being limited to one of purification : 'Playing Mozart is a kind of absolution. After a murder, tenderness and grace are soothing. The blood of the hostages is washed away! But what the barbarian cannot do is create. Where is the music from Hitler's Germany? Where are its poets?'[40] This configuration around the possibility and impossibility of creation usually centres on music, writing and art, but in 'Le Comédien homme libre' (The Actor a Free Man), it is the actor who is seen in similar terms. Having established that his creation springs from his solitude, and the necessary interdependence of his solitude and his freedom, it continues:

How are we now to think of this man, this living unit, in the political system our green visitors practise and praise? In this dictatorial regime from which the divine imagination is excluded, free will banned, non-conformity deported, how can the actor, this sensitive vagabond, who by definition and by design, is and wishes to remain free, how can he 'be'? He is no more. He has become one of the numerical pawns on the board, (...) a dead puppet in the impatient fingers of a tyrant.[41]

None of this constitutes a renewal of the vision of the artist, but is rather a reinforcement of certain elements within a traditional image. As a unique individual, the artist is seen to be drawing from within himself, through a process of gestation, pain and birth, the work which bears witness to his creative force and as such he is threatened by 'this barbaric and mindless *uniformity*'.[42] But he also exists in a wider context, as a creative genius, the embodiment of Art – and therefore in a similar relation as the individual is to Man – one of the highest achievements of the human spirit which is particularly threatened by the destructive and deadly forces of Nazism opposed to it. Nazism as sterility halts the constant process of creation and recreation which is necessarily inscribed within a continuity. Like the notion of France and the value of *témoignage*, creation and creativity are therefore also structured within time.

There are three central characters in Claude Morgan's *La Marque de l'homme*;[43] the narrator Jean Bermont, his wife Claire and their close friend whom Claire has known since childhood, Jacques Fontanier. Jean and Jacques find themselves in the same prisoner of war camp after the defeat of France and correspond with Claire, who is having to share her home with German officers. The first part concentrates on the prisoner of war camp, brings to the fore the differences between Jean and Jacques, especially in relation to Claire's letters, and ends with Jacques's death. This period is returned to in the second part when Jean discovers Claire's diary which gives a full account of her daily dealings with the Germans and her reactions to letters from himself and Jacques. This second and longer part deals primarily with the question of whether to become involved in Resistance work. Having engineered his release from the prisoner of war camp Jean does finally engage in Resistance activity, is arrested and held in prison. After his release he learns Claire has followed the same path and is being held in the women's prison at Romainville. There is another shift backwards in time with the discovery of a further section of Claire's diary, restarted after his return home, and ending abruptly with her fears of arrest. As many of the differences between Jean and Claire and their views of Resistance turn on their attitudes to Jacques, he remains a central figure after his death, through constant invocations by the other characters and through the device of the diary.

This novel aims to produce a recognition of responsibility and of the necessity for action but this is not the point of issue now. Here it will be a matter of tracing the importance of the figure of the artist. *La Marque de l'homme* is peopled with intellectuals, poets, musicians, and the artist as visionary is a key figure, both custodian and transmitter of the positive values of humanism. That Jacques is a composer, that the major German character is a musician, that Claire herself plays to a high standard means that the debate about culture is articulated through the action of the narrative: Art is essential to the characterisation of Jacques and crucial to the narrative problem of recognition of the enemy by Claire.

An early exchange between Jean and Jacques in the camp is a telling example of culture being defined in relation to its opposite, the non-human. Jean believes his friend is thinking of his music, while Jacques angrily replies that music and creativity are incompatible with the spectacle of oppression and degradation which surrounds them. Jean's incomprehension and misunderstanding enable Jacques to expound his knowledge; this dialogue is but one of many moments establishing the differences between the two and marking Jean as ignorant. Jacques goes on to explain why the German musical heritage is no longer relevant: 'Both the musician and the poet are forbidden to express the truth of the times we are living in. If a Goya were to appear, he would be shot. A Voltaire – shot. A Hugo, shot. Against culture, and so against man, a terrifying battle of annihilation is being waged.'[44] The radical discontinuity in the present between the inhuman experience of the camps and the possibility of its artistic expression is thus restated in relation to the Germans specifically, in the break between their cultural past and their present behaviour which even closes the possibility at this time of the historically precedented artistic responses of vehement anger and indignation. 'The annihilation of man' therefore covers both the actual experience of degradation and the threat to Art as transcendent value.

A similar distinction is found at the level of the manifestation of culture, in the context of attitudes to continuity and change. Claire and Jean believe that in spite of the tragedy of defeat and occupation, art, literature, music and the great monuments of France itself remain to give hope for the future, whereas Jacques insists that the artefacts of culture cannot continue divorced from their humanist context; they cannot 'live' without men.[45] For Jacques it is the transcendent value which gives meaning to any particular expression which otherwise is literally devoid of meaning (or, even worse, takes on a negative value, as we shall see later). This dislocation between the transcendent and the tangible, between Art and its manifestation, is the means by which the problem of the 'barbarian artist' can be confronted: 'I know only too well how music can act like opium on the mind, not the music one composes, but the music played with others. (...) It is an alibi and an absolution.'[46] What is important is that *creation* is explicitly exempted from this instability around the notion of artistic activity. These manifestations, divorced from a creative source, are characterised by a dissipation of energy, a weakening of the will, especially dangerous in the case of the 'barbarian' in its effects on others. It is tempting to read the gap between 'opium' and 'absolution' as semantically bridged by the unspoken phrase 'religion is the opium of the people', turning their minds elsewhere, obscuring the perception of reality. 'I refuse to be decieved', Jacques continues: in other words, the barbarian uses Art in order to confuse. 'The real barbarian is the one who knows he's a barbarian', writes Claire in her diary, 'Who uses Mozart as if for absolution (...) who deliberately annuls the many-layered sediment of human thought deposited over the centuries.'[47] The negative use of Art is thus caught in the sterility of the moment, denying the past which is constituted not by the moment, but by the continuity of duration, that which is, has been and will be.[48] At every point the individual and the particular moment are caught up in the movement to the transcendental ideal. The creative artist, the prophet of the future, is the privileged figure of this 'tension towards', this going beyond.[49] In total opposition to the soporific effect of a negative Art, creativity unites energy, passion and the will in one single direction, towards the future, and the narrative paradigm of this figure at the vanguard of the struggle for Man is Jacques, around whose name accumulate its specific characteristics: 'His thoughts remained turned towards the future with an anxious, feverish tension.'[50] 'He was a poet, and had a prophetic awareness (prescience) of the future.'[51] Jacques is opposed to Jean in this too, for he has to learn to go beyond himself as an individual and translate Jacques's vision into action, but the truly negative counterpoint to Jacques, the mirror image who deceives Claire until the demonic basis of his art is made clear, is the German officer and musician, Kurt von Stum.

Claire's return to Paris with her son after the defeat to find her home occupied by German soldiers is the start of the now familiar narrative schema establishing proximity and contact in order to examine the relation with the enemy, and because of the limited number of possible oppositions within such a schema on which to base the narrative options (communication/silence, group/individual, friend/foe, French/German, national/political) there are many echoes here of both *Le Silence de la mer* and *Le Tilleul*. However, unlike the niece in *Le Silence de la mer*, Claire is marked by a certain ambivalence in relation to the question of whether the Germans are friends or foes. She feels no hatred as they are 'people like us'[52] nor any spirit of resistance, as 'Germany seems invincible'.[53] On the other hand, she enjoys ironically pointing out the illogicalities in German propaganda, the brutalities of their actions. The result of this is that it is the soldier Werner who is reduced to (or takes refuge in) silence, which provokes a disturbance of the communication/silence opposition. He also fluctuates across the friend/foe opposition, for example in accepting German propaganda about being 'invited' into lands they invade, yet being sensitive to the sensibilities of the occupied. This is allied to a fluctuation across the national/political opposition: 'he assures me he is a sensitive, peace-loving man who does not believe in the happiness of imperialism'[54] and is fighting only for the Fatherland. Until his satisfaction with German victories in the East and the loss of individuality as he once more puts on his uniform, the dividing line between the German as individual and as military invader has been quite unstable. Werner also has artistic leanings which are briefly mentioned only to be dismissed as unoriginal,[55] and which are important from the narrative point of view as a forerunner of the more complex artistry of von Stum who will be less easy to deal with.

When we come to von Stum, it is difficult to avoid being constantly aware of the figure of von Ebrennac: 'He likes to take up position against the bookcase, flicking through books and commenting on them aloud. He is very curious about our country and seeks to learn about it by getting me to talk. At ten o'clock precisely I rise and he ceremoniously takes his leave.'[56] There are many similar details which appear to create von Stum as an ironic rejoinder to von Ebrennac. Ironic, because of the shift attendant upon the one major change – von Stum is in favour of war: 'We can fight and still love each other, no?'[57] is a far cry from 'We shall fight no more. We shall marry!'[58] For von Stum, 'men lose their creative tension in peace-time'.[59] He is also an enthusiastic supporter of national socialism.[60] The result of this is that, unlike von Ebrennac, von Stum is *unlikeable*. The disturbance is not effected by any personal qualities or attraction; the entire burden of this is therefore borne by the German as artist. He and Claire frequently play together: 'I have to open my eyes wide to convince myself it is not Jacques in front of me, but this stranger.'[61] 'As God is my witness, I am indifferent to the man. But the artist makes me forget the enemy. The artist makes me ask why I should think of this man as a barbarian.'[62] This mirroring of Jacques in the

communicative power of music is therefore the sole factor preventing the recognition of von Stum as an enemy.

As with Werner, with whom communication was broken at the
mention of German aggression, so with von Stum: the invasion of
Russia provokes the first, if temporary disturbance of their
'communication', playing together, because, in *La Marque de
l'homme*, spiritual grandeur is not resumed under France;[63]
France and Germany are opposed in so far as they are embo-
diments of a greater opposition, that of the forces for and against
man. If Russia is the country of the brotherhood of man, then
Russia is the ultimate enemy of this military crusade, revealing
once and for all its anti-humanist nature, the moment when the
meaning of the war becomes clear.[64] The definitive breakdown in
communication is effected by the shooting of hostages, the first
act of aggression mentioned within France: now it is Claire who
retreats into silence.

The appeal to the 'historical real' has removed the very basis of
the music; it no longer has the power to efface the world, even less
'the blood on their hands and which they cannot remove'.[65] It
remains for a letter from Jacques to destroy the figure of von
Stum as artist, to separate artistic expression from its creative
source, providing a negative image of the true artist previously
discussed. To single out just one point: the illumination of the
visionary artist is lost in the artificial fog projected by the artist
who has separated his art from its humanist source: 'Any cultured
assassin can restore his purity by playing Mozart.'[66]

Vercors's *Les Mots*[67] is a post-war text displaying many of the
features characteristic of persuasive writing. It is engaging with
the debate on the nature of poetry, and ends with a clear refusal
of literature as an end in itself, and of poetry as a hermetic,
self-sufficient art. Its interest here lies in its use of the figure of the
artist.

After the massacre of the inhabitants of a nearby village, Luc,
the central character and a poet, is no longer able to maintain his
art as a formal research into language deliberately divorced from
meaning, nor his refusal of any social or emotional content, for he
is a witness, not only to the deaths of the villagers, but also to the
painting of a beautiful picture by the German officer in charge,

who sets up his easel in front of Luc's house and takes no part in the killings, the sounds of which are clearly heard. It is the juxtaposition of aesthetics and horror which effects the change in Luc, since neither the officer's status as artist nor the quality of his art are challenged. On the contrary, the characteristics of the figure of the artist in this text are shared by both Luc and the officer,[68] and necessarily so in order to allow the nature of that art to be called into question. Luc defines his art as 'the authentic interplay of pure thought'[69] whose process is governed not by logic or reason but by 'a kind of inner illumination'[70] serving as a guide distinguishing between the important values of language and the inappropriate question of morality, institutions, economy and politics'.[71] This distinction proves to be less straightforward under the Occupation than before. He maintains his 'inner purity', by following events but refusing them access to his 'inner realm'.[72] However, the process is marked by a tension, as excluding the non-spiritual demands constant effort, constant soul-searching as to whether he is being sincere or merely taking the easy way out.[73] The story starts with this question, and much of the first part forms a reflection and explanation of his position,[74] bearing the hallmarks of the 'examination of conscience' which reiterates his belief in the possibility of maintaining 'what is most precious' even under Nazi rule and of refusing all commitment in poetry.

The similarity between the officer and Luc is immediately marked by the former's joy at the view in front of Luc's house, as this was the very reason Luc moved in to that house, but it is also made explicit, as Luc detects a 'secret affinity' between their work.[75] The officer keeps his back turned to the village below and shows no sign of being at all disturbed by the sounds of the dreadful scenes there, accounts of which intersperse the descriptions of the progress of the painting. But the reality of the massacre belies his intentions and throws to the fore the crucial question of sincerity as earlier defined by Luc, since the officer also believes art and war should be kept separate. '[Today] I've enriched humanity with a beautiful creation. (...) The rest is silence.'[76]. But that is precisely what it is not for Luc. As he searches through the unrecognisable remains of those burnt and killed, words come rushing forth in spite of himself, each one 'a torture and a relief'.[77] And they are the words he had banned, charged with a social and an emotional meaning.

This has been effected because at the level of the narrative function of the artist, the German is substituted for Luc, who is removed to the sidelines as onlooker while the two elements of the opposition Life/Art are displayed before him (at which point he faints, which could be read metonymically as an effacement of this 'Luc'). Luc can therefore return to the centre of the action as a figure who is inscribed within both orders.

In *L'Impuissance*, also by Vercors[78], the report of the massacre in Oradour and the death in a concentration camp of Bernard Meyer, a mutual friend of the narrator and the central character, Reynaud, call into question the status of Art itself. Here it is not a question of a negative Art serving as alibi and absolution, but, for Reynaud, all artistic endeavours. His rejection is absolute as he piles up all his cultural possessions in order to burn them. The humanist belief in Man, bearer of the virtues of civilisation, universal essence of humanity in which all men partake, is by the end of the Occupation[79] finding it difficult to accommodate acts defined as inhuman and retain its universalist basis. The fear of evil as a contaminating force is having far-reaching effects, and *L'Impuissance* is pointing towards the post-war preoccupation with moral uncertainties; here Art is denounced as camouflaging from the individual the essentially 'bestial' nature of Man. It is not the fact of the individual's relation to a universal human nature which has changed, but its content. Art is the focus of Reynaud's attack as the supreme expression of a supposedly civilised humanity, and thus, for Reynaud, its supreme alibi. It should however be mentioned that his violent and unambiguous rejection of Art and all it stands for can in part be explained by elements in his own character (and is thus reminiscent of the fluctuation around Thomas's passion for France in *La Marche à l'étoile*). Reynaud is 'always ready to load onto his own shoulders the weight of any injustice – always ready to be the one to pay for the sins of the world'.[80] though the reference to the Occupation as years spent 'in the depths of the catacombs' probably suggests the parallel intended is the early Christian martyrs rather than with Christ himself.

The narrator's final comments which form a kind of codicil to the narrative reverse the terms exactly. Reynaud cannot redeem the world and Man by immolating Art, precisely because 'man is a pretty nasty brute. Luckily art and disinterested thought redeem him.'[81] On the other hand, the relation of the individual to Art has indeed been disturbed and become suspect. The restriction of this feeling of suspicion to the narrator alone sounds more like denegation than conviction, though one could argue that, as in *La Marche à l'étoile*, it serves to distinguish and preserve Art as transcendent value: 'And yet, since that day, I've lost my love of reading. But it's me, not the books: I'm the one who has a guilty conscience.'[82] The narrator thus internalises Reynaud's message on the baseness of men by realigning the set of relations constituted by *Art – Man – men* and transposing it to a religious framework, where Art is superior to Man who is in need of redemption. As an individual man, then, the narrator does not reject Art, but knows he is unworthy of it. Unfortunately, art and thought thus seem to be completely taken out of the human sphere of action, and certainly this conclusion cannot be considered positive in the sense I have used the term of the 'persuasive' text. It ends with a statement of the value of Art, not with a lesson for the future. This is therefore a transitional[83] text, endorsing neither the certainties of humanism nor their outright rejection.

L'Impuissance is further evidence of the way in which events such as Oradour are undermining the central tenets of humanism, particularly the faith in Man and belief in a common humanity, towards the end of the Occupation. But this is not to say that these kinds of question are entirely absent from the fiction of the Resistance. The narrator of *Le Puits des miracles* insistently asks: 'What kind of men have we become?' in the face of the material and 'spiritual' degradation imposed by Vichy. In *La Marque de l'homme*, the humiliation of being a prisoner is mentioned as one of the main sources of suffering in the camp. But this can only be taken as evidence of such questions being a constant preoccupation or indeed characteristic of Resistance literature when the demands of the structure of narrative are ignored. Any particular narrative problem must inevitably contain the possibility of more than one development in order that it may constitute a real dilemma which can be solved. If this is true of realist fiction in general, it is especially true of 'persuasive' fiction. To recall a most obvious example: there would be no danger of von Ebrennac not being taken for an enemy unless he were constructed as good and likeable, or, more to the point perhaps, seductive. But it would be misleading to deduce from this that the text is not concerned with the recognition of the enemy. In the same way, the narrator's meeting in the courtyard at the end of *Le Puits des miracles* with those preparing for Resistance by hiding a gun for future use is an effective answer to the earlier question, and the fears of passive adjustment to any situation it implies.[84] In *La Marche à l'étoile* the degradation imposed by the Occupation cannot be read outside the eternal France/present France opposition which articulates it, nor the fact that here identification of this degradation is *necessary* in order to surmount it. All these stories therefore exemplify the structures of *littérature de témoignage*, in the way they produce a pro-Resistance interpretation of the Occupation, and in their positive affirmation of the values of humanism.

Notes

1 Part of his argument is a political critique of the assumption of the notion of 'culture' and its universalist basis by the anti-fascist movement, and its failure to elaborate a politics of culture. See also Fortini, 'The Writer's Mandate', *Screen*, Spring 1974, pp. 33–70.

2 Mario Cannella, 'Ideology and Aesthetic Hypotheses in the Criticism of Neo-Realism', *Screen*, Winter 1973–74, vol. 14, no. 4, p. 28.

3 J. Guéhenno, *Journal des années noires*, p. 196.

4 'Subject' here being used in the narrow political sense. Cf. British subject.

5 Cannella, pp. 34–5.

6 Quoted in 'Pages choisies de Jacques Decour', *LF*, no. 14, mars 1944, p. 8.

7 *NRF*, vol. 13.1, 1919, p. 45.

8 P. 46n.

9 Forez (pseudonym of François Mauriac), 1943.

10 *LF*, no. 10, octobre 1943, p. 3.

11 *In the Service of the People*, London, 1945, p. 13.

12 'Domaine français', *LF*, no.18, juillet 1944, p.3.

13 *Ibid.*

14 *Opéra*, Journal de tous les arts, avril–mai 1944, p. 1.

15 'Les Fusillés d'Ascq', *LF*, no. 16, mai 1944, p. 4.

16 'Le Crime contre l'esprit', *LF*, no. 16, mai 1944, p. 8.

17 *La Nuit finira*, p. 184. His answer is: 'One could only reply with

reference to the eternal values which, I told myself, France must personify if she is not to deny herself.'
18 P. 92
19 *LF*, no. 13, février 1944, p. 4.
20 P. 93
21 On the narrative level this also serves to close any possibility of escape from their situation.
22 P. 9.
23 P. 8.
24 P. 10.
25 P. 11.
26 *Ibid.*
27 *Ibid.*
28 P. 12.
29 P. 13.
30 'Domaine interdit', *LF*, no. 14, mars 1944, p. 7.
31 'Un homme, un art ne valent que par la puissance de vie qu'ils projettent.' P.S. (Pierre Seghers), *Poésie 42*, V, novembre–décembre 1942, no. 11, p. 91.
32 See Pierre Emmanuel, 'Le Poète et son public', *Poésie 45*, janvier 1945, no. 22, p. 131. The post-war date shows (a) the continuity of vision concerning the nature of poetry and (b) that poets are still *arguing* for a particular kind of poetry to be accepted.
33 Georges Meyzargues (pseudonym of Aragon), in *Poésie 43*, XII, janvier–février 1943, pp. 3–12.
34 Claude Jacquier (pseudonym of Georges Sadoul), 'A travers la presse littéraire', *Poésie 42*, novembre–décembre 1942, no. 11, p. 71.
35 'Signaux de Suisse', *Poésie 42*, II, février–mars 1942, no. 8, p. 82.
36 In *Poésie 42*, II, p.4.
37 The intellectual importance of North Africa was of course immense at this time.
38 Pp. 4–5.
39 P. 5.
40 'Domaine interdit', *LF*, no. 14, mars 1944, p. 7.
41 *LF*, no. 15, avril 1944, p. 5.
42 *Ibid.* Emphasis added.
43 Paris, 1946, p. 19.
44 Pp. 19–20.
45 P. 69.
46 P. 67 (Jacques speaking).
47 Pp. 229–30 (Claire's diary).
48 Cf. Jacques's fear that France/Claire is goiing to 'renier son passé, se renier elle-même'.
49 See p. 185.
50 P. 19. And see also p. 132 and p. 134.
51 P. 230.
52 P. 137.
53 P. 139.

54 Pp.140–1.
55 P. 141.
56 Pp. 145–6.
57 P. 145.
58 *Le Silence*, p. 40.
59 P. 145.
60 See p. 147.
61 P. 146.
62 Pp. 147–8. This accent on von Stum's lack of attraction is also overdetermined from a narrative point of view by the primary conflict between Jean and Jacques. Jean reacts to Claire's letters about von Stum with jealousy and fears she might be betraying him. Jacques, for whom Claire represents France ('à travers elle je voyais la France elle-même', p. 66), fears she is betraying herself. By these phrases Jacques's interpretation once again is proved to be superior to Jean's.

63 Comparing this to *Le Silence de la mer* demonstrates most clearly how far the logic of the narrative is dependent on the perspective which informs it. In *Le Silence* it is an important constituent element of the German, contributing also to the blurring of the friend/foe opposition that Werner von Ebrennac is a musician, but it does not trouble the cultural supremacy of France within the French/German opposition. Von Ebrennac himself accuses German music of being 'inhumaine' (p. 44).

64 'Je pense intensément à toi, Jacques, qui attendais cette heure. *L'heure où la guerre prend un sens*. L'heure de l'épanouissement, de l'Apocalypse.' p. 146. Emphasis added.

65 P. 151.
66 Pp. 150–1.
67 *Les Mots*, 1947.
68 See p. 46.
69 P. 18.
70 P. 15.
71 Pp. 15–16.
72 P. 22.
73 P. 18.

74 He has been asking this question 'for four years' (p. 13). Therefore these questions are dated at the end of the Occupation. (The massacre of the village recalls Oradour.) The imperfect dominates. From the section starting 'Il se réveilla' (p. 25) on what will be the day of the massacre, narrative time and action coincide, and the past historic dominates.

75 Pp. 34–5.
76 Pp. 42–3.
77 P. 49.
78 In *Le Silence de la mer et autres récits*, pp. 113–30.
79 This text is internally dated: 'these four years France has spent in the depths of the catacombs', p. 117. The writing is dated July 1944.
80 P. 117.

81 Pp. 129–30.

82 P. 130.

83 I.e. between the structures of unity of the 'persuasive' writing of the Resistance and the structures of ambiguity characteristic of the post-war novel.

84 It might be possible to read the shift towards the expression of violent and bloody revenge in the later edition, quite similar to some passages in Audisio, as part of the movement away from the optimistic belief in the brotherhood of man.

Chapter three

The figure of the individual; responsibility, action and choice

One received opinion of the war years in France is that they were a time of clear-cut moral choices: Resistance or collaboration, for or against the Germans. Sartre tells Camus that 'Political choice went without saying for Frenchmen like ourselves.'[1] Camus too, in his first 'Réponse à Emmanuel d'Astier', writes that to ask why he joined the Resistance was for him a meaningless question – it was just impossible for him to imagine himself not being on that side.[2] So for many the response was fairly uncomplicated and the Occupation was a time of moral certainties. Oliver Barrot contrasts 'the straightforward conflict under the Occupation with the uneasy times of the cold war'.[3] Yet for S.B. John, the Occupation is rather characterised by 'the profound sense of ambiguity which so frequently penetrates the loyalties and the moral and political choices of French society at this time.[4] And it is difficult not to agree with Claude Roy that the signposts clearly indicating the paths to honour or dishonour are to a great extent the projections of hindsight: 'In October 1940 I discovered, in occupied Paris, this simple fact – in histories written after the event, even if the heroes do not always know where they are going, we know it for them. But I did not have a clue where I was going.'[5] In the post-war period, the dynamics of the nationalist and patriotic discourses tended to produce a picture of the Occupation polarised into a battle between the Resistance, spearhead of the nation, and the Germans and traitors, a view which coexisted with a fictional production whose preferred subject was the ambiguity of daily life under the Occupation. In a sense, therefore, the kind of choice – simple or complex – which is revealed depends on whether the accent is placed on the Occupation as ordinary routine living, or the Occupation as war, in which case, quite tautologically, the choices were pure and unequivocal for those who knew where the battle lines were, who had effectively already chosen.

Simone de Beauvoir sums up this difference, referring to Sartre's difficulty in translating 'the clearcut antagonisms of a prisoner of war'[6] into civilian life in Paris, where 'just the fact of breathing was compromising'.[7] Even those who knew precisely which war they were still fighting did not find it easy to incorporate this into an Occupation which is as much a civilian as a military experience; in far greater numbers were those who followed Vichy in considering the defeat as the end of the war, and who would have to be persuaded, by personal experience[8], argument and exhortation, to join or support the active opposition. In an interview first published in 1969, Sartre blames his belief in an absolute freedom of individual choice on the experience of the Resistance.[9] But *Les Lettres françaises* still found it necessary to *argue* the point in 1942: 'No more room for ifs and buts, for waiting or playing a double game (...) There are only two attitudes possible now: treason or joining the fight.'[10] A clear indication of the at best simplistic nature of the model pitching the whole nation into war is that such efforts at persuasion continue to the very end of the Occupation.

The question of choice and responsibility, dictating commitment to the Resistance cause, is present in nearly all Resistance novels, though in many it does not constitute a narrative dilemma. In *Le Silence de la mer* the silence which greets the German officer is not itself the subject of any previous deliberation. In *Veillée*, one of the stories in *Contes d'Auxois*, Appolonie and Marie who dream of peace and happiness do not understand why Marie's husband Jean should leave the house every night, but the reader is left in no doubt as to his reasons, the importance of the battle for the future and the necessity to be involved in its preparations. In *A l'appel de la liberté* by George Adam, the situation is clarified for the main character Antoine who has just escaped from a prisoner of war camp, when he listens for the first time to a broadcast from London, and he returns to Paris to continue the fight and to lead others into 'seeing clearly into themselves and doing the same'.[11] The exemplary story of Antoine constitutes one step in this direction.

The clandestine press is also exhorting the French to move to action. It seeks to reduce the apparent complexity of the situation to what it considers to be its true simplicity: 'submission or resistance to the enemy',[12] and also rhetorically claims that this is no choice at all: 'It is not easy to deliberately parachute out of a plane. But when the plane carrying you is in danger, in a nose dive and about to crash, there is no alternative. And that is the situation we are in.'[13] Richard Cobb believes that, in the north, because of its geographical situation and First World War experiences, 'there could be no *équivoque*, for there existed no choice'.[14] The efforts of the press are directed towards persuading the French that this is true for them all.

A choice so inevitable as to hardly merit the name is further determined by the fact that any attempt to evade committing onself in itself constitutes a choice, but for the other side. 'Not to fight is to help the enemy', proclaims *L'Humanité* of 18 August 1944.[15] Opposition to the *Service du Travail Obligatoire* provokes similar appeals that 'inaction is a crime'.[16] 'Autour d'une batteuse' (Around a threshing machine), a short story in the ninth issue of *Les Lettres françaises*, sets out to demonstrate the importance of solidarity in resisting enemy demands (in this case, for wheat) and the limitations of a selfish attitude. The farmer in question cannot see why just doing his job could help the enemy, but he falls in line with the rest of the village and the moral of the story is clearly spelt out; it may be taking unprecedented forms, but this is still a war.[17]

Individual responsibility does not stop with the right attitude. Knowing where one's duty lies is not enough; there is a further demand, to do something about it. 'We will judge men by their actions alone.'[18] 'France is at war', proclaims *Défense de la France*, and those who are only concerned with personal safety are 'deserters'.[19] Just as the *relève* and the *STO* are polite words for deportation, as far as the Resistance is concerned, so 'Occupation' is a polite word for 'war'. Once this is realised, all areas of social and private existence are changed: the notions of responsibility, action and choice are structurally interdependent, but equally dependent on the figure of the enemy. The constitution of the individual as Resister and the recognition of the enemy are two elements of the same movement. This point will be further developed later.

It has often been emphasised that the Resistance was a volunteer, not a conscript force, and this may go some way towards explaining the stylistic features of the call to action, based on a direct appeal to each individual:

Heroism is that instant when a decision is reached (...) that minute when you hear the call and must answer (...) PRESENT.[20]

Nothing must stop you acting. We need no other call up than that of our own conscience.[21]

The convergence of military and quasi-religious vocabulary produces a strict voluntarism which cannot be evaded. Vailland's description of the Occupation as 'that peremptory demand to take sides',[22] is particularly apt when applied to the imperative nature of the address to the individual: 'We must each recognise our responsibility and act accordingly.'[23] And this commitment must be constantly reaffirmed in a veritable examination of conscience: 'Wherever you are, you must not let a single day go by without asking yourself: "Today, what will I do; today, what have I done for my liberation?".'[24] As the above quotations show, this is particularly acute from spring 1944 onwards as the final battle approaches, and is also operating around another major event of the Occupation, the attitude and action to take in the face of the *Relève* and the *STO*. Quéval's comment after the war is a fair reflection of the Resistance position: 'The yardstick of patriotism under the Occupation is there. Anyone who resisted deportation did their duty. Anyone who abetted it is excluded from the national community.'[25] There was a great campaign throughout the clandestine press against the *Relève* and the *STO*; Kedward comments that 'it is clear from the tone of the arguments that some workers are allowing themselves to be attracted by the scheme'.[26] *La Relève*, one of the *Contes d'Auxois*, is part of this campaign, and also is a clear example of the manner in which the question of choice is constructed as an individual dilemma.

The story opens with two conflicting imperatives, one addressed to a group, the other to a singular, indeterminate subject, which constitute the terms of the dilemma:

In the newspapers, it said 'Workers, leave (*partez*) for Germany. For those who did not experience the prisoner of war camps, it is a duty to relieve those who have been anxiously waiting, for months, behind barbed wire. It is your duty.'

And the banned radio intoned with a mysterious, commanding voice which embedded itself in people's heads: 'Germany, don't go, Germany, don't go (*ne va pas*).'[27]

These two commands install a number of specific elements (imperative, singular and plural, the verbs *aller* and *partir*) which generate and continue to structure the development of the story. The first part presents the reactions of a group of workers to the official demands; the second concentrates upon the case of one particular worker, Robert Basin, who has been called up for the STO. The shift from the group to the individual, in part demanded by the imperatives at the beginning, is effected by the issuing of individual papers for the STO, giving a particular urgency to the singular imperative from the Resistance, 'ne va pas'.

The group of workers addressed by the *Relève* feel they can choose whether to go or not, a choice which is then placed within a historical context, a political context, as a continuity is established with strike action and struggles against oppression in the past. Translating this struggle into the context of the Occupation entails a rejection of the official pronouncement. The way the discussion of the responses of the workers (two of whom are tempted by the personalised basis of the appeal) is developed is therefore ordered within the opposition between 'leave' and 'do not leave'. A further division between the workers and the official pronouncement appears in the difference between their knowledge of the failure of the *Relève* and newspaper reports of its success. Their knowledge is confirmed by the replacement of the volunteer system by the STO, creating the category of 'obligatory volunteers'.[28] But the ending of the volunteer system and the issuing of the individual papers means that the choice can no longer operate within 'leave'/'not leave', indicated by the fact that the use of the singular, tied to 'go', reappears at this point:

– What will you do if you're picked out? (...)
– I'm not leaving.
– That's easy to say. But where will you go (*où vas-tu*)?[29]

As staying would mean being arrested, negation of the affirmative order 'leave' is no longer sufficient, but neither is acceptance of the negative order 'don't go', as its prescription of immobility allows no response to 'what will you do?' or 'where will you go?'

The switch to the particular case of Robert Basin will produce the solution. As individual worker, he functions as addressee of both imperatives, being the unifying focus by which the narrative articulates them; Robert Basin is also a named individual with a personal history and this will enable the new elements to be introduced which will reconcile the conflicts. Robert examines, and cannot resolve, his dilemma. He goes to see his girlfriend Simone who states the only possible outcome to the conflict in the terms within which it has been posed up to now: 'You're leaving, she said.'[30] 'Don't go' has proved ineffective against the individualised order of the STO. Simone, the only character not addressed by, and therefore not subordinated to either imperative, is the element which will allow 'don't go' to be realised. She is placed in opposition to the offical imperative ('You must not leave', she says)[31] and, within the psychology of the couple, has already helped Robert towards attitudes incompatible with passive submission. She issues the third imperative and provides the solution:

Don't leave, she said for the third time.
How, he said.
I'll hide you.[32]

The addressee of this third imperative can submit to it and the story ends by opening on to a positive future as the hint of selfish motives such as personal safety is set aside, and the negative 'you must not leave' is replaced by an affirmative: 'Men must stay here.'[33] Finally the future is governed by the affirmative imperative replacing 'don't go': 'When the time comes to take out the rifles and machine guns, then go (*alors, va*) I won't hold you back.'[34]

In 'La Relève' the question of choice is subsumed under the possibility of action. Although Robert Basin already knows which side he is on, and therefore does not want to go to Germany, since 'if it serves their interests, then ours are the exact opposite'[35], he cannot translate that decision into action. Schematic as it is, 'Autour d'une batteuse' mentioned earlier is more typical of the stories dealing particularly with individual dilemmas, both in its emphasis on the question of choice and the kind of opposition which structures it; it is also constructed on the basis of the response to an order, but one order only, from the Resistance, and the farmer has to decide whether to please himself or to submit and be inconvenienced. The important factor here is the presence of a wider group, the village as a whole, which overrides personal considerations, a new feeling of solidarity binding him in spite of himself. If the possibility of the individual choosing to pass to action is inseparable from the recognition of the enemy, it is also inseparable from the recognition of belonging to a wider group. Wilkinson writes that 'refusal to obey despotic power was the duty of every *résistant*. Yet at the same time, a purely solipsistic view of the individual as an end in himself was rejected by the Resistance in the interests of group solidarity.'[36] Throughout the pages of *Les Lettres françaises* the notion of the individual is articulated with that of a totality, and individual responsibility therefore has a social dimension.

Gillois informs his readers of the process of becoming an active Resister in a manner very similar to the schemas of the stories which will be considered here:

> Those who have become active before you were men and women like you, your neighbours, your fellows.
>   Their greatness is to have done simply what it seemed to them impossible not to do. Perhaps they hesitated at the last minute. Perhaps, indeed doubtless, they were sometimes afraid. Conquer as they did your feelings of fear and doubt.[37]

But if a couple of sentences in a broadcast are enough to refer to and thus dispose of any potential problems, in the fiction the fears, doubts, hesitations and outright refusals expand to form the very stuff of the narrative.

In most of the novels and stories concentrating specifically on various kinds of hesitation about active involvement, action, given the importance of the recognition of a *de facto* state of war, means ultimately only one thing: to kill.[38] Also, all the doubts which the main characters experience are finally overcome after the death or imprisonment (operating as a virtual death) of another main character with whom relations have been both close and full of conflict; but this death is always the occasion of a new reconciliation between them: 'Just when I find her again, they take her away from me'[39] are the words of the main character of *La Marque de l'homme* and a particularly clear demonstration of the structure. There are two points to be made about this. Firstly, since these novels equate action against the enemy with an acceptance of killing and being killed, it is quite logical that this aggression, which functions as the positive resolution of the conflicts of the narrative, does not surface *ex nihilo*, directed at the enemy alone, but is structured into the development of the novel, extending to the whole network of relations. Secondly, given the frequency with which this entails the death of a friend, wife or lover, it is a reasonable hypothesis that such a death is structurally determined by those relations of aggression and therefore necessary *in order that* the main character may move to action.

In 'Les Rencontres' (Chance Meetings), by Aragon,[40] the main character who cannot bring himself to join the active Resistance in the *maquis* is a journalist, Pierre Vandermeulen, who is generally known by the name he writes under, Julep. The title refers to his meetings over a period of ten years with various members of a working-class family, notably Emile Dorin, a metal worker. The contrasting evolutions of Julep and Emile, specifically in relation to major political events (February 1934, the strikes of 1936, Spain, the defeat of France and the Occupation) form the basis of the story, the point of which is to take the journalist into active participation in the Resistance. That he is in fact split across two names is extremely important, for each connotes a different set of values. He signs 'Vandermeulen' for his serious writings , 'Julep' for the frivolous pieces. However, the latter are more successful, Julep becomes famous and Pierre Vandermeulen slowly disappears. Moreover, under the Occupation, he uses several other pseudonyms, and receives a set of false papers in the name of Jacques Denis, but Julep dominates by the frequent meetings with Emile who always calls him 'Monsieur Julep'. 'Vandermeulen' is therefore also effaced in the network of narrative relationships. He fights the war as 'Lieutenant Vandermeulen', and so this name is marked as 'serious' and 'military'. Equally importantly, the dilemmas and conflicts in relation to action are focused on 'Julep'.

Julep first meets Emile and his wife Rosette at a cycle race at the *Vélodrome d'Hiver*, introduced by Emile's sister Yvonne who works at the same newspaper. Julep is sent to major sporting events, although not at all interested in sport, to write about the atmosphere. He notices a young enthusiast who turns out to be Emile. The connection between them continues on the basis of Julep's work – he interviews Emile when he has to report on the political opinions of the 'man in the street'. On this occasion Julep also meets Rosette's sister and brother-in-law, who both work at Renault. Neither are named and the sister is never mentioned again. The brother-in-law will be important 'because he was obviously a Communist and we clashed over one or two things, of course'.[41]. From the strikes of 1936 Emile becomes more and more politically involved, an evolution Julep does not follow and furthermore blames on the brother-in-law. Emile is cast in the role of educator, explaining why he is on strike, or later, why he and Rosette, with two children already, wish to adopt a Spanish refugee child (the brother-in-law himself is fighting in Spain). The working relationship also breaks down. Emile's comments on Munich, even watered down by Julep, are too extreme to be printed.

The first meeting at the *Vélodrome d'Hiver* can be seen as a paradigm for their subsequent meetings and their attitudes to the Occupation. Julep, as a journalist who knows nothing about sport, is an ignorant observer. Emile is passionately involved both with the race and anything to do with bikes, he is therefore both knowledgeable and a participant. The structure remains with the shift to political matters: Julep interrogates, Emile informs. Under the Occupation, the political knowledge and activities of the family are tranlsated immediately into action against the Germans. The brother-in-law is brutally killed by the Germans during a strike, Rosette is deported to Silesia and Yvonne arrested and held in a camp. Emile joins the *maquis* and is finally caught and executed. Julep undergoes a slow political and intellectual evolution from his initial position on the side of law and order. He chronicles the shift of public opinion away from Vichy, is approached several times by the Resistance, but continues to earn his living as before, which now means writing in the collaborationist press. One crucial element of change for Julep is coming personally into contact with the *maquis* after taking part in a mass escape from prison: after Yvonne's arrest, he decides to hide a Jewish colleague, but the poorly made false identity papers lead to them both being arrested. He meets Emile in prison, and it is

Emile who makes sure he is included in the escape, having significantly asked him his name. It is as 'Vandermeulen' that he escapes, placed on the list of political prisoners and counted as a patriot. He now defends the *maquis* against anti-communist friends, and himself learns to overcome his past attitudes. He finally accepts fully his personal responsibility: 'Did the brother-in-law, or Yvonne, or Rosette wait for the Allied landings? I will have to join in. It's not possible to let things go on like this, without joining in.'[42] But the decision to do something about it only occurs with the news of Emile's death:

> Someone must give me weapons. I was a lieutenant, for God's sake, in the French Army. I too would know how to train the men in the *maquis* to use arms (...) I am Lieutenant Vandermeulen, not that spineless Jacques Denis, not that egoist Julep. (...)
> My dear Emile. On this very day. This final meeting is for eternity, Emile.
> Today Lieutenant Pierre Vandermeulen starts his new life. You can't betray your friends.
> And when one falls, ten more must rise.[43]

Vandermeulen, as he must now be called, can start to act, a part of the group he recognises himself as belonging to, with Emile whose work he continues.

In this story, there surfaces none of the overt aggression between the two main protagonists which I have indicated as characteristic of these novels. Indeed, it may seem perverse not to take the final note of unity at face value, especially as the alliance forged beyond death with those killed or executed, who live on in those who continue their action, is a theme often found in Resistance poetry. But there are hints that the relation between Emile and Julep is more complex than the major opposition which I have outlined above, and that Emile's death is not solely contingent upon being caught by a German patrol.

One can understand this more clearly by drawing on material in another story in the same collection, 'Les Jeunes Gens'(The Young Men), a story of three young men. Elisée, who is executed as a *dénonciateur* by the other two, uses dreams to compensate for his miserable existence: 'He dreamt only of himself. Let the world perish, let his family, all others perish, so he might, even momentarily, shine, triumph, live.'[44] This is extremely similar to the construction of 'Julep', the name tied to fame and success. Elisée is self-centred, like Julep 'the egoist'. His dreams avenge him for his own inadequacies, he is ineffectual like 'Jacques Denis'. Through his dreams, Elisée can recreate himself, but for that he has to purge more than his own hated self: 'all the people Elisée knew were dying violent deaths (...) It was not important how: but in the end, a new life was starting, with Elisée cleansed of all the filth of the past.'[45] Vandermeulen in 'Les Rencontres' also starts a new life: Julep and all who knew him are destroyed, specifically Emile who refused to call him by any other name.

The first clear sign of Julep being imbricated in aggressive structures marked by killing occurs towards the end of the story, in a dream which ends with an image of Emile and a *milicien* of the village where he is staying: 'He was aiming at Emile. I wanted to cry out. (...) but Emile was the one who had fired and the *milicien* on the road, was bleeding, bleeding... I awoke with a start, frightened at myself. Did I really wish a man's death?'[46] It is difficult not to suspect here a certain ambiguity as to *which* man's death he wanted, the one who was shot or the one he failed to warn. Certainly before the dream he is becoming increasingly at risk from the Resistance, always focused on and therefore equated with Emile. A 'youth camp' he is visiting is raided by a group from the *maquis*, all armed and 'aiming at us'[47] one of whom turns out to be Emile, who also becomes omnipresent in the increasing number of explosions in the region: 'It's silly, but I have the impression it is always Emile who is behind them.'[48] And if Elisée's selfishness takes the form of a generalised hatred and persecution ('he did not like gun shots. He always, in his dream, felt he was the one being fired at'),[49] Julep seems to be cast in the same mould, as part of the dream shows: 'Suddenly, gunshots, and men who had done nothing but be there, fell to the ground'.[50] echoing up the earlier incident in the youth camp.

Further evidence of an ambivalence on Julep's part towards Emile can be seen if we consider his relations to the family, excluding Rosette whom he describes but has no specific reactions to. Julep is gradually more and more attracted to Yvonne, and regrets not having married her; twice he notes her physical resemblance to Emile. The brother-in-law to whom Emile draws politically closer provokes great antagonism[51] and of them all is the one to undergo the violent death Elisée dreams of inflicting. So Emile is flanked by two characters, each of whom he resembles, each marked by either strong attraction or hostility. This ambivalence, which explains how Emile can be both emulated and eliminated from the narrative, finds its counterpart in the differences, the structural significance of which can now be realised, between Julep and Vandermeulen. Emile's death, inscribed within the narrative structures, is necessary in order that the shift between them may be effected.

In 'La Relève', the dilemma which inhibits the possibility of action is centred on the individual, but there is no suggestion of a negatively connoted self-centredness being a contributory factor, mainly because the recognition of a group identity is not in doubt. The two stories by Aragon discussed above are more typical, since in many Resistance stories selfishness in a leading character fulfils the function of blocking the recognition of responsibility and action.

There are of course many variations on this pattern. An egocentrism which is not overcome can lead directly to collaboration. This is what underpins the portrayal of Elisée in 'Les Jeunes Gens'; he lives out his fantasy of himself against the world he knows by aligning himself, under the Occupation, with the Germans, identifying with their apparently unlimited power, as they are the enemies of his enemies. This psychological portrait of a traitor finds its political equivalent in *Le Puits des miracles* where the unbridled selfishness of the ruling group has its roots in their opposition to the Popular Front and explains the welcome they extend to the more powerful invaders. That this particular psychological trait should occur so often indicates its value in the system. The reason it is such an effective and economical means of portraying attitudes which are construed as negative, in that the priority it accords to exclusively personal concerns is an outright rejection of a common national or political good greater than the individual, lies in the structural importance of the figure of the individual. Self-centredness or active Resistance, the former closed in upon itself, the latter open, as by osmosis, to a collective identity, constitute the two primary narrative options in relation to the appeal to action which is predicated upon an individual response. The figure of the individual ensures a structural homogeneity which is essential if a particular character is to

pass from exclusive individualism to Resistance without disturbing the overall coherence of the narrative.

For action which can be described as pro-Resistance to occur,
the two elements of the oppositional structure schematically
described as the one *versus* the other, relying on the figures of the
individual and the enemy, must be aligned on the axis constructed by us *versus* them to which they are metonymically and
often metaphorically related; for example the French pair in *Le
Silence de la mer* are *part of* a wider French identity which they also
represent. (These structures will be discussed further in the next
chapter.) In novels where it is precisely the question of action
which is in doubt, these two structures fail to coincide: the one
versus the other is, on the one side of the opposition at least, a
literal rather than a schematic rendering of the relationship, since
the structure operating in these novels is that of 'I *versus* all of
them'. But this means that the shift to 'us *versus* them' (reduced to
a definite enemy) necessary to achieve a positive ending, can be
accommodated without altering the structure.[52] In other words,
the nature of the opposition retarding the positive ending is in
fact generated by the nature of the ending to be achieved.

In the first part of *La Marque de l'homme* many minor differences
are developed between the narrator Jean Bermont and Jacques
Fontanier which culminate in their differing attitudes to Jean's
wife Claire. For Jean this takes the form of an obsessive jealousy
which becomes particularly acute after Jacques escapes from the
prisoner of war camp. But for Jacques this jealousy reveals a
possessive kind of love symptomatic of a general egoism: 'You
think you are the centre of the world',[53] a phrase which continues
to haunt the narrator after Jacques's death, and which sums up
the manner in which he is shown to have adapted to the harshness
and isolation of the prison camp by hanging on to the notion of
personal happiness. In this novel, this purely personal response is
opposed to belief in a transcendent ideal which not only overrides personal considerations but offers a kind of salvation for
some, as another prisoner, Costes, explains: 'Captivity is not the
same test for all (...) To a certain extent, Fontanier was protected
from its worst features because he believes in man. The Christian
also escapes them. But the man who does not believe in man and
does not believe in God, who has only himself and is his own god,
if he is lucid – like you for example, Bermont – he suffers more

than the others and starts hating the whole world.'[54] This is an accurate description of the kind of state Jean was in while Jacques was away from the camp, which meant that for Jean the outside world was filled with a hostile presence bent on taking Claire from him. The culmination of his selfish state, it is characterised by feeling hostility being directed towards him (and internalised to the extent that he longs for his own death) and also by hatred, the recognition of which is, like his conversation with Costes, part of his long process of self-analysis and change.[55] What is striking about it is that he fails, when admitting how hatred has ruled him, to mention directly any hostility towards Jacques, who was the main focus for his anger. The structures of aggression under-pinning the relations between the central characters are played down as Jean moves towards an acceptance of active Resistance involvement. This is however less an overcoming of aggression than a rechannelling of it in a different direction.

The primary opposition between selfish and unselfish attitudes which dictate behaviour under the Occupation structures all the major themes of this novel – love, death and action – and also the very mode of being of the individual. Jacques, motivated by a defence of France and of man, 'rises beyond his own limits'.[56] Saubret, a former colleague of Jean's who preaches a philosophy of detachment, is a grotesque parody of this: 'a slave of his own self, a monster swollen to the skies'.[57] This is precisely the path Jean is taking in the camp, obsessed by the jealousy inherent to selfish love: 'I had my anguish which kept me alive, which swelled out to a grotesque size, monstrous and insatiable'.[58] and which leads to his generalised feelings of hatred. Attitudes to death constitute another essential element of differentiation between the selfish personality and the active Resister. The latter accepts his death in the name of a greater ideal, but as his life is a perpetual going beyond the limits of his own self, so his death too takes him to new heights: 'For the believer, by which I mean the believer in a religion or a set of ideas, Christian, Communist or just patriotic – death can be an achievement, a blossoming, an explosion of life at its summit.'[59] Acceptance of death resides in the access to a collective identity in which the fighter lives on, whereas, even in the battle for France, self-protection, 'putting my life above my ideal',[60] was Jean's primary concern.

The diegetic development is governed by the account of Jean's evolution towards a full acceptance of his own death, and also of those close to him. The first break with the structures of hatred opposing Jean and Jacques occurs with the introduction of the enemy as a specific figure in the text. Jean is summoned before the commander of the camp to tell what he knows of Jacques's escape, and he desperately wants to do so in order to prevent Jacques reaching Claire. Significantly, this is the first time Jean is named: 'I', the subject of the narration, becomes Jean Bermont, the object of a command. The hatred directed towards Jacques is interrupted by a more powerful, implicitly hostile presence, and this is one of the clearest examples that the recognition of individual responsibility, founded on a group identity, and recognition of the enemy form part of the same movement. Claire later goes through the same process when for the first time she experiences hatred for the 'barbarians': 'My personal wretchedness takes me out of my solitude and into a feeling of solidarity with this oppressed people. It makes me, in my turn, a fighter (*une combattante*).'[61]

The generalised hostility between the self and others has focused specifically on relations between Jean and Jacques and therefore one could argue that the logic of the narrative demands the elimination of the latter in order to eliminate the conflict for which it has been the vehicle. As Costes later says to Jean: 'Fontanier's death, all it taught you about yourself, changed you again, one could say it *released* you.'[62] This has a specific meaning within the context of this narrative[63] but also admirably describes the process whereby the deaths of important characters are inscribed within the network of relations as a necessary part of the active commitment of the main character. After Jacques's death the primary opposition between the active and the inactive is carried by the relations between Jean and Claire. On his return from the camp, Jean has been transformed into an apprentice Jacques,[64] whereas Claire has now developed the kind of selfish love which is the focus of an obliquely expressed antagonism. For Jean, the only way forward is 'the fight or suicide',[65] the latter in response to Claire's possessiveness, thus renewing the internalised aggression combined with hatred experienced in the prison camp. This culminates in Jean's refusal in prison to talk to the interrogator who threatens to arrest Claire, in spite of the fact that 'my refusal condemned my family',[66] a dilemma within the interpersonal structures which has been indirectly announced by Claire's anger that the husband of a friend might be shot as a hostage because of Resistance actions, while Jean justified them as necessary whatever the consequences. Sartre considered that under the Occupation, 'the real drama is that of the terrorist who, shooting Germans in the street, provokes the execution of 50 hostages'.[67] Throughout the clandestine press, responsibility for these executions is laid firmly at the Germans' door, who thereby reveal themselves as the real terrorists. But in *La Marque de l'homme*, and even more so in *Le Sang des autres*, the question of these deaths is indubitably linked to that of the individual responsibility of the Resister. Within the narrative schema, then, the drama of the hostages being raised in this manner fulfils two functions, both closely linked. The Resister has to face the possibility of causing deaths *other than* those of the enemy – this is Claire's accusation, and also that of Jean Blomart's mother in *Le Sang des autres*; but because this is discussed in relation to a separate group, the fact that these are precisely the relations pertaining between the main characters themselves is obscured.

It is hardly surprising to find an existentialist novel such as *Le Sang des autres* under the heading of responsibility, action and choice, for in a philosophy of the subject which rejects notions of external necessity or pre-ordained sets of values in order to bring to the fore the idea of individual freedom, in both the philosophical and moral senses of the word, such themes are particularly important, as are relations with others. Simone de Beauvoir singled out this latter question as her primary motivation in writing the novel,[68] and felt that the use of the Resistance was rather unhappily tacked on in order to provide the necessary social dimension. It is certainly true that the novel is heavily marked by its existentialist perspective and vocabulary. The structures of recognition, for example, signalling the collective identity underpinning the possibility of action, are cast in a specifically philosophical context in the author's summary of the book: 'In the generosity of comradeship and action, [Hélène] finally won that recognition – in the Hegelian sense of the word – which saves men from immanence and contingency.'[69] Yet this does not lessen the novel's striking similarity to other Resistance novels which take as their subject the problems of action, and especially to *La Marque de l'homme*. In both, the central conflicts become gradually focused on the relations between a man and a woman; both use the technique of differing narrative viewpoints in order that the central character, subject of the narration, becomes the object of a different subject's narration.[70] In both – and this they share with 'Les Rencontres' – the problem posed by the deaths of those marginal to the particular action of the protagonists is an important dimension of the primary opposition. It is thus apparent that, whether an author's intention is to demonstrate the necessity of action under the Occupation or to examine interpersonal relations of conflict, once this is translated into narrative terms it becomes subordinated to a set of structural constraints which means that there is little trace, in the end product, of which point in the structure was the author's starting point. Given that the central dilemma of whether or not to act is inseparable from the equation between action and killing, then structures of aggression must underpin the refusal of action as much as the action finally undertaken. In the case of *Le Sang des autres*, the problems raised by the executions of hostages, in reprisal for the kind of action against the Germans carried out by the main protagonists, is the primary reference of the title, but, as will be seen, the death of others commands the various narrative dilemmas of the pre-war historical development, in both personal and political spheres. The Occupation and the Resistance provide the context, the culmination and the finally positive solution to conflicts which are inherent in the narrative as a whole.

In *La Force des choses*, Beauvoir reiterated her annoyance that *Le Sang des autres* was acclaimed as a Resistance novel, a fact she attributed to the timing of its publication,[71] and stressed that its main theme was 'the paradox of existence lived by me as my freedom and grasped as an object by those near to me'.[72] But the important point in relation to the structure of unity is not so much the existential structure of this paradox but rather its precise content, since the realisation of the self as other takes place in the context of death and separation.

A connection between death and relations with the other can already be found in Beauvoir's discussion of the subject of *L'Invitée* (She Came to Stay). The existence of the consciousness of the other was, she says, 'as scandalous as death'[73] and in the same passage she explains that 'crime was one of my habitual fanta-sies';[74] to stand as the accused in the witness box is to realise a total personal responsibility. At a time when she sees herself trans-ferring reponsibility for her life to Sartre, 'only a crime could return me to my solitude'.[75]. By interweaving these themes she produces an imaginary scenario which, allowing for some changes of emphasis, serves as an admirably neat analysis of the dynamics of the oppositions found in the Resistance fiction con-cerned with the dilemmas of action: 'A consciousness revealed itself to me, in its irreducible presence; through jealousy, through envy, I committed a fault which placed me in its power (*à sa merci*): *my salvation lay in annihilating it*.'[76] The choice of violent attacks and reprisals under the Occupation must therefore be con-sidered to be a *motivated* one: as *La Marque de l'homme* and *Drôle de jeu* demonstrate, the dangers of action can be rendered by involvement in a clandestine newspaper or intelligence gather-ing, which the risks of arrest, torture and execution imbricate just as effectively in structures of violence. In *Le Sang des autres*, however, the elements inhibiting action cannot be resolved by Blomart facing arrest and execution but by coming to terms with himself as a murderer; the relation of the main character to killing is therefore much more direct.

The whole of the novel is organised to produce the answer to the simple choice with which it opens, whether or not the Resistance group will carry out their planned attack on the follow-ing day:

When he opened the door, all eyes turned to him.
'What do you want of me?' he said.
'I need to know if it's on or not for tomorrow.' said Laurent.[77]

The manner in which the question and answer are posed itself points to the terms which are at the heart of the dilemma: 'want' (*vouloir*) as opposed to 'need' (*falloir*), or, to put it another way, desire as opposed to fatality. It is across these terms that the self will be constructed as both desiring subject and necessarily fatal object (the pun is deliberate) for the other.

Laurent is supposed to be planting a bomb at the 'antibolchevik exhibition'; as leader of the group Jean is not allowed to take part in these expeditions, but has to take the decisions concerning them, and Hélène's fatal injury means he no longer feels capable of doing so. He puts it off until the morning, which establishes the temporal structures of the novel. Hélène will not survive the night but for Jean and the others the concerns of the immediate future dominate the present. By deferring the crucial decision until the following morning a finality is explicitly introduced into the narrative process in which past, present and future are implicated. It is the narration of the night, substantially the narration of Jean and Hélène's past (which is also the past of the other members of the group) which must produce the way out of Jean's present dilemma.

The history of Jean Blomart is typical of the retrospective history of the political Resistance literature, where the struggle against fascism is projected back into the inter-war years, with the Popular Front, the fight against the fascists in France and the Spanish Civil War constituting the main elements in a chain which leads to the present, and implicitly final, battle. Blomart leaves his bourgeois home and becomes a political activist, involving street battles against the Right. When Jacques, the younger brother of his friend Marcel, who has come under his influence, is killed, he drops all these activities. His choices have led to the death of another, destroying his view of himself as a pure liberty in control of his actions and their consequences. So he becomes a trade union militant, refusing all possibility of violent action; the Popular Front is the realisation of his hopes: 'the reconciliation of all men in the free recognition of their future'.[78] However, such harmony is always articulated with the separation which the novel presents as being at the heart of human existence: 'All were singing in unison. *As if we did not each occupy a separate place on earth; as if we had not each been this barrier for the other; that is each one for himself alone, existing next to others forever separated from them: another.*'[79] Blomart maintains his principle of non-violent action during the Spanish Civil War and the Munich crisis. This is the same historical itinerary and the same perspective as that of *Les Chemins de la liberté*: refusal to intervene is revealed as another kind of intervention which maintains an intolerable situation – they may feel like Parisians enjoying a stroll, doing no harm to anyone. For the Spanish they were 'de beaux salauds' (proper bastards).[80] That this is one element of a sequence is underlined by the narrative in the references to the future which are in fact already realised, as this is all in flashback: 'Do you think Hitler will stop with Austria? France's turn will come.'[81] Jean's political itinerary has led him full circle; there is no possibility of retreating into a self-centred, self-sufficient existence, nor of avoiding the essentially antagonistic relations with others.

The main reason for the central position of Blomart's relations with others being founded on death and separation is that it is overtly presented as structuring all his personal relationships as well as his political stances. *Le Sang des autres* is unusual in that it returns to the childhood of the main character, and although Jacques's death is the first consequent upon political action, it is not the first that he has had to come to terms with. When he was eight, the child of Louise, a poor woman his mother used to visit, died.[82] This episode is important, not only for its function in the novel, introducing Jean to the scandal of death and the impossibility of living another's experience, the first lesson on his journey to knowledge about the nature of human existence, but also for the particular grouping of themes which sustain it. The event is irremediable, but the trauma it produces cannot last forever, and Jean's attempt to suffer as Louise is suffering is doomed to failure. More interestingly, the notion of life continuing for the living is rendered by a resurgence of desire, and desire is characterised as aggressive: 'desire to bite into their creamy arms, to plunge his face into their hair, to crumple their light silks like a petal'.[83] Ultimately this is what underpins the feelings of guilt and remorse; that the death and suffering of the other were wished for. The blood of others is a scandal not just because they die, but because they are killed, which is to say that the question of responsibility is an essential element of the deaths themselves.

Much of the pain of separation and death stems from the difficulty of deciding just who is the instigator, and who is the victim of it. Louise's child (*le petit de Louise*) and his mother both appear to be absolute victims. But Jacques takes a gun to the demonstration where he is shot and Blomart hears the cry: 'C'est le petit qui a tiré le premier' (The child fired first),[84] a choice of words which suggests that blame and remorse are fluctuating across the characters who are all constructed within the structures of aggression. Blomart's mother tells him of Louise's tragedy with a expression on her face which is difficult to visualise: 'full of reproach and apology',[85] but which admirably sums up the ambivalence concerning the responsibility for the evil of separation

and death. My argument is then that Louise and the dead child
present one variation of the complex pattern of 'the child as
victim of the mother/the child as victim of its own aggression
towards the mother', and the apparently contradictory expression describing Jean's mother is indicative of this. This is particularly clear in the episode when Jean eventually leaves home and
therefore his mother, for the question of who *wishes* the separation (that is, the continuing ambivalence of *vouloir*, desire equated
with aggression) is explicitly formulated.[86]

The death of Louise's child is typical in other ways. Separation
or death often occur in the context of the mother-child relationship: as obvious examples, one can list Jean, Yvonne (a friend
of Hélène who has to look after her hypochondriac mother; they
are Jewish and the Occupation separates them), Ruth (the child
Hélène sees being taken from her mother during a round-up of
Jews in the street) and their mothers. The all-pervasive importance of the connection between mothers, children and death can
be seen in the way it generates certain descriptive features:
'Besides, who was he, the man I was calmly beginning to assassi-
nate by the pond where a swan was floating, under the placid gaze
of mothers of children? (*des mères de famille*)',[87] comments Blomart
about his growing friendship with Jacques.

Another structural element found throught the novel is the
'vigil by the bedside' (*veillée*).[88] Jean's night at Hélène's bedside
while his friends wait in the next room forms the framework of
the narrative. This is partly repeated in the night of Hélène's
abortion which he spends at her bedside, which is a veritable *mise
en abyme*, both of the formal organisation and of the structures of
aggression of the novel, and serves to place the relationship
between Jean and Hélène within the complex of mothers and
children, separation and death. It is also found in transposed
form in Yvonne's situation who spends night after night looking
after her mother. Their relationship appears a cruel parody of
the image of suffering motherhood watching over the dying child
for which Louise is the prototype, since Yvonne's mother is a
malade imaginaire, and Yvonne, unable to leave her, is her victim,
for Hélène at least.[89] The reversal of Louise's situation produces
a nightmare: separation of mothers and children in this novel is
always traumatic, but so is the one instance where they remain
together, another indication that separation is as necessary as it is

painful.

The lesson Jean learns from his childhood and youth is that any direct intervention in the lives of others will have necessarily fatal consequences. 'He has always been convinced that everything he does kills someone', remarks Marcel.[90] His attempt to be completely self-sufficient, to suppress dangerous wishes and desires by suppressing all relations with others which cannot be controlled by his will, is the particular form egocentrism takes in this novel.[91] 'You spend too much time on yourself',[92] another friend later reproaches him. If Jean Bermont in *La Marque de l'homme* seeks personal happiness above all else, Jean Blomart's hopes, paralleling his fears of personal aggression again articulated through the term *vouloir*, are for peace. And like Bermont, it is only in an acceptance of killing and being killed that he discovers he can give meaning to his life. As war approaches, he is still debating the question: 'So busy announcing why we did not *want to die*, did we give a thought to knowing why we were still living?'[93] 'Was it necessary to lose our freedom because we had refused slavery, to dirty ourselves with a thousand crimes because we had not *wanted to kill*?'[94] The declaration of war supersedes Jean's personal dilemma by eliminating the personal dimension: 'Wanting war; not wanting war. Now the answer was meaningless. War was there.'[95] He is a cog in a war machine; fighting a battle does not involve interpersonal relations. Under the Occupation the action of killing can also be voluntarily undertaken because it is still action against the enemy. The presence of the Germans means that 'I' is opposed specifically to 'they', thus entering into a relation of similarity with the other, and from this similarity a unity between subjects can be built. The antagonism between 'I' and 'they', the Germans, causes no problems, since they do not enter into the interpersonal structures of the text; they are characterised by the sound of their boots, the colour of their uniform and their lack of individuality: 'I walked cheerfully through the streets of Clichy, those deaths did not weigh me down.'[96] The political context also annuls the personal difficulties in relation to killing those who are not the enemy, the hostages. Firstly because, in order that the enemy be perceived as such, the state of war must be maintained; the deaths of hostages are therefore *necessary*, the question of personal desires becomes secondary as 'want' is effaced by 'need' ('We need French blood to flow.'[97]). Secondly Jean's knowledge of the violence inherent in inaction, and the inescapability of the criminal, essentially murderous nature of man, means that this particular violence can be accepted. It is when the deaths of others are reintegrated into the interpersonal structures that Blomart's inhibitions return, that he is once more constituted as other, in relation to his mother and finally Hélène, the two major figures in the complex of themes of death and separation.

A red poster goes up in the Métro informing of the executions of twelve hostages, immediately after the attack Blomart helped carry out. Before the German threat of a further twelve executions in three days' time, his mother's reaction is one of anger and silent accusation. He remembers, not just Jacques's death but significantly that of Louise's baby, for this is the occasion of the final separation with his mother: 'she will die without having forgiven me'.[98] Feelings of anguish return, he is again the wilful assassin. But the necessity of his action means he must continue if he is not to fall back into the contingent and the arbitrary and this can now be combined with the inner motivation articulated through 'want': 'I knew it. I wanted it. We shall continue tomorrow.'[99] As stated earlier, separation of mother and child proves necessary. The affect of horror within personal structures, which has resurfaced with the fatal wounding of Hélène, must however still be overcome for a successful conclusion to be reached. Hélène wakes up before dying to allow the question to be resolved. She reaffirms her own liberty, her freedom of choice and responsibility for what has happened to her.[100] This does not remove the opposition between the self and others, but in the definitive assertion of *falloir*, it has removed from that structure the intention of killing. Blomart has not killed Hélène, she has chosen her own death. The removal of implicit antagonism between the two major figures in the novel means that Blomart is no longer the active murderer of the hostages, he has become a 'blind force of fatality', [101] and the narrative can end by the assertion of the continuation of the struggle. The decision posed at the outset is now taken positively.

It is no accident that *La Marque de l'homme* combines the question of the nature of the artist with the necessity for active commitment to the Resistance, for the underlying dichotomy between a Resistance embodying humanist values and a profoundly anti-humanist enemy means that belief in justice, freedom and the individual demands direct action to sustain these values, and a refusal of Resistance is a retreat from the world as well as a rejection of the notions of human solidarity and fraternity. The transition to direct action is effected by the recognition of the enemy which at the same time founds the individual as Resister, partaking of a group identity. The options of retreating from the world into purely individual concerns, into personal relationships, into art conceived as its own justification, are progressively eliminated to close the possibility of any private haven free from disruption or aggression. All the novels I have dealt with in this chapter focus upon the moment of choice itself, on how the individual constructed by the narrative moves from a general to a specific hostility. To transfer from the opposition of 'I *versus* them' to that of 'us *versus* them' does not eliminate the mechanism of antagonism and hatred, the vocabulary of menace and threat, the desire to eliminate a hostile presence, and the fear of the power of that presence as constituted by prisons, torture and executions. This explains why this literature is successful, by which I mean that the negative elements and the conflicts are successfully eliminated, and that the narrative can order its themes to a positive end. Resistance literature in general aims to produce or reinforce hostility towards the Germans. The novels which concentrate on the individual, which take as their subject the elaboration of the process by which that hostility is produced, are able to end with a recognition or reaffirmation of the Resistance precisely because both the negative and positive elements are operating within the structures of hostility. *Le Sang des autres* does not end with mothers and children joyfully and permanently united, but in two out of the three cases (Yvonne, Ruth), it is the Germans who are the hateful presence separating them. The oppositions on the basis of which the narrative has been constructed do not change; the positive ending can be accommodated within the structures of hostility because this is the means whereby the Occupation can be presented as being in fact the continuation of a war.

Notes

1 'Réponse à Albert Camus', *Les Temps modernes*, no. 82, août 1952, p. 336.

2 In King (ed.), *Selected Political Writings*, p. 102.

3 'L'Ecran français', p. 357. James Wilkinson makes a similar point, stating that from August 1944, 'certainties became blurred in a complex pattern of conflicting rights and interests', *The Intellectual Resistance in Europe*, Cambridge, Mass., 1981, p. 50.

4 'Vichy France 1940–1944: The Literary Image', in *French Literature and its Background*, 6, p. 203.

5 *Moi je*, Paris, 1969, p. 295.

6 *La Force de l'âge*, 1970, p. 553.

7 *Ibid.*

8 It is not surprising that Kedward found that 'individual Resisters, discussing their motivations, invariably emphasise the strength of feeling which marked their reaction to a particular event or experience and which was significant in their decision to resist' (*Resistance in Vichy France*, p.186), for such experiences either reveal the battle lines, or prove to be the decisive spur to action. Camus informs d'Astier that reading of the execution of Gabriel Péri, the Communist *député*, was such a moment for him (King (ed.), *Albert Camus: Selected Political Writings*, London, 1981, p. 102). Throughout the fiction of the Resistance, revelation occurs in a particular situation, the dynamics of which will be discussed later. To take just two examples here: a Vichy policeman in *L'Armée des ombres* working for the Resistance dates his commitment from the day when, helping the Germans search for Resisters, he is berated by one of the victims and *sees* what he is doing for the first time (p. 125). The final scene of Aragon's 'Le Collaborateur' ends with a child, the beloved grandson of the collaborator of the title, being shot for running out into the street and 'breaking' the recently imposed curfew. There is no indication of the grandfather's reaction, but as his 'collaboration' consists mainly in his public expression of support for Vichy and the German presence, the need for law and order, and the view that those who are arrested for opposing it are only getting their just deserts, the 'revelatory' intention of the *dénouement* is clear.

9 'Sartre par Sartre', *Situations IX*, Paris, 1972, p. 100. Emphasis added.

10 'La Leçon de Toulon', *LF*, no. 4, décembre 1942, p. 2.

11 1944, p.79.

12 'La France nouvelle', *Résistance*, no. 4, 13 décembre 1942, p. 1.

13 'Dialogue sur l'action', *LF*, no. 1, p. 5.

14 *French and Germans, Germans and French*, Hanover and London, 1983, p.54.

15 Reproduced in Tollet, *La Classe ouvrière dans la Résistance*, p. 302.

16 'Sauver notre jeunesse', *LF*, no. 6, avril 1943, p. 1.

17 *LF* no.9, août 1943, p. 2.

18 'La Leçon de Toulon', *LF*, no. 4, décembre 1942, p. 2.

19 'La France est en guerre', *Défense de la France*, 15 janvier 1944, in *Nous sommes les rebelles*, pp. 39–41.

20 Gillois, *De la Résistance à l'insurrection*, Lyon, n.d., p. 180. Broadcast of 3 June 1944.

21 'La Guerre, rien que la guerre, tout pour la guerre', *LF*, no. 16, mai 1944, p. 2.

22 *Le Surréalisme contre la révolution*, Oeuvres complètes, vol. 8, p. 265.

23 'La comédie Française à l'honneur', *LF*, no. 16, mai 1944, p. 3.

24 Gillois, *op.cit.*, p. 192, broadcast of 21 June 1944. See also pp. 195, 284.

25 Quéval, *Première page cinquième colonne*, Paris, 1945, p. 232.

26 Kedward, *Resistance in Vichy France*, p. 225. Azéma estimates there were 40,000 volunteers and about 650,000 sent under the STO scheme by 1944 in Germany, *De Munich à la Libération*, p. 212.

27 *La Relève*, p. 15.

28 p. 18.

29 *Ibid.*

30 P. 21.

31 *Ibid.*

32 P. 22.

33 *Ibid.*

34 *Ibid.*

35 P. 20.

36 *The Intellectual Resistance in Europe*, p. 73.

37 *De la Résistance à l'insurrection*, pp. 179–80.

38 This is quite explicit in *Le Sang des autres*, where clandestine meetings or writings are described as 'des semblants d'action' by the main character who insists they undertake 'de vrais actes', i.e. direct attacks on the Germans (p. 178).

39 P. 232.

40 In *Servitude et grandeur des Français*, Paris, 1945, pp. 7–38.

41 P. 10.

42 P. 36.

43 Pp. 37–8.

44 P. 135.

45 P. 137.

46 P. 34.

47 P. 29.

48 P. 32.

49 P. 138.

50 P. 33.

51 One can perhaps trace a certain battle with the brother-in-law for Emile on Julep's part in the repetition of his almost hopeful questions to Emile: 'Tiens, tiens, brouillés?' (p. 12) and 'Vous êtes fâchés ensemble?' (p. 19).

52 Cf. 'La Vie privée ou Alexis Slavsky, artiste-peintre', by Elsa Triolet (*Le Premier Accroc coûte deux cents francs*, 1945, pp. 83–232), where hostility and aggression govern Alexis's relations to the world, until a shift to the collective life of the Resistance in the village overcomes the 'je/ ils' opposition, demonstrating the importance of the recognition of the state of war and the enemy in order to pass beyond a purely selfish stance. It is interesting that Elsa Triolet later wrote (in 'Préface à la clandestinité', Introduction to Folio edition, p. 18), that she regretted not ending the story with Alexis being captured and tortured (in order to show the overriding importance painting had for him); its similarity with the novels in this section show how feasible such an ending would have been.

53 P. 29 See also pp. 27–8.

54 Pp. 71–2.

55 See p. 72.

56 P. 112.

57 P. 115.

58 P. 51.

59 P. 186.

60 P. 111.

61 Pp. 226–7.

62 P. 83. Emphasis added. And this is all the more true of the clandestine short story which ends with Jacques's death.

63 And is dependent on the cultural perspective of the novel, uniting the Christian and the Communist in their belief in man. The images of Christianity accentuated in the novel are those of the Christian martyrs put to death for their belief, and of Christ on the cross, dying to save man. The deaths of Resisters reveal the same power to communicate their faith through the sacrifice of their lives.

64 His evolution will be a gradual fusion with all the Resistance activists he has met and whom he now metonymically represents. See pp. 202, 219.

65 P. 155.

66 P. 200.

67 Interview in *Carrefour*, no.3, 9 septembre 1944. Quoted in Contat and Rybalka, *Les Ecrits de Sartre*, p. 90.

68 *La Force de l'âge*, p. 623.

69 P. 625.

70 This is achieved in *La Marque de l'homme* by interspersing the first person narrative of Jean Bermont with long extracts from Claire's diary. *Le Sang des autres* is altogether more complex. The action in the present which forms the framework to the narrative is a single night during the Occupation. Several members of a Resistance group are gathered together, while in the next room one of them, Hélène, lies fatally injured. Her friend and lover Jean Blomart is spending the night at her bedside. The events and dialogue of this night are related using the classic third person narration. During the night Blomart recalls his past, from his childhood to the events of the previous evening. This is juxtaposed, in alternate chapters, with the past seen from Hélène's point of view (using third person narration). There are frequent shifts between first and third person narration in the chapters told from Jean's point of view, and Simone de Beauvoir established the following distinction: 'He spoke of himself in the first person, when reliving the past from his point of view, and in the third person when considering from a distance his appearance for others' (*La Force de l'âge*, p. 626). This is combined with his 'monologue intérieur' in the present, giving his thoughts and reactions about decisions to be made, and pursuing a one-sided dialogue with the unconscious Hélène. His judgements on the past, which interrupt his narration of it, are put in italics.

71 Of course, if a section had been published, as she says it was going to be (*La Force de l'âge*, p. 650) by the Editions de Minuit, the identification would have been all the stronger. An extract did appear in *La Patrie se fait tous les jours*, under the title 'La Rafle'(The Raid). But there are other reasons for dissenting from her judgment in this matter. Apart from the questions of structural coherence established by the all-important question of the death of others, the fact that the Occupation and Resistance constitute the present of the narrative, whose substance is therefore constructed in flashback, necessarily places the preoccupations of the past within the context of the present to which constant reference is made.

72 *La Force des choses*, p. 59.

73 *La Force de l'âge*, p. 364. She comments in a footnote: 'I was unaware at the time of Hegel's phrase: "Each consciousness seeks the death of the other." I only read it in 1940'.

74 P. 364.

75 P. 365.

76 *Ibid*. Emphasis added.

77 *Le Sang des autres*, p. 9.

78 P. 63.

79 *Ibid*.

80 P. 112.

81 P. 114.

82 Beauvoir is drawing heavily on autobiographical material in this novel. She relates in *Mémoires d'une jeune fille rangée*, Paris, 1969, that two women figured prominently in her life, her mother and a kind of nanny called Louise. Louise eventually left to get married, and they visited her in the *chambre de sixième* where she lived. Her baby dies and the young Simone is heartbroken, pp. 6–7, 135, 183–4.

83 P. 14.

84 P. 34.

85 P. 12.

86 See p. 26, 'Elle l'aura voulu', and p. 27, 'Je ne voulais pas sa souffrance.'

87 P. 23. Cf. also a minor character described as having 'a fixed smile like a child or a corpse'(p. 189); or, as dawn breaks at the end of the novel: 'Five o'clock. The first doors are opening. The doctor and the midwife run to the bed of the ill man and the woman confined to her bed' (p. 222). The doors opening inevitably recall previous references to prison cell doors and the hostages being taken out to be shot, especially as two sentences later we read: '*They are lined up against the wall*' (p. 223).

Hélène's abortion also enters this complex of themes.

88 Cf. a phrase occuring in the context of the irremediable nature of the child's death: 'my mother could keep her vigil at the bedside night after night' (p. 13).

89 Hélène tells her that her mother's actions are explained by 'the pleasure of persecuting you' (p. 73). Yvonne sees her situation as necessary ('Il faut ce qu'il faut' p. 74). This is also organised with *vouloir/falloir*, where *vouloir* equals aggression.

90 P. 114.

91 Jean's self-sufficiency is matched by Hélène's selfishness which takes an overtly aggressive and individualistic form.

92 P. 209.

93 P. 126. Emphasis added.

94 P. 147. Emphasis added.

95 P. 150.

96 P. 211.

97 P. 179. Jean speaking.

98 P. 213.

99 P. 212.

100 Hélène's itinerary is very similar to that of Claire in *La Marque de l'homme*. Her egocentrism characterised by the self against the world (see p. 165), combined with her attempt to live through Blomart and place their relationship above all else, leads to open hostility between them. Her attitude of indifference under the Occupation ends when she finally recognises the German officer she is associating with as the enemy, and simultaneously her responsibility for what is happening to France (pp. 202–3). She joins Jean's Resistance group and accedes to the collective identity forged through solidarity (p. 222).

Chapter four

Unity

If Resistance fiction as a whole relies on a structure of unity; if, that is, the positive resolution of the narrative conflicts depends on a well-defined and homogeneous group distinct from the enemy, the dynamics of this structure are very clearly revealed in the statements on unity in Resistance writing and in those stories where it is the opposition of unity and disunity which forms the primary narrative conflict. It is well known that the Resistance was a coalition of forces united in their aim of national liberation but with very different perceptions of the nature of the war being waged and of the kind of future which victory might bring. The theme of unity returns time and again in Resistance writing, not only as an attempt to spread the Resistance message, but also as an expression of the movement towards unity which characterised the history of the Resistance.[1] Jean Moulin, de Gaulle's representative, arrived in France at the beginning of 1942. At the beginning of 1943, Fernand Grenier went to London as representative of the Communist Party and the *Francs-Tireurs et Partisans*. In January 1943 also, *Libération-Sud*, *Combat*, and *Franc-Tireur* formed the *Mouvements Unis de la Résistance* in the south, becoming the *Mouvement de Libération Nationale* in December 1943, when joined by movements in the north. The *Conseil National de la Résistance*, founded in May 1943, grouped movements and parties.

Yet that the appeal to unity is a constant in the Resistance and in Vichy as well is itself symptomatic of the important divisions present, not only between the Resistance and Vichy but also between Resisters and non-Resisters and within the Resistance itself (tensions between *la France libre* and the *Résistance intérieure*, between movements and parties,etc.). This means that unity is either a goal to be achieved or a state of affairs which is under threat, from the divisive tactics of the enemy, for example.[2] In each case it is operating on the mode of the imperative, in order that the enemy may be defeated, or that disunity may be averted. In other words, the appeal to unity is inseparable from the identification of the forces of disunity and the figure of the enemy is essential to this structure. The clearest expression of this lies in the slogans where identification of the enemy is, explicitly or implicitly, the basis of unity : 'One enemy only, the invader';[3] 'One leader: de Gaulle. One fight: for our freedom';[4] 'One enemy only: the foreign oppressor. One desire only: the liberation of France.'[5] The three elements involved – the absence of unity, unity as project (to achieve or maintain), and opposition to the enemy – mean that unity is always 'purposeful' and thereby necessarily summons up the enemy.

Jean Touchard stresses the importance of the theme of unity in de Gaulle's writings: 'the words "one", "same", "alone", "indivisible" are the fundamental words of the time for de Gaulle',[6] and *L'Unité* is the title of the second volume of his *Mémoires de guerre*.[7] For Vichy too, the strength of the appeal to unity is in direct proportion to its fragility: 'The Pétainist Nation is an irreducible and unanimous grouping (ensemble), it is by definition the *entire* Nation. (...) At the same time, it is constantly being challenged: a threat might be *fatal* to it, and specifically the *class* struggle.'[8] One can see the imperative nature of unity in Pétain's speech of 30 October 1940 (after the meeting with Hitler at Montoire): 'It is with honour and *in order to maintain* French unity – ten centuries of unity in the context of action constructing the new European order – that today I embark on the path of collaboration.'[9]

The appeal to unity very often takes the form of an invocation of a greater entity, usually the nation, which the Resistance (or de Gaulle and *La France libre*) incarnates: 'The Fighting French are France'; 'The Resistance is France.'[10] The same is true of Vichy, calling for the union of all Frenchmen around their leader Pétain: 'Pétain is France; and France, today, is Pétain.'[11] As far as the *Résistance intérieure* and de Gaulle are concerned, this culminates quite logically in the conflicting stances of 25 August 1944, which at least shows discourses do have material effects. De Gaulle, having disapproved of Leclerc allowing Rol-Tanguy

(Communist leader of the *Forces Françaises de l'Intérieur* in Paris) to have his signature added to the document of German surrender, then clinches the argument by showing Leclerc 'the proclamation published that very morning by the *Conseil national de la Résistance*, presenting itself as "the French nation" and not mentioning the government or de Gaulle. Leclerc immediately understood.'[12] De Gaulle goes on to make his speech at the Hôtel de Ville without, as Azéma points out,[13] mentioning the CNR once.

In this patriotic context, the linguistic markers of unity which Touchard noted in de Gaulle's writings are found throughout the clandestine press. In *Les Lettres françaises*, for example, every issue bar two carried some form of appeal to unity, and several articles take unity as their theme.[14] Together with 'alone', typical of the call to unity here is the vocabulary of totality; 'all', 'each', 'the whole' 'entire'. Another frequent device is that of 'unity in diversity', an enumeration of the different backgrounds and allegiances of Resisters. An early example is found in the 'Manifeste du Front national': 'Representatives of all political tendencies and all faiths; Gaullists, Communists, democrats, Catholics, Protestants, we have come together to form the FRONT NATIONAL DES ECRIVAINS.'[15] Or: 'In the factories the workers' militias will protect the Gaullist boss as much as the Resistance engineers and workers.'[16] This device is certainly symptomatic of the 'unitary strategy'[17] of the *Front national* and the PCF, but will also be found in the fiction of unity.

In view of the priority given to national liberation and the concerted effort of all Resistance forces to that end, it is not surprising that expressions of a purely political unity are therefore diachronic rather than synchronic, as can be traced in the unity of purpose underlying the expression of the continuity of the struggle against fascism.[18] The call to unity is the call to unite the nation; differences of opinion on fundamental political or religious matters are mentioned in order to underline the strength of this patriotic bond. Similarly the great divide between Catholics and Communists is bridged by the faith in man which inspires them both. This is not to say everything is subsumed under a national configuration. What is being forged through the appeal to unity is a composite enemy. As Kedward points out, 'the acceptance of several enemies was part of the gathering strength of Resistance', citing the tracts in the southern zone in October

1942 against the Relève, signed by both Resistance movements and the PCF: 'It was a significant feature of Resistance in the southern zone that it should first proclaim its unity (...) to support action which was anti-German, anti-Vichy and anti-capitalist at the same time.'[19] Above and beyond this, it is in the logic of both the national and anti-fascist positions, as we have seen, that they can unite in opposition to 'the barbarian' and 'the invader'. The important point here in relation to the fiction is that, except in those stories written against this overriding enemy (of which *La Marque de l'homme* is a good example), and *a fortiori* those concerned specifically with unity, the novels and stories of the Resistance are inscribed within either a political or a national perspective in accordance with the kind of enemy identified.

Servitude et grandeur des Français (Servitude and Greatness of the French), by Louis Aragon,[20] is a collection of short stories written under the Occupation which, as the subtitle 'Scènes des années terribles' (Scenes of the terrible years) indicates, is aiming at a kind of fresco of these years. The reference to Vigny's *Servitude et grandeur militaires* in the title, and perhaps also to Balzac's *La Comédie humaine* in the subtitle, places the collection within a French literary heritage, in line with Aragon's insistence on a return to rhyme and the troubadour traditions in his poetry of the time. The patriotic defence of France and the union of all Frenchmen informs all the work of this writer who chose François la Colère as one of his pseudonyms, and several of these stories display the devices which invoke the Resistance as totality. The representatives of the forces of order are often used to draw attention, in spite of themselves, to the magnitude of the Resistance. The policeman in 'Les Bons Voisins' (The Good Neighbours), for example, trying to get a couple to admit to listening to foreign broadcasts: 'You're not a conspirator because you listen to foreign radio broadcasts. Otherwise you'd have to say the whole of France was conspiring.',[21] or the German judge, the commandant von Lüttwitz-Randau, who sentences Resisters: 'It's enough to make you think the whole of France is beginning to rise against us.'[22] Aragon is writing within the *Front National* perspective where patriotism is not dependent on a purely national identity but aims to forge alliances across political, class and national boundaries. The device of 'unity in diversity' is used to this effect:

The comrades... One comes from the lands of the hop (...), another had
never left the smoke and the sirens, he's a child of the black towns... that's
a son of the bourgeoisie who had never cooked an egg before... the other
one fought in Spain with the legendary Brigades... and even a German,
yes a German they had tortured, his own people, in the last corpse-mak-
ing factory in Dachau; beaten, skinned alive, and yet he escaped... A
German who speaks in sad tones of Germany... another Germany.[23]

This alliance can also underpin an entire story as a post-war
reviewer points out: ' "Pénitent 43" would merely be an anecdote
– a priest saves an atheist "terrorist" who had hidden in his
confessional from the Gestapo. But read the anecdote more
carefully, this sudden intimacy between "The one who believed in
heaven, the one who did not believe in it." '[24] There are similar
devices in *L'Armée des ombres*: an aristocrat who had been fiercely
anti-Republican before the war now works with a tradeunionist in
the Resistance. But this is a unity forged under the Occupation
specifically against the Germans (there are many references to a
new, changed France), and as such is closer to the national than to
the political, anti-fascist configuration.

The primary narrative dilemma of *L'Armée des ombres* is focused
on the question of survival of the individual and also of the group,
and all the stories and most of the anecdotes are concerned with
arrests, prisons and escapes. But the strength of the Resistance as
such is not in doubt: 'The enemy can no longer hope to suppress
the resistance. (...) There are too many organisers, assistant
organisers, volunteers and accomplices.'[25] 'Accomplices' is a key
term, for by using a technique of 'complicity', the unity of all the
French against the occupiers is demonstrated. Complicity enters
into the narrative structures as the means by which the protagonists escape arrest, and thus continue to survive. There are anecdotes of train journeys, for example, where all the travellers in a
compartment are made aware that one of their number is
engaged in illegal activities and yet say nothing to the German
soldiers present. A 'garde mobile' sent by Vichy to hunt down
members of the *maquis* informs one of their leaders: 'Have no
fear. I was an officer in the Republican Guard. I have sworn to
guard the Republic. Today the Republic is in the *maquis*. I am
guarding her.'[26] There are countless other anecdotes relaying
commitment to the Resistance cause from those not actively
involved[27] which serve to present the Resistance as a national

struggle, and which therefore become anecdotes which are *typical* of that struggle. Similarly the active Resistance members are representative of thousands more. At a meeting of the leaders of fourteen Resistance organisations, one of them says: 'We are only 14 but we are carried by thousands and probably millions of men (...) Our army is an army of shadows. The miraculous army of love and misfortune. I have become aware here that we are only the shadows of these shadows and the reflection of this love and this misfortune.'[28] This is further reinforced by the particular stress placed on the named characters in this group of stories where they provide the main link from one chapter to the next. The hero of Chapter I, 'L'Evasion', is Legrain, who refuses to escape from the camp with Gerbier because his serious illness would prevent him taking an active part and make him a burden on Resistance resources. In the second chapter, Félix appears. In the third chapter, Félix tells Gerbier how ill his son is, but angrily refuses money to have him taken care of, at which point Gerbier recalls Legrain: 'The same dignity, the same sense of honour.'[29] By this means, Félix's reaction is taken beyond the realm of the psychology of an individual character and becomes representative of the nobility of motives inspiring those involved in Resistance. This continuity of spirit is all the more striking in a narrative which is discontinuous on the level of the action.

Complicity, unity in diversity and invocation of a totality are important mechanisms found in varying combinations in the fiction. In terms of the structure of the narrative, this involves a cast of characters distributed across a three-tier system – the named protagonists of the Resistance group, a much larger number of others who may or may not be named, who appear just once or twice, and the thousands (or the totality) invoked. The function of the second two levels is to forge the collectivity which underpins the actions of the Resistance group and to which it stands in metaphoric and metonymic relation. By their importance as protagonists (for the episodes in which others appear are organised around them) and their named status, they stand out as embodying the Resistance (here, we feel, are its actions, its dangers, its routine), or symbolising its ideals; on the other hand they are also shown to be part of a greater whole, as demonstrated in the cast of thousands.[30] This structure is apparent in *F.T.P.*

A short story in the *Contes d'Auxois, F.T.P.* is a clear example of the use of metonymy and metaphor to link the main group of the story, through solidarity and symbolisation, to a wider Resistance. It concentrates upon the *Francs-Tireurs et Partisans*, the Communist movement who waged armed struggle against the Germans. The attack upon the German train related is typical of the kind of warfare involved. This incident constitutes the action of the narrative in three stages; the information about the train, the preparations and the attack itself. It is also explicitly designed to convey something of the nature of the F.T.P who were branded as gangsters and terrorists. The story therefore accentuates the ideals which motivate the group of six men involved and also, true to the *Front National* politics of patriotic alliance, the diversity of their social positions, and their identity as Frenchmen, living in the same town (which thus functions as a microcosm of France). Furthermore, a quotation from *La Chanson de Roland* is set above the opening lines: 'Franceis i unt ferut de cor et de vigur' (The French struck with heart and vigour).

The main event of the narrative is introduced with the opening lines, when 'they' ('on') come to warn 'him' that a train carrying German soldiers will pass through that night. 'He' calculates when the train will reach the forest. 'However, he went to the small café, by the station, where René usually has lunch.'³¹ The use of 'they' already carries implications of anonymity and conspiracy, suggesting a more general background. The reason for the use of 'however' only becomes clear much later; in spite of the information received, the anonymous man, later named as Paul, still wants corroboration of the time from René who works at the station. The extradiegetic function of the passage introduced by 'however' is to show the conspiracy in action and to place the two men within the social context of the small town. They act out their encounter in the café as a casual affair, and the causal links implicit in the series of juxtaposed actions emphasise their conspiratorial status which, by ordering the sequence of events, emerges as the most important factor in the narrative. By means of an old woman who comments on them as they walk down the street, their situation in the town is given (where they work, and live, whether married or single), as well as some of their personal history. A few details which seem insignificant – that Paul has planted potatoes and spinach in his garden – serve the same function, of building up a picture of René and Paul as part of the life of the town, and so place them firmly within a civilian context. The forces to which they are opposed are ironically indicated, to underline the ignorance of the woman who now abandons her position at the window, and to draw the reader into the conspiracy, since the fact that something *is* happening has been the basis for the relation of the events: 'Nothing worth watching ever happens in this street. It's not as if I lived in the main square with all the comings and goings of the market and the Kommandantur, which has taken over the town hall, or even rue de la République which they've now called rue du Maréchal Pétain. Paul is going home and René is going with him, because they've always been friends, that's all.'[32]

Further developments continue to juxtapose military action and civilian context. There are four other men to be informed, and Paul's wife Alice contacts two of them. Alice's function is to register the danger of the action and the courage of the men, especially Paul, and to be the pivot for the co-presence of the two terms of the opposition of the normal (peace, domesticity) and abnormal (war, danger), and the means whereby the latter is affirmed: 'she knows (...) there is no happiness, however simple, however humble, *at the moment*, without lies and selfishness'.[33] That concern at the danger is expressed by Alice (in terms of stereotyped images of brave men and anxious women) allows the narrative to avoid the elements of insensitivity and heartlessness which could have been contained in the reference to the *Chanson de Roland* and which are explicitly set aside: 'She was not made to hold out a shield to her husband or her son and say: "Come back on it or under it." '[34] The narrative can therefore concentrate on the portrayal of the almost epic assurance of the men themselves.

The men gather in the night at the appointed meeting-place and move towards the railway. It is at this point that the reasons for their actions are enumerated: 'And why are they there, this evening, the six lads, instead of dozing in the sleepy gloom of the little town?'[35] The context within which their activity is placed is constituted by the struggle for liberation, the value of action and commitment to a new society. The fact that different reasons are given for each man is another example of 'unity in diversity'. For one of them, action is placed in the context of the specifically national struggle: 'And there is Robert, who is here because he refuses to admit his country can be defeated and do nothing to regain its independence.'[36] The others convey reasons which are not reducible to the Occupation alone. One of them enjoys fights. For the rest, this action is part of a social or political commitment to change. Paul-le-Grand has learnt you have to fight for 'the disappearance of injustice, for plenty, peace and joy'.[37] René was brought up in an orphanage and is also fighting for justice. Paul promotes action as a means of creating values and dominating history. In nearly every case, each man is placed metyonymically in relation to a larger group: 'This is why he is with those who know what they want'; 'This is why he is on the side of those who (...) are fighting now for the liberation of his country'; 'And there is Louis, a time-served tanner, who is here in order to be with the workers and peasants of the U.S.S.R.'[38] This rhetorical use of repetition, and especially that of certain key words – *know, want, have learnt* – which eliminate for the reader all possibility of questioning their authority, gives to each man an epic stature. The implications of their action extend far beyond the destruction of one train, for the next stage of the narrative raises them to the level of symbolic representation of Resistance as an absolute. Their concerted action acts as a vehicle for the unity of all those referred to, or more accurately, whom they now encompass. They are no longer socially situated individuals, Paul the bank clerk, Paul-le-Grand the cobbler, whose action is one among many, but figures in whom all other Resisters are present. In relation to the beginning of the story, they have been depersonalised. The description of the laying of the explosives which follows this major sequence interrupts their epic anonymity but does not break it. Indicative of this is the sudden use of 'on', reminiscent of the opening sentence, at the moment of the attack, and the detached attitude as they shoot down the German soldiers connoted by the use of 'with no more hatred than a surgeon would feel'. The final sentences, dominated by 'on', present them as a homogeneous unit, which in its indeterminacy is able once more to suggest the whole Resistance.

Drôle de jeu also ends by subsuming the actions of the Resistance group under resistance as a general moral force; commitment to political change, too, is at the heart of this novel, structuring the kind of Resistance portrayed. The novel was begun in spring 1944, when Roger Vailland, who was working for the Bureau

Central de Renseignements et d'Action in London, found himself cut off from his Resistance network. It was well received on publication[39] as an irreverent, even cynical view of Resistance which some found shocking[40] firstly by its title, the metaphor of the game suggesting the Resistance was not to be taken seriously. The precise weight to accord to this seemingly ironic title divides critical opinion. Claude-Edmonde Magny records Vailland's protests that the expression had been taken from 'drôle de guerre' to indicate that 'it involved a game which was no game, (...) which was even the exact opposite of a game'.[41] Bertrand d'Astorg seems to agree. For him, it is the risk (*l'enjeu*) of arrest, torture and death 'which gives it weight and price to this phoney game',[42], whereas for François Bott, Marat, the central character, 'risks his life unstintingly, but with a *dilettante* attitude, as one would play. The title says it well. Marat *gambles his life*, but he is *gambling* (Marat *joue sa vie* mais il *joue*'[43]). Likewise Michel Picard insists on the cynical view of the Resistance as an absurd enterprise put forward in a whole series of metaphors around the idea of the game by another important character, Annie.[44]

Shocking also was the atmosphere evoked in the novel. For d'Astorg, in both characterisation and plot, it contrasted with 'the myth of a Resistance full of heroes with clean hands'.[45] Jean-Pierre Tusseau compares *Drôle de jeu* to the film *Le Chagrin et la pitié* in its portrayal of the less heroic aspects of the times, with the black market bars, restaurants and night clubs, a world of luxury and decadence. He also thinks the French come out badly from this novel, 'a lucid portrait of a resigned people', 'the diagnostic of a "heroic" people who had to be forced to fight',[46] and joins d'Astorg in his overall judgement: '*Drôle de jeu* destroys the Resistance myth even before it was institutionalised.'[47] It all adds up to a novel which sounds closer to the ambiguous vision of the post-war period than to Resistance fiction with its proclamation of the positive virtues of the Resistance. There is even doubt as to whether it is 'about' the Resistance at all. Vailland himself wrote : 'It is not an *historical novel* (...) *Drôle de jeu* is not a novel *on* the Resistance (...) Any historical or political argument one tried to extract from it would by definition be worthless.'[48] He later argued that: 'my relations to *Drôle de jeu* are those of a dreamer to his dream'.[49] And this is a view which has prevailed. Vailland's work is read as wish-fulfilment, with the characters as vehicles for negative and positive figures, the deaths, assassinations and castrations being so many exorcisms, and characters such as Marat projections of what he wished to be.[50]

Now there is no doubt that Vailland's work lends itself to being treated as a whole. Jacques Charmatz has written of the novels displaying Vailland's 'personal mythologies'.[51] It is certainly possible, as the major critics of his work convincingly demonstrate, to group the characters of the novels according to an overall typology where each novel is placed in relation to the *corpus* and of course to the author. *Drôle de jeu* receives particular attention as the first in the sequence, and is read for what it reveals of the overall structures of that sequence. Despite some reservations,[52] my argument here is not that such an approach leads to a misreading of *Drôle de jeu*, but that an analysis of this novel in relation to the structures of Resistance fiction will reveal it to share the characteristic features of persuasive fiction in its delimitation of the enemy, and its positive resolution of its conflicts and dilemmas. For all critics of his work, the opposition inclusion/exclusion is the dominant one, both in Vailland's work and his life; it is probably no coincidence, therefore, that this novel of the Resistance is concerned, both thematically and structurally (at the level of the major oppositions and narrative finality), with unity. J.E. Flower makes the point that the characters of this novel 'fall into two distinct categories: representatives of the French population in general, and a small group directly involved with Resistance'.[53] I would argue that the three-tier pattern discussed earlier is more accurate,[54] but the important point is that in situating the Resistance group in relation to a wider group, *Drôle de jeu* uses the structure typical of the novels concerned with unity.

Caracalla is the young leader of the network, and seconded by Chloé; Marat/Lamballe ('Marat', like 'Caracalla', is a pseudonym) and Rodrigue, his 'lieutenant', are attached to the network but their relations to it are never very clear. In the first chapter, Frédéric arrives from Toulouse, having narrowly escaped from the Gestapo. He was denounced by the father of his fiancée Annie, whom we meet in the third chapter and who herself then comes to Paris. Mathilde, a friend of Marat from before the war also becomes involved with the group (though not with its work), as her young lover, Dani, who was one of their radio operators, has been arrested and she is looking for ways to free him. The episodic structure of the novel (centred on Marat whom we follow through his days of clandestine meetings, trips to the country, journeys through Paris, discussions with other members of the group, meals, etc.) introduces a wide variety of other characters, primarily those of collaborationist Paris encountered in black market restaurants, night clubs and during an evening with Elvire, another pre-war friend of Marat; and those involved in Resistance, providing information, or organising a derailment by the *maquis*. The diverse background and political allegiances of the Resisters convey the unity of the patriotic alliance: Caracalla, one of the first to have defected to England, is rumoured to have been a member of *Action française* before the war; Rodrigue and Frédéric are Communists; Marat a fellow traveller. This is the mechanism of 'unity in diversity' and extended, through the episodic structure, to the various kinds of people Marat works with. But the importance of collaboration and the occasional strong reminders that the coalition within the Resistance is above all temporary make it clear that this is a novel of political, not national, unity. In fact there are very few Germans in this novel; they are present in the many references to arrest, prison, to raids in Paris and patrols in the country, but appear as characters only in the night clubs, part of the collaborationist scene. In other writings on this period, Vailland emphasised the dual nature of the enemy 'Franco–German occupying forces'; to grasp the serious nature of Resistance in *Drôle de jeu*, as well as the reasons for its ironic tone, it is necessary to examine this political context in which it is placed.

In direct contrast to pre-war times, the war is presented as a privileged time, politically, for intellectuals. This is a theme Vailland treated often. In both *L'Homme mystifié*[55] and *Le Surréalisme contre la Révolution*[56] Vailland describes the pre-war period as 'le temps du dérisoire' (time of pointlessness). The artist, divorced from a public and marginalised, saw any kind of official career as *derisory*; the same vocabulary is used of the pre-war group Marat belong to : '*We all shared the inability to take bourgeois values seriously.*'[57] And so a sense of gratuitousness pervades all their activities as they flaunt their marginality and cultivate irrationality, a sense of despair, black humour and elegant suicides. Nothing matters, and revolt becomes an absolute value. Although

' "tempted" by communism',[58] they could take the opposite direction: 'If revolt is not integrated into class consciousness, it leads as easily to fascism as to communism.'[59] Lucid in their denunciation of the bourgeoisie ('From the surrealist period we at least hope to retain the *virtuoso* use of insult'[60]), they nonetheless had no awareness of their own privileged position within it. Their feelings of being derisory were as much as anything the expression of the ineffective nature of a revolt which has no solid political basis – they were, he says, condemned to the permanent irresponsibility of childhood. Parasites of the bourgeoisie whom they denounced, their sense of gratuitousness corresponded to a profound lack of necessity. The worker, on the other hand, is in a situation where he necessarily has to take a stand: 'He accords himself no rights of neutrality. The one who does not go on strike is a strike-breaker.'[61] Exclusive and excluded, the intellectuals were 'out of work' (*en chômage*) and 'an intellectual who is permanently out of work cannot join a strike.'[62] By the nature of their situation unable to realise this fact, they mistake the derisory nature of their existence for existence itself. They sought to give an universal dimension to their own particular situation, and thus, victims of a *mystification*, were further prevented from gaining knowledge about social processes and their position within them.

Paralleling the situation of the worker, the war is a time of demystification and of necessity: 'The war and the Occupation, as time has gone on, have finally put each French person in the *situation* of the worker who becomes a *strike-breaker* if he does not strike.'[63] The war is therefore a crucial time for Marat, not least, as he explains to Rodrigue, as it has produced at last the possibility of action: 'You will never know to what extent, for a certain number of men, there was *nothing to do* between 1930 and 1940. Now we are fighting, hope is very near, we are going to change the face of the world, open the cocoon where a new man is trembling.'[64] The Resistance is inscribed within the movement towards a new political future, and only thus can its promise be fulfilled, but it is also liberation in its own right; Marat recalls a conversation with a man in Spain in 1940 who remembered the civil war as a good time, for at least there was the possibility of change and victory. Marat compares France and Spain: 'Before '39, France, it was not the *nevermore* of the defeated man in

Spain but a perpetual *not yet.*'[65] The Resistance, breaking with the time of inaction, has at last allowed the dislocation maintained by the *nevermore* and the *not yet* to be superseded by *now*. Picard believes that the doubts expressed about the success of the revolution maintain the 'not yet' as a pole of Marat's personal dilemma.[66] Yet I would argue that 'nevermore' and 'not yet' are anchored around the notion of action, not revolution. The tensions about the future are aroused by the fear that it may herald a return to the *past*, that is to the pre-war situation. 'If all fails' is doubled by 'suppose it all starts again like before'. The whole experience of the war has been centred on its opposition to the pre-war situation ; the return of 'Lamballe' would indeed be traumatic as it implies, among other problems, the return of the 'nevermore'/'not yet' paralysis. It is in this perspective that one must place the temptation presented by the death of Lorca which, as Picard rightly says,[67] fixes the perfect moment (*maintenant*) for eternity, and avoids the prospect that the future may be no more than the past reborn. And yet Marat remains on the whole optimistic about the future. The notion of failure – the return of the past, continuing dominance of the past – is presented and rejected, it has on the whole no more than a hypothetical status. To become 'Marat' is to be born to a new life. He is no longer 'marginal' but coincides completely with his Resistance activities: 'Life in the service and my own life (...) are one and the same life.'[68]

The political importance and function of the Resistance is revealed quite clearly at the end of the novel. Marat is alone in a hotel room, reading *Anabasis* by Xenophon. The small army of the Greeks is in a parlous state, isolated, without provisions, and surrounded by enemies. Marat reflects: *'The indigenous body which is giving way, this is the inert mass of the French who keep saying "We must accept the inevitable, we must not forget we are defeated."* '[69] This is echoing an earlier conversation between Marat and a priest in the country, where the priest tells Marat: 'The country is giving way. (...) The Allied attack is too long in coming. (...) The half-hearted, terrified by the harshness of the repression, are once more starting to say, like in 1940, "We must not forget we are defeated." '[70] In other words, the novel, situated in March–April 1944, is deliberately set at a time when the French people is undergoing a sort of *induced* passivity, due to the failure to capitalise on the political change of 1943: 'We should have started direct armed action, as soon as the first *maquis* were formed, without waiting for the English, like Yugoslavia.'[71] The point is that, with the importance of Resistance as preparation for the Revolution, and the *imminence* of the last battle of the Resistance, which must therefore be pivotal, this is a crucial time, and, far from aiming to denounce a fraudulent heroism that never was, or revealing a French nation that had to be forced to fight, Vailland is pointing the finger at those who are holding back from direct action and general insurrection. Such sentiments are found throughout the Communist clandestine press.[72]

The effect of this is to throw into relief the *heroic* nature of the Resistance in this novel. Vailland wrote in 1951 that all his novels could be grouped under the general title : 'In Search of Heroism' (he also describes them as presenting various aspects of the struggle between St George (Progress) and the Dragon (Reaction)).[73] He defines the hero in a Cornelian sense,[74] categorically denying that a collectivity can be heroic, for heroes have a specific function: '*Loin de Moscou* (Far From Moscow) tells the epic story, I repeat, epic, of a small group of heroes animating and transforming a *mass* of men initially *inert and demoralised*.'[75] The function of the heroic Resistance group is to act as a catalyst to change the 'inert mass' of the French nation. Its relation to the nation therefore parallels that of Xenophon's army: 'We have to behave as courageous men and exhort others to imitate us.'[76]

But the hero for Vailland is not restricted to the man of action, and this because action is placed in a political perspective: it serves a cause, that of the Revolution, and aims to achieve greater happiness and freedom. Time and again, in various articles, he points out the limitations of action for action's sake, or action undertaken for individual satisfaction, calling it 'a nonsense, an empty notion, (...) a mystification'.[77] Mystification, for Vailland, is the means by which the forces in power maintain their position. To mystify is to substitute nature for politics, to convince men that their particular circumstances are part of the human condition and cannot be changed. Demystification is therefore a political act, and the struggle between Progress and Reaction is doubled by 'the struggle between reason and the sacred'.[78] The libertine is as much a 'hero', in Vailland's sense, as the man of action. This goes a long way to explaining the particular form of *Drôle de jeu*, where

reflection is as important as action. The long conversations Marat
has with many of the younger characters about the nature of the
war, love, religion, money and the importance of the Resistance,
are each in turn *didactic* sessions where the knowledgeable Marat
seeks to demystify his comrades in order to free them from
attitudes which hamper the ushering in of the new world as much
as the defeat of the Resistance would. *Drôle de jeu* can be read as a
deciphering of the 'text' of Resistance and Occupation,[79] giving
the state of play at this particular moment between the forces of
reaction and mystification, and those of progress. The prize,
politically, goes to the Communist Party :'Only the Communists
have at their disposal a doctrine which allows them to make a
coherent interpretation of events',[80] but within the dynamics of
the action, Marat the libertine–hero has the key role. This is also
reproduced at the level of the structure; the resemblance of *Drôle
de jeu* to a detective story is unmistakable, as Marat seeks to
understand the mystery of Mathilde's behaviour : 'seeking the
explanation which will turn a succession of apparently incoherent
acts into logical behaviour'.[81] The pursuit of coherence over
fragmentation, both thematically and structurally, is yet another
symptom of the drive towards unity at the heart of this novel.

The ironic tone of large parts of the novel can therefore in no
way be read as cynicism towards Resistance as such, even less to
the Resistance as political project. *Drôle de jeu* can be set alongside
other Resistance novels and writings whose target is as much the
internal as the external enemy. To see it as destroying the myth of
the Resistance is to miss the political myth which informs it, which
surfaces in the first place in what is explictly set aside in the
Avertissement mentioned earlier. Far from engaging with questions of documentary realism, as superficially it may appear to do,
the *Avertissement* aims to present a particular vision of Resistance
which, in sentiment, could have come straight out of *Les Lettres
françaises*:

> This is not a *historical novel*. If I had wanted to draw a picture of the
> Resistance, it would be inaccurate and incomplete as I do not portray
> either the *maquisards* or the saboteurs in the factories (among other
> examples) who were some of the most disinterested and purest heroes of
> the Resistance.[82]

Quite logically, *Drôle de jeu* cannot be an historical novel if
the forces of history and the Resistance proper are absent. No

debunking of myths here. But then the novelist who writes in 1948 that the Communist Party was 'the only French political party which, from 1940 to 1944, engaged totally in *direct action* against Hitler and against Pétain, against the Franco–German occupying forces',[83] is fairly selective in his iconoclasm! A complete, accurate picture would include both groups, the *Avertissement* tells us, both the Intelligence group of the novel and the men of (direct) action, but there is no doubt which, so admiringly described, is the more *serious*, precisely because the Resistance is a transitional phase on the road to Revolution whose real value lies in the fact that the action has commenced. Marat hammers home this political message in the novel, and the gap at the level of the *énoncé* between his political motivation and the particular kind of Resistance work he does is a first explanation of the pervasive irony, for it is plain that, if we draw together the value of action and of the 'direct action' of the PCF, it is the pure and disinterested 'maquisards' and 'saboteurs' who embody it, rather than an information network run from London whose activists, a rather motley crew in comparison, have no political unity of purpose and no action as a group. The political myth, conferring value on one kind of Resistance activity, is operating at the level of the *énonciation* to inevitably cast the members of the information group in a rather ironic light.[84]

With the emphasis it places on the struggle against the taboos of reaction, the convergence of political action and personal salvation reminiscent of Malraux's *La Condition humaine*, and its ironic tone, *Drôle de jeu* does at first sight appear marginal to the majority of Resistance fiction. But in the political themes which inform it, including Marat's reaffirmation of Man as supreme value in the final pages, and in the reconciliation effected between Frédéric and Marat in the recognition of the enemy,[85] *Drôle de jeu* deploys the major themes of Resistance fiction and is indubitably governed by the structure of unity.

Notes

1 Which Azéma describes as 'le temps des confluences', *De Munich à la Libération*, p. 264.

2 Many examples of protests at attempts, mainly by Vichy, to divide Communists and non-Communists, or to divide the FTP from the population under the denomination of 'bandits' or 'terrorists'. Occasionally

tensions within the Resistance surface: 'A grave danger threatens the French Resistance, of degenerating into a political operation. (...) We are referring to those who would seek to use this suffering, to use the risks others are facing, the deaths of others, for personal or partisan ends.' It goes on to blame those who are seeking personal reward and 'who are quick to call themselves fighters' and 'the gangsters who want to monopolise the Resistance in order to control things later'(pour ensuite avoir les places) 'Etre forts', *Défense de la France*, 20 septembre, 1943, in Indomitus, *Nous sommes les rebelles*, p. 31.

3 At the heading of the paper *Valmy*.

4 *Combat* heading.

5 *L'Université libre*, numéro spécial, sept.–oct. 1941.

6 *Le Gaullisme*, p. 54.

7 *L'Unité 1942–1944*, Paris, 1956, p. 3. But only in the triumphal walk down the Champs Elysées on 25 August 1944, in the mutual recognition of leader and people, is unity achieved (and even then, in these *Mémoires* composed after the event, indications of future political discord abound).

8 Miller, *Les Pousse-au-jouir du maréchal Pétain*, Paris, 1975, p. 94. Kedward makes a similar point in relation to the divisive nature of many of Vichy's laws: 'All were advanced as measures to unite the country, since by the logic of the nationalist position the declared aim of Jews, Freemasons, trade-unionists, Marxists and anticlericals, all those under legislative attack, had been to divide and fragment the nation', *Resistance in Vichy France*, p. 89.

9 Quoted in Aron, *Histoire de Vichy*, Paris, I, 1973, p. 424. Emphasis added.

10 Michel, *Les Courants de pensée de la Résistance*, pp. 53–5, 433–4.

11 Cardinal Gerlier's famous pronouncement quoted in Duquesne, *Les Catholiques français sous l'Occupation*, Paris, 1966, p. 46.

12 *L'Unité*, p. 306.

13 Azéma, *De Munich à la Libération*, p. 351, and see *L'Unité*, pp. 709–10.

14 'L'Union pour la victoire', *LF*, no. 5; 'L'Unité de la France', *LF*, no. 7; 'Une seule France', *LF*, no. 11; 'Un seul et même peuple', *LF*, no. 17.

15 *LF*, no. 1, septembre 1942, p. 1.

16 'Défense de l'intelligence', *LF*, no. 13, février 1944, p. 2.

17 Azéma, *De Munich à la Libération*, p. 354, and see chapter above, 'Les Lettres françaises'.

18 See the discussion in previous chapters of the references back to 1934, the Spanish Civil War, etc. Robrieux, in *Histoire intérieure du parti communiste*, Vol. I, Paris, 1980, chronicles the importance of anti-fascism in the PCF, and the hostility to any 'arrangement with or concession to the Nazi occupier' among the rank and file members in 1940: 'For them it was the same war being waged against the same enemy, the Spanish civil war being continued in France, against a supine bourgeoisie prepared to team up with Hitler; against rulers who preferred to make pacts with the fascists rather than leave the working class to get on with it', p. 515.

19 *Resistance in Vichy France*, p. 243.

20 Paris, 1945.

21 P. 53.

22 'Le Droit romain n'est plus', p. 182.

23 P. 220.

24 Review of *Servitude et grandeur des Français* in *Poésie 45*, no. 25, juin–juillet 1945, p. 119. The reference is to the Aragon poem, 'Celui qui croyait au ciel, celui qui ne croyait pas'.

25 P. 97.

26 P. 92.

27 It might be argued that the suggestion is that they are already actively involved in the Resistance, in other organisations. However, the confrontation between the named characters of the story and the anonymous characters referred to only by function (the 'garde mobile' quoted above; a hairdresser who gives Jean-François a coat to hide his torn clothes (pp. 99–101); a 'concierge' who 'has never been one of us, and knows nothing of our business' (p. 112) and yet manages to warn the main character the Germans are waiting for him) is to promote a picture of general support with people ready to help actively when necessary.

28 Pp. 131–2.

29 P. 58.

30 It could be argued that the same structure governs the relations, in non-fictional writing, of de Gaulle, or the Resistance, or Pétain to France, which they incarnate and which transcends them.

31 P. 51.

32 P. 52.

33 See p. 56.

34 Pp. 55–6.

35 P. 58.

36 P. 58. France's independence is constantly stressed throughout Resistance writings, and is often an important goal of unity. In the context of the Front National, it is also a political statement, in its refusal to accept subordination to the Allies or *La France libre*. Cf. Charles Tillon's comment: 'From a military point of view (...) squeezing the trigger of a firearm is a perfectly 'legal' action. Whereas that of a patriot in civilian clothes, armed with a bludgeon in the absence of pistol, will be considered until the Liberation as the action of an outlaw. In fact the dilemma is already the following: whether to fight to rebuild an army of Frenchmen in France, or to wait for a liberation which has been prepared outside France...' *Les F.T.P.*, Paris, 1962, 10/18, p. 99

37 P. 58.

38 *Ibid.*

39 It was awarded the Prix Interallié.

40 'Vailland, lieutenant de la Résistance: témoignage de Robert Lupezza', in Max Chaleil (ed.), *Roger Vailland: Entretiens*, Paris, 1970, p. 80.

41 Claude-Edmonde Magny, 'Les Romans', *Poésie 46*, no. 30, février–mars 1946, p. 76.

42   *Aspects de la littérature européenne depuis 1945*, Paris, 1952, p. 72.

43   *Les Saisons de Roger Vailland*, Paris, 1969, p. 110.

44   *Libertinage et tragique dans l'oeuvre de Roger Vailland*, Paris, 1972, p. 102.

45   D'Astorg, *op.cit.*, p. 72.

46   *Roger Vailland: un écrivain au service du peuple*, Paris, 1976, p. 32.

47   *Ibid.*, p. 107.

48   Avertissement, *DDJ*, p. 7. Picard has made the point that Vailland does claim historical verisimilitude for *DDJ* in the prologue to *Bon pied bon oeil*.

49   'Projet inédit de préface', 1947, quoted Picard, *op.cit*, p. 197.

50   See Recanati's notes to the *Ecrits intimes*, Paris, 1968 (hereafter *EI*), especially pp. 79–80 on *DDJ* and Resistance.

51   'L'Economie romanesque' in *Entretiens*, p. 125. The singularity of this personal mythology is well recognised, to the extent that a Livre de poche edition of *Les Mauvais coups* proclaims on its back cover: 'Le plus "Vailland" des romans de Vailland.' The same is true of the non-fiction too.

52   Some of the characters of *DDJ* return in Vailland's third novel, *Bon Pied bon oeil*, which opens in March 1948; fictional devices of verisimilitude, and the reading of both novels in relation to the development of the one author, establish a continuity between the two. Rodrigue is now a committed Communist Party activist, François Lamballe/Marat, after a stint as a war correspondent during which he was wounded (and, it is revealed at the end, rendered impotent, which is read as a psychic castration), is breeding bulls in the country. But the fact that 'Marat' now belongs to the past itself indicates a profound disturbance of the structures of *DDJ*. Rodrigue, the hero, is opposed to Lamballe the uncommitted, with Marat constituting their common past. The whole economy of the novel is different to *DDJ*. Furthermore, the *discontinuity* between Marat/Lamballe and Lamballe/Marat is symptomatically revealed in a lapsus in the Prologue where the author brings the reader up to date from 'the day in June 1943 when *Drôle de jeu* ended'. All the action of *DDJ* takes place from March to April 1944. Picard notes this as a mistake (p. 551, note 48) and also that Marat is made much older than the Marat of *DDJ* would be, which he considers highly significant. (His argument is that Marat/Lamballe is now split into Rodrigue and Lamballe, p.166.) But the error with dates is no less significant, for, as will be shown, the choice of dating is extremely important. By moving it *back*, Vailland effectively annuls his previous novel in order to rewrite it into a different sequence.

53   *Roger Vailland, the Man and His Masks*, London, 1975, p. 38.

54   M. Sidoine, for example, whose psychology, home situation, etc., are established, is not on a par with the anonymous dentist who is just referred to.

55   1947. An introduction for a projected series of pamphlets and critical essays which did not come off. Hereafter *HM*, in *EI*, pp. 122–7.

56   1947. *Oeuvres complètes* (hereafter *OC*), vol.8, pp. 231–82.

Hereafter *SR*.

57 *DDJ*, p. 26 (Marat's 'monologue' is always signalled by italics).
58 *SR*, p. 259.
59 *DDJ*, p. 29.
60 *HM*, p. 127.
61 *SR*, p. 263.
62 *Ibid.*, p. 264, and see DDJ, p. 22.
63 *SR*, p. 265.
64 *DDJ*, p. 158. And to realise how far the *Front National* politics informs *Drôle de jeu*, one has only to compare this to the comment in *F.T.P.* that the action of the six men is a step towards 'Man, who as yet they are not, but who will be tomorrow' (l'Homme qu'ils ne sont pas encore mais qui sera demain), p.59.
65 *DDJ*, p. 158. The two English terms are both used.
66 *Libertinage et tragique*, pp. 97–8.
67 *Ibid.*, p. 99.
68 P. 304.
69 P. 430.
70 P. 212.
71 *DDJ*, p. 213.
72 I am therefore disagreeing with Professor Flower that the novel's period of time is 'selected almost at random' (*The Man and His Masks*, p. 38), and with Colin Nettlebeck's interpretation of 'inert mass' ('Getting the Story Right: Narratives of World War II in Post-1968 France', *Journal of European Studies*, vol. 15, Part 2, no. 58, June 1985, p. 88). In both cases I would argue the importance of narrative structure has been overlooked.
73 *EI*, pp. 443, 446, 448.
74 The frequency of references to Corneille in Vailland's novels is often commented on. Indeed, in the passage quoted above, he is defending himself against the charge that his Communists are too Cornelian.
75 *EI*, p. 444. Emphasis added.
76 *DDJ*, p. 429.
77 *EI*, p. 446.
78 *SR*, pp. 272–3. The major and still valid contribution of the Surrealists, for Vailland, was their onslaught on taboos. But because, caught in their contradictory position, there was no political purpose to the demystification, they were themselves, like the exponents of action for action's sake, mystified (and see *DDJ*, p. 301).
79 Cf. François Bott, *Les Saisons de Roger Vailland*, p. 47: 'Vailland never stops *explicating* the text of his life, the text of our lives.'
80 *DDJ*, p. 110.
81 P. 346.
82 *DDJ*, p. 7.
83 *SR*, p. 281.
84 That the political project is structuring the novel at the level of the *énonciation* can also be traced in the shifts in tenses which occasionally reveal a transcendent narrator whose comments are made from the

point of view of the Revolution. For example when Frédéric analyses for other young Communists, and with great authority, recent productions of Racine, Corneille, Marivaux: 'The others listened respectfully. (...) We will have to wait until the Revolution has produced its own culture for them to judge objectively certain superstitions', pp. 180–1.

85   Frédéric is arrested by the Gestapo, which, in a manner recalling Jean Bermont being summoned by the camp commander mentioned in the previous chapter, allows Marat to stress what unites them, rather than the disagreements which have been dominant in the course of the narrative.

Conclusion

We have seen in the discussion of *littérature de témoignage* that the fiction written within the structure of unity can be characterised as 'literature of persuasion', committed to speaking the truth of the Occupation. In the pages of *Les Lettres françaises*, as well as the outright denunciations of official distortions, the Resistance knowledge is conveyed through the procedures of 'the historical real' and contextualisation, which are the means of 'speaking the unspoken'. The similarities between Sartre's definition of committed literature and the Resistance *littérature de témoignage*, particularly in relation to the explicit assumption of a social and political engagement, has also been noted. Literature should produce the possibility of a reading of the world, and this, under the Occupation, means combating the silences and distortions of official discourse as well as presenting the positive values the Resistance is defending. The 'historical real' is an important mechanism in the fiction too, in articulating the reality of the war, but perhaps the most immediately apparent feature, specific to the fiction, of the persuasive mode of writing is the structuring of characters across ignorance and knowledge.

Many of these narratives involve a transition from ignorance to knowledge, through the development of a leading character or across several characters; they present the inadequacy of the reading of the world held by the ignorant, and the superiority of the alternative reading which is therefore confirmed as knowledgeable. In *Le Silence de la mer* the narrative function of ignorance is fulfilled by von Ebrennac. The cultural division between the values of Prussian honour and Nazi barbarism allow him to be a credible military figure in complete ignorance of the military and ideological realities, and we follow his process of disillusion. By their silence the French couple signal their knowledge of von Ebrennac as enemy, which is confirmed when he too recognises the fact. The German soldier in *Le Tilleul*, the Resistance group in *Les Amants d'Avignon* (as opposed to the rest of the country which is only gradually coming to understand what is really going on), André in *Yvette* are all knowledgeable characters in dialogue with the ignorant. In other words, knowledge is not handed down from on high by an extra-diegetic narrator, but structured into the development of the major narrative dilemmas.

Sartre argued that the world in crisis was producing 'novels of *situation*, without internal narrators or omnipotent witnesses',[1] and Resistance literature certainly exemplifies this in the sense he was using it, that is to say without an omniscient spectator *outside* the action. On the other hand, all narration implies a narrator who is the subject of the *énonciation*, and therefore structurally in a position of superiority over the characters in the story being told. There are two points to be made about this in relation to Resistance fiction: firstly, the large number of first person narratives which apparently reduce to a minimum the gap between the *énonciation* and the *énoncé*, and secondly, that the superiority of the extra-diegetic narrator is consistently exploited to voice the 'historical real' of the text. *Le Puits des miracles*, *La Marche à l'étoile*, *La Marque de l'homme* and *Le Sang des autres* are all first-person narratives where it is the narrator who is the focus of the transition to knowledge;[2] the development of the narrative is at the same time the account of the narrator, who is both ignorant and puzzled, coming to understand either the true relations of power pertaining in Vichy France in the case of *Le Puits des miracles*, or the necessity for action in *La Marque de l'homme* and *Le Sang des autres*. This means that the dilemmas of the narrative are presented as they are 'lived' by the narrator–character, and the extra-diegetic narrator is not a separate voice commenting on the action. The same is true of the third person narratives of *Contes d'Auxois*, when the narration switches away from the main character, from whose point of view the story is being told, in order to voice the greater knowledge of, for example, the women in the queue in *Les Moules et le professeur*.

The effect of knowledge being integrated into the action in this way is to place *de facto* the reader in a position of knowledge. The clearest example here is perhaps the opening of 'F.T.P.', where the reader, after the meeting of Paul and René about the train, is *necessarily* in a greater position of knowledge than the old woman who sees the two men walking down the street and thinks there is nothing happening. It is through this very same mechanism that, in *Le Puits des miracles*, and in several of Aragon's short stories, the reader is obliged to be knowledgeable about the 'historical real' which the narrator or main characters are conveying in spite of themselves. And as the narrative achieves its positive ending and the ignorant finally understand what is really happening, the content of that knowledge is inevitably encoded as the truth of the situation.

To designate Resistance fiction as literature of persuasion is not to pre-empt discussion as to whether it is convincing, but to elucidate the devices whereby it realises its own mission as *littérature de combat*. Any individual reader can refuse its equation of narrative knowledge and historical truth, but that is not the point. What is important is the way these narratives impel the reader into the position of knowledge about the alternative, Resistance, truth, while still dictating the nature of the knowledge the reader is constructing. As will be seen, the structures of knowledge could not be more different in the novel of ambiguity.

Notes

1 *Situations II*, p.252.
2 In many respects the narrator of *La Marche à l'étoile* is more knowledgeable than Thomas, but, like all Frenchmen, he has to learn the truth of the degraded France through Thomas' story in order that France may be purified.

Part Three
Novels of ambiguity

Introduction

It would not be difficult to take de Gaulle's triumphal walk through Paris on 26 August 1944 as the end of the Occupation, but the shots fired on that occasion, and the German bombings in Paris the same night are sufficient reminders that it was not quite over. In fact, fighting continued in the east of France until March 1945. But by the end of September 1944, only 3.5 per cent of the country was still occupied by the Germans,[1] and for the vast majority of French people the problems to be faced are those of 'l'après-Libération';[2] the material difficulties which loom large, and all the questions attendant upon the transition of power and the new kind of society to be ushered in. Attention is now centred upon France itself.

As was stated earlier, there never was one single Resistance. After the defeat of the Germans, a task which had given its unity of purpose to this coalition of very diverse forces, divergences and latent conflicts which were never far from the surface now come into the open. As early as September 1943 Viannay in *Défense de la France* is warning that the Resistance is in danger of degenerating into a narrowly political operation, and denouncing those 'who seek to use the dangers and deaths of other Resisters for personal and partisan ends'.[3] A few months later, he is expressing the open hostility of many in the Resistance movements to the rising ascendancy of the political parties which are controversially represented in Algiers.[4] As Touchard commented: 'The period 1944–46 is one of "the breakdown of unity".'[5] Another major source of bitterness and recrimination is the well-documented break between de Gaulle and the internal Resistance. Jean-Pierre Rioux, in a map detailing the state of the battle in the areas liberated from the Germans at the end of August 1944,[6] with two large areas liberated by the Allies and two by the *Forces Françaises de l'Intérieur*, provides an immediate visual snapshot of the 'dual power'.[7] A clash between them was no doubt inevitable. The internal Resistance was united as much against Vichy as against the Germans, was committed to sweeping social and political changes of which the ridding of Vichyist elements was one essential part. De Gaulle and the Allies, particularly worried about the dominant position of the Communists in the Resistance organisations (a worry shared by some within the Resistance) and their prestige, were above all concerned to avoid the danger of civil war.[8] This meant they were perceived by many Resisters as being hostile to the political aims of the Resistance and ideologically in sympathy with the men and forces represented by Vichy.[9]

The process of *épuration* (purging of collaborators), too brutal, ill thought-out and indiscriminate for some, too indulgent and incomplete for others, was the central focus, and indeed a weapon, in these arguments.[10] Many reasons underlie the atmosphere of bitterness and disaffection surrounding the *épuration*, as Marcel Baudot explains in *L'Opinion publique sous l'Occupation*:[11] the courts being swamped by vast numbers of denunciations, both serious and trivial, making it very difficult to expedite matters; the patent unfairness of a system which left the 'economic collaborators' relatively unscathed, and was often seen to be slow in arresting powerful figures. The post-Liberation *Lettres françaises* is continually drawing attention to the 'sabotage of the *épuration*': 'It's the small fry of collaboration who are crowding the prisons, while the real culprits escape punishment.'[12]

Attitudes to Vichy are another cause of acrimonious debate. Both the Gaullists and the Communists are stressing that France, apart from a small group of traitors, found its unity in the Resistance, and the logic of their positions could be crudely summarised as: to be against the Resistance was to be against France; Vichy was against the Resistance; Vichy was guilty of treason. It was argued that although people might have been sincerely misled by Vichy in the early part of the Occupation, after 1942 no error was possible and the CNE publish their judgement that 'supporting the Maréchal's policies after the occupation of the southern zone is considered to be a case of national disgrace' (*indignité nationale*).[13] Within this perspective the battles of the Resistance still have to be fought, so that justice would finally be done, and so that the equation between the Resistance and France defining all others as traitors can be sustained. But this blanket assimilation of Vichy and collaboration to treason has the effect of preventing any real analysis either of what Vichy was or of the difference between Vichy and collaboration,[14] and of produing a general feeling of culpabilisation. Luc Estang argued: 'The man in the street who, without being a traitor, was not necessarily a Resistance hero, is developing an inferiority complex about it. And this is being reinforced as he is given to understand he is to be on the receiving end of lessons in moral rectitude.'[15] Many others argue against what they see as the excesses of the *épuration*,[16] express anxiety that the Resistance is showing itself to be identical to the enemy it is combating,[17] or attack what is in their view a misplaced moralism which seeks to fix a purity of choice for all time;[18] all of which will be summed up in the pejorative term of 'résistantialisme'.[19]

The post-war period therefore presents a rather contradictory picture of many different positions and attitudes feeding into a battle for the *meaning* of the Occupation years and the various political options within them.[20] *Les Lettres françaises* welcomes the republication of the clandestine texts of *Les Editions de minuit* 'which are as relevant today as they ever were',[21] and Max-Pol Fouchet salutes *le Puits des miracles* as 'a book which avenges us' in its demonstration that Vichy was the real enemy.[22] Those who are on the receiving end of the justice of the *épuration* are also defending themselves and organising 'a "national opposition" against blind democracy being manipulated by Communism'.[23] The political parties are playing the Resistance card for all it is worth, yet Baudot notes the general failure of the attempts by the *Conseil National de la Résistance* to present its own candidates at the elections or to manage to get them elected: 'This disaffection of the electorate for the militants of the Resistance stems both from the propaganda of the re-emerging political parties and from mass suspicion towards the inflating numbers of Resisters whose clandestine activity, by necessity not well known, is rightly or wrongly considered dubious.'[24] To which he adds the suspicion that the Resisters are using their reputation to 'grab key positions and satisfy petty resentments at the expense of decent folk who can only be reproached with having naively had confidence in the old Maréchal'.[25] It is clear that the myth of the Resistance and the accusations of 'résistantialisme' are strictly contemporaneous.

The primary contradiction between the complex social and political realities of the Occupation years and the simplistic confrontation between heroes and villains, the Resistance and the rest, notably Vichy, will be the very stuff of the novels of ambiguity. The effect of these novels of the immediate post-war period is on the whole to frustrate the attempt to make unequivocal moral judgements according to political allegiance, which distinguishes them from some of the films and novels of *la mode rétro* which, it has often been noted, tend to reverse the terms of the Resistance myth in substituting a handful of Resisters for the handful of traitors. *Le Chagrin et la pitié* has rightly been seen as reopening a debate about these years, mounting a direct attack on the grossly inaccurate myth that France was – apart from its handful of traitors – solidly behind de Gaulle. But that it is also operating within a framework equating moral righteousness with the Resistance can be seen in the fact that it fails absolutely to *explain* Vichy, to contribute an analysis for the reasons for Pétain's popularity or to bring out the fact that Vichy was a contradictory amalgam of many different forces. Support for Vichy is still, in this film, morally tainted, as the interview with Mme Solange the hairdresser shows, where the interviewer ensures she 'admits' her support for Pétain.[26]

The post-war novel of the Occupation which, it will be seen, can hardly be enrolled into the service of the Gaullist or Communist myths either, is concerned above all to demonstrate the ambiguity of the times, and this will be traced in the fragmentation of the categories constituting the structure of unity, that is, the figure of the enemy and the figure of the individual, and in the irony which at all levels of the narrative is a distinguishing feature of this writing.

Notes

1 Noguères, *Histoire de la Résistance en France*, 5, Paris, 1981, p. 760.
2 *Ibid.*, p. 799.
3 'Etre forts', 20 septembre 1943, in *Nous sommes les rebelles*, p.31.
4 *Ibid.*, pp.37–9.
5 *Le Gaullisme*, p.74.

6 Jean-Pierre Rioux, *La France de la IVe République*, 1, Paris, 1980, p.12.

7 'La dualité des pouvoirs', Grégoire Madjarian, *Conflits, pouvoirs et société à la Libération*, Paris, 1980, pp.75–102.

8 See Baudot, 'La Résistance française face aux problèmes de répression et d'épuration', *Revue française de la deuxième guerre mondiale*, vol.21, no.81, janvier 1971, pp.23–47.

9 cf. 'Le Grand Divorce', and 'La Restauration' in Bourdet, *L'Aventure incertaine*, Paris, 1975; Pierre Hervé, *La Libération trahie*, Paris, 1945; 'Retrouvailles des bien-pensants' in Charles Tillon, *F.T.P.*

10 This is particularly notable in the contradictory figures brought forward in relation to the numbers killed and the so-called 'blood-bath'. See Noguères, *Histoire de la Résistance*, pp.764–8; Baudot, 'La Résistance française face aux problèmes de répression et d'épuration', pp.37–8.

11 Paris, PUF, 1960, pp.210–13.

12 *LF*, 4 novembre 1944, p.1.

13 *LF*, 7 octobre 1944, p.5. 'L'Indignité nationale' is the phrase which appears in the 'Ordonnance du 18 novembre 1944 instituant une haute cour de justice' of the *Gouvernement provisoire* (L. Duguit, H. Monnier, R. Bonnard, *Les Constitutions et les principales lois politiques de la France depuis 1789*, Paris, 1952, p.469).

14 See Rioux, *La France de la IVe République*, pp.61–7.

15 'A travers la presse littéraire', *Poésie 45*, no.23, février–mars 1945, p.118.

16 See Rioux, *op.cit*, pp.61–2.

17 See Robert Morel's poem 'Liberté' and Vercors's reply in Vercors, *Le Sable du temps*.

18 Cf. Paulhan, *Lettre ouverte aux directeurs de la Résistance*, Paris, 1951, which restates many of these arguments.

19 Cf. Rioux, *op.cit*, p.62, on l'Abbé Desgranges, *Les Crimes masqués du résistantialisme*, published in 1948.

20 *Les Fantômes armés*, by Elsa Triolet (Paris, 1947), much of which is set in occupied Germany, is an example in fiction of this continuing battle of the Resistance.

21 *LF*, 28 octobre 1944, p.5.

22 *LF*, 12 décembre 1945, p.3.

23 *La France de la IVe République*, pp.61–2. See also Claude Bellanger's description of 'L'opposition "révisionniste" ' in his contribution to *Histoire générale de la presse française*, Tome IV: De 1940 à 1958 (Bellanger *et al.*, eds.), Paris, 1975, pp. 310–11.

24 *L'Opinion publique sous l'Occupation*, Paris, PUF, 1960, p.213.

25 *Ibid.*, pp.213–14.

26 *Le Chagrin et la pitié*, *Avant-scène Cinéma*, nos 127/8, juillet–septembre 1972, pp.64–5.

Chapter one

Changing narrative structures: the figure of the enemy

Les Forêts de la nuit is a clear demonstration that the various characters who, sociologically speaking, could be described as the enemy – the German soldiers, the sadistic torturer Merkel from the 'Gestapo française', even the right-wing pro-German bourgeois epitomised by Madame Costellot – are not in any sense forged by a structural figure of the enemy of which they would diegetically be the various manifestations, nor are they opposed by a homogeneous Resistance group which is unequivocally positive. One of the German soldiers is certainly far more sympathetic a character than Darricade, the careerist Resister. Fragmentation affects both terms of the previous opposition.

Les Forêts de la nuit draws on many of the schemas and mechanisms, especially in relation to the German soldier, which are already familiar from Resistance fiction. Similarly the depiction of the wealthy pro-German milieu as represented by Madame Costellot recalls characters from Resistance novels which include the internal enemy – *Le Puits des miracles* or *Alexis Slavsky*, for example. But in a narrative whose finality is constituted not by the possibility of future Resistance victory but by the sad chaos of the Liberation and the subsequent triumph of the completely amoral characters, these elements have a very different function, namely to project the superficiality and futility of moral judgements and principles into the Ocupation years.

The billeting of German soldiers on individual homes[1] again figures prominently as the vehicle for establishing certain sets of relations between the French and the Germans (and other Germans are mentioned; Werner, with whom Fernande Arréguy is having an affair, and the nightly patrols, frequently referred to as robots, which are conveyed by the sounds of their boots on the streets). Very friendly relations are established between Cécile Delahaye and Friedrich Rustiger, a musician who knows one of the works composed by her late husband. The Costellots are also on friendly terms with von Brackner, an important officer at the *Kommandatur*. Unlike equivalent examples in Resistance fiction, the Germans are shown to be integrated into the life of the French town.

Conventional characteristics of the German in French literature are spread across these two soldiers. Rustiger, having made a rather ironical comment on Hitler's mustical taste, is hailed by Balansun as 'a spiritual son of Goethe, out of place in the barbarian hordes of the Third Reich'.[2] He thus contrasts with the aristocratic von Brackner, who takes every opportunity to gain information about the local Resistance and arrange their capture by the 'Gestapo française' group led by Merkel. The attitudes of the two Frenchwomen with whom they are staying are also clearly differentiated. Mme Delahaye is a gentle, inoffensive woman who would never dream of being rude to this good German who could also be described as the first victim of von Brackner; when it is discovered he has a Jewish grandmother he is sent to the Russian front. He blames von Brackner for this, calls him 'a real Nazi', giving the following warning which functions partly as an *annonce*, that is, anticipating later developments: 'You must be very wary of him... He also knows all that goes on at Saint-Clar. I don't know how he knows it all.'[3] From several previous incidents, however, the reader is fairly certain of the importance of Mme Costellot in this respect. In the following chapter she arranges for von Brackner to interview Berthe, the disaffected and vengeful servant of the Delahaye, and a compulsive eavesdropper, whom Gérard has finally sacked, in order that she can recount the conversations betwen M. de Balansun and Mme Delahaye about Francis's clandestine activities.

The use of the billeted German schema presents an obvious contrast between the two women, but it also serves several other narrative functions, firstly through their different fates at the Liberation. Mme Delahaye is taken by a crowd led by Berthe, who has widely related the affectionate farewell to Rustiger, and has her head shaved, or at least is undergoing this until M. de Balansun rescues her. Mme Costellot escapes to a neighbouring town, much to the fury of the crowd. That Mme Delahaye, whose good faith has never been questioned, should be a victim of the *épuration*, feeds into one of the theses of the book, that the mass demonstrations of the Liberation blindly fastened on scapegoats and dissipated the energies which might have produced the 'magnificent leap'[4] which was hoped for. Furthermore, the hysterical nature of these demonstrations involved many who were last-minute converts covering up their own anti-Resistance attitudes; for example, M. Lardenne tells anyone who will listen that their family sheltered an English airman whom Jacques brought home for a night. At the time none of the others realised who he was, and were quite horrified when they found out. It is clear that the Liberation scenes are intended to demonstrate the poverty of moral judgments concerning what constituted pro-German behaviour. On the other hand, it is difficult to argue that the sympathy for Mme Delahaye should not be extended to Rustiger. He is narratively important as a counterpart to von Brackner, and first demonstrates the latter's ruthlessness. He is very grateful for the kindness shown him in spite, as he says, of being their enemy.[5] In effect, he is as much a victim of circumstance as Mme Delahaye and M. de Balansun. His presence means that the Germans as such do not constitute the enemy in the sense of the negative 'other' of the text.

Mme Costellot's case may appear more straightforward in that she directly contributes to Francis's death and actively supports the German presence as the only bulwark against the working classes, and far more acceptable than the Anglo-American domination which she says would replace it. Yet she feels unhappy about her role in denouncing Francis and makes von Brackner repeat his promise that no harm will come to the young man. Like virtually everyone else she remains ignorant of what really happened to him,[6] and readily accepts that he must have been deported to Germany. Added to this is the fact that great emphasis is given to her own character and psychological motivation. Social snobbery is her major trait, and the fact that she was snubbed by the English gentry at Biarritz in pre-war times makes her a ready believer in the New Order and its denunciations of Anglo-Saxon capitalism, and all the more flattered by the attentions of the aristocratic von Brackner. But she is never perceived as an enemy by any of the other characters, and the shifting narrative viewpoints which afford as much insight into her psychology and idiosyncracies as to the others' means that finally she has more in common with Berthe than von Brackner: she is constructed as limited and petty, her actions in relation to Francis going far beyond anything she imagined, and finally she is just one more example of the universal stupidity of the times.

The direct responsibility for the death of Francis lies with the group of the 'Gestapo française', but indirectly is, again, also caused by several chains of psychological factors. Because, once Francis had explained his Resistance involvement, his father converts from a pompous espousal of Vichy to theatrically outspoken hostility, Berthe has something concrete on which to build her accusations; because Mme Delahaye does not know how to deal firmly with Berthe, the latter delights in telling tales about her employer. Within the 'Gestapo française', Merkel remembers Hélène's surname when Philippe is having an affair with her, and therefore particularly chooses this Bordeaux case for the sadistic pleasure of involving Philippe. This is not unlike the complex plotting of *Drôle de jeu*, but here the two directly responsible, Merkel and von Brackner, just disappear from the story without anyone discovering their role in it all, or, in Merkel's case, ever guessing he is in the 'Gestapo française'. Nor is there any Marat-like sleuth to piece together the information, identify and eliminate the guilty.

Les Forêts de la nuit thus presents one major process fracturing the figure of the enemy and preventing the installation of the structure of 'us *versus* them' characteristic of the novels of unity. *La Peste* is the most famous example of another process which installs relations of ambiguity across the oppositional structure, by assimilating the enemy to the *combattant*.

In a letter to Roland Barthes in 1955, Camus wrote that '*La Peste*'s obvious content is the fight of the European Resistance against Nazism',[7] and he was perfectly right. It is impossible to read this novel after other Resistance and post-war novels on this period without being constantly aware not only of the deliberate reference to the Occupation, but also its similarity to other post-war novels about the Occupation, in both structure and choice of themes. This is due to two primary reasons: the familiarity of the metaphor of the plague, and the particular referential system of the novel.

The use of the plague to represent the war met with some criticism. Simone de Beauvoir wrote: 'To assimilate the Occupation to a natural scourge was another way of avoiding History and the real problems.'[8] Sartre clearly saw the mechanism underlying the equation, although his conclusion seems rather harsh: 'In choosing injustice, of his own free will the German placed himself with the blind forces of nature, and you were able, in *La Peste*, to have his part played by microbes without anyone noticing the mystification involved.'[9] The comparison with the Occupation is so obvious, not because of a particular sleight of hand thought up by Camus alone, but because the descriptions of the Germans and Nazis in terms of disease and plague had become something of a cultural cliché, generated, as Sartre saw, by humanist discourse identifying them as anti-human and beyond rationality. Daniel Guérin's title *La Peste brune* (The brown plague) is an early example in the context of fascism, although in 1930 Norton Cru already describes war as 'a disease like the plague'.[10] During the Occupation the metaphor returns time and again; of Chardonne's conversion to Nazism the *Cahiers de Libération* asks: 'By what secret wound had the microbe entered this organism and infected it?'[11] It will be recalled that the Resistants in 'F.T.P.' shoot down the ambushed Germans 'with no more hatred than a surgeon'. *La Sombre Route*, by Robert Heim, a strongly worded attack on the Germans, is shot through with medical and biological vocabulary epitomised in the phrase: 'in Germanism there is *germ*'.[12] Camus's originality[13] was to take the figure of speech literally in order to generate the fictional narrative of the plague in Oran. It is difficult to see why he should be considered more guilty of mystification than the countless others for whom the metaphors of disease and plague were common currency; it might more accurately be argued that it is the systematic exploitation over the length of a novel of this extended metaphor, plus his own particular thesis of the value of revolt over revolution, which has laid bare very clearly the ahistorical nature of the comparison.

The medical vocabulary which connoted the non-human nature of Nazism also extended very easily to encompass the contaminatory effect of the evil unleashed. As late as 1962 l'Abbé Popot wrote: 'The Nazis, (...) since they were unable to conquer us, inoculated us with a horrible virus capable of contaminating all men.'[14] The image of the plague is therefore admirably suited to a novel about the war which also seeks to elucidate the nature of that war, to place it in a general framework of moral reflection on evil in the world. Indeed, it is for its metaphysical dimension above all that *La Peste* has been admired or criticised, and it is read primarily as an expression of Camus's philosophy rather than as a novel of the Occupation. But to classify *La Peste* as an allegory of the Occupation sustained by specific references, for example to the black market, rationing, the blackout, and dominated by its symbolic meanings, is to underestimate the importance of the referential system of the novel and the precise functioning of the metaphor of the plague.

The quotation from Defoe, placed as an epigraph to the book, which introduces ideas of substitution and of the representation of the real by the fictional is generally recognised as a signal to the multiple levels the novel simultaneously sustains. The first lines of the novel confirm not only the substitution indicated in the epigraph, but its nature: 'The curious events which are the subject of this chronicle took place in 194., in Oran. By general agreement they were out of place, departing somewhat from the norm.'[15] The manner of indicating the date is crucial. The suppression of a final figure in order to denote historical vagueness and thus, given the Defoe quotation, connote a fictional, allegorical status, is certainly fulfilling its connotative function, but is also historically quite precise. To have chosen 'in 19..', for example. would have confused the reader who could not be presumed to know there had never been a plague in North Africa this century; the connotation of substitution would have been obscured. Even if it had been clearer, the intended referent, given the length of time involved, would not have been grasped. On the other hand, to supply a final figure and restrict the date to a particular year would have abolished the connotative function and integrated the date into the purely fictional account of the plague,[16] in the way the town of Oran is.[17] In other words, the final choice of date makes it clear that the substitution will be an historical one and that the events of the plague are to be read historically as the events of the war. This reveals the mechanism by which the narrative can sustain simultaneously its two levels, fictional and historical, or the historical real and the narrative real of the text. Obviously in a novel published after the war this does not have the same *function* as in Resistance fiction, that is, articulating what is officially suppressed. However, in the dislocation of the narrative and historical realities of the text, it is a mechanism identical to that of *Les Mouches* for example. And indeed the extract of *La Peste* published in *Domaine français* does read above all as 'contraband' writing.[18] The mode of dating therefore serves to index the Occupation and the war as the historical reality of the text, and structurally *La Peste* depends on the same kind of referential system used in all straightforward realist novels to establish their historical credibility.

The mode of narration chosen for the fictional plague, that of the chronicle, is a further adjunct, and perhaps a necessary one, to the intertwining of the two kinds of realities sustained by the narrative. The conventional hallmarks of a chronicle – the absence of fabulation, the eye-witness account – which serve to mark its veracity are faithfully adhered to, as is an internally coherent referential system: the sequence of events dependent on the progression of the plague and the medical descriptions. Formally the referential system of a text is 'reality blind', in that it can index a purely fictional reality as successfully as an historically attested one (science fiction would be the most obvious example). On the other hand, this documentary writing is the perfect vehicle for the documented reality which is also being indexed by the very same referential system. It does so in several ways. The first chapters, detailing the official reluctance to recognise the presence of the plague, could be read as the equivalent of the phoney war, especially given the note 'la drôle de peste' (the phoney plague) in the *Carnets*.[19] The introduction of *le fléau* (scourge) as a generic term of which war and plagues are specific examples also facilitates the interchangeability of these phenomena, as well as preparing the general reflection on the nature of the *fléau* in the world and human reaction to it.[20] The patrols at night, the sounds of shooting, particular terms such as *four crématoire* (crematory oven), the establishment of the camps, the black market, the curfew, reduced lighting, lack of paper, radio contacts with the outside world, are all examples of the metonymic procedures described above in relation to the presence of the Germans. These references are sustaining the internal reality of the events of the plague and the historical reality of the war, and it is because of these mechanisms that that reference is so obvious:

countless novels of and about the Occupation use the sounds of
the patrols at night, for example, to index the Occupation as the
historical reality of the text. Where there is no linguistic or other
identity between the two systems, then the reference is supported
by further comment. The 'formations sanitaires' (sanitary teams)
is a case in point here: 'The intention of the narrator is however
not to give these sanitary teams more importance than they had.
In his stead, it is true that many of our fellow citizens would today
succumb to the temptation of exaggerating their role.'[21] Finally,
in addition to the use of referential systems, *La Peste* also suggests
parallels by the use of a 'discursive homology', in Paneloux's
speech, in the plague newspapers and the descriptions of the
'nouveaux moralistes', a mechanism which again recalls primarily
Les Mouches.

Many of the above references are clearly drawing on the
Resistance statements on the nature of the war. Pouillon said of
La Peste: 'It is the novel of the Resistance such as one would have
wished it to be. The struggle of a diverse group, but united
against an external enemy.'[22] It may seem strange therefore that
it is classed here as a novel of ambiguity, especially as it is precisely
for the oversimplification imposed by the metaphor of the plague, eliminating the social and political conflicts within France
and within the Resistance, that the novel has been consistently
criticised.[23] Moreover, its metaphysical statements on the nature
of the human condition and its moral message that 'there are in
men more things to admire than to despise'[24] are not in themselves at all ambiguous. But if one follows through the development of the plague[25] it can be seen that the differentiation
between this external menace and those struggling against it
completely breaks down, thus clearly distinguishing *La Peste* from
the novels of unity of the Resistance.

The passage where the plague is subsumed under the more
general category of *le fléau* is a crucial moment opening the door
to the metaphysical dimensions of the plague: 'Scourges are not
something that man can encompass ('à la mesure de l'homme'),
one tells oneself therefore that scourges are unreal, a bad dream
which will pass. (...) [Our fellow citizens] thought themselves free
and no-one will ever be free as long as there are scourges.'[26]
Plagues and wars are the specific, exceptional, astounding manifestations of this banal phenomenon ('Scourges are, indeed, a

common event'[27]) – a distinction which is structured by one of the major oppositions of the novel between 'surprise' and 'habit/ banality' – and its inhuman, nightmarish qualities are described in order to underline the fact that it lies beyond both the social order and modern science. Indeed, it could be argued that much of the development of the novel is generated by the attempts to impose some kind of human order on the plague, through the compiling of statistics, the bureaucratic organisations (the very ambiguous nature of these attempts will be discussed later). More importantly, once the disease has taken on the dual nature of the plague (war)-scourge, chronicle and comment become difficult to separate, since the chronological development of the medical plague in Oran and the reactions of the inhabitants is also a moral reflection on the presence and effects of the *fléau* in the world. It is the function of the conversations between Rieux and Tarrou to define more precisely its nature.

Their first conversation shows the plague to be an 'extreme situation' revelatory of the human condition, and demonstrates the metaphysical status of the medical profession. Death constitutes 'the order of the world'[28] and therefore like *fléau* falls under the discourse of banality and habit. Rieux is placed in total opposition to this discourse: 'I am still not *accustomed* to seeing people die.'[29] His medical activities to prevent deaths therefore imply a metaphysical stance against the human condition. The second major conversation is dominated by Tarrou and takes this one step further. The two men go up to a terrace overlooking the town. 'It is as though the plague had never climbed up there', says Rieux.[30] And the function of this conversation, by dwelling on the aspects of the metaphysical plague not specific to the town or the disease, will be to generalise the plague in the narrative development, beyond the town, beyond the 'narrative real' from which it can then disappear.[31] In this episode the meaning of the metaphysical plague is extended to encompass human justice and injustice, and human responsibility for death in the world. Tarrou realises his involvement in political movements attempting to change a social order which could condemn men to death brought him once more on to the side of the executioners. Finally he knows that the plague in all its aspects is, like the human condition, inescapable: 'I know for a definite fact (yes, Rieux, I know everything about life as you can see) that *each of us carries the plague* in themselves, because nobody, no, nobody in the world, is immune.'[32] And it is here that the structure of unity can be seen to have been irrevocably changed, in that those who are struggling against the plague are as likely as a Cottard to disseminate it.[33] Their value, which for Camus was immense, lies in their attitudes and actions against the plague, but it is certainly difficult to see them as united against the 'external enemy' of which Pouillon wrote.[34] Though it takes a very different form, *La Peste* breaks down the unambiguous structure of the one *versus* the other as effectively as does *Les Forêts de la nuit*. One has only to recall the end of *F.T.P.* and the impossibility within that story of suggesting that the men who kill 'with no more hatred than a surgeon' might be carriers of the evil they eliminate, to realise the distance travelled.

The fragmentation of the structure of the one *versus* the other also entails a fundamental change in the structures of recognition and aggression which, underpinning the themes of responsibility, action and choice, were shown in the novels of unity to be the basis for the constitution of the figure of the individual. What the post-war novel highlights time and again is the impossibility of the recognition of the enemy as other, and, no doubt necessarily, a concomitant accentuation of interpersonal aggression which can be neither transcended nor reorientated, as will be seen in the next chapter.

There are scenes in several of the novels which dramatise the resemblances between the opposing forces. The village of Jumainville in *Mon Village à l'heure allemande* has received various contingents of foreign soldiers, Austrian and German, which it remembers when the *milice* arrive: 'Those *miliciens* are French, paid by Hitler to kill French people. This is the real enemy (...) I feel the Germans as foreign bodies. I don't digest them. But this lot of scum are real poison. They're bawling something. Odd, we understand. Might it be French?'[35] The replacement of the Germans by the French has crucially disturbed the absolute otherness of the enemy; that this is not sociologically inevitable can be seen by reference to *Le Puits des miracles* where the arrival of the German soldiers clarifies the absolute otherness of the French ruling clique. It is not surprising that it is Auguste, one of the villagers in the *milice*, rather than the German officer Siegried

Bachmann, who starts killing the villagers. Bachmann is shown to be more bothered by the amount of paperwork he has to do rather than by active repression. When Auguste's black market dealings risk becoming embarrassingly public, Bachmann, who is in fact as skilled a black marketeer as Auguste, feels harassed by Auguste's father whom he only imperfectly understands: 'What is he asking? That I don't have his son shot? That I just frighten him? We'll see. After all, I don't care whether he's shot or not.'[36] The final comment obviously adds to the stereotyped portrait of the heartless administrator, but also by its very indifference places him outside the relations of hostility which in this novel determine the relations between the French.

In the novels of unity the direct encounter with the enemy is often the occasion for the definitive moment of recognition; in the novels under consideration here it retains its importance as a crucial episode in the narrative structure, but without the function of realigning the relations of aggression in order to concentrate them on the enemy and the individual. In *Le Royaume de l'homme* (The Realm of Man), by Edmond Buchet,[37] a novel which charts the different political paths taken under the Occupation by a group linked by ties of friendship and marriage, Sébastien, a former protestant priest who is now the leader of a *maquis*, decides to execute personally a *milicien* who has been condemned to death by the group, and takes him off alone. However, he wishes the man to agree to his own conception of death as an act, and not passively submit to it. 'One would think, said the other, that we were talking about your own death',[38] and indeed the whole dynamic of this scene is to produce an identity between the two. In a not dissimilar scene in the definitive version of *L'Education européenne* by Romain Gary,[39] the impossibility of seeing the enemy soldier as different adds an important dimension to the lesson learnt by the main protagonist, Janek: 'In the end, all this famous European education teaches you is how to find the courage and some good, valid, clean reasons, to kill a man who has done you no harm.'[40] This definition of 'European education' is replaced by a less negative vision at the very end of the book, but it nonetheless constitutes a break from his earlier perception of the war. Janek, who joined the *maquis* as a child, is now fifteen, and keen to prove himself the equal of his companions. He manages to become friendly with a group of German soldiers whom he plans to kill, but their kindness towards him causes the first problems: 'It took an effort of imagination to remind himself that these young men were his mortal enemies.'[41] After the fatal explosion he engineers, Janek has to kill a soldier who happened to be away from the camp, skating on an improvised rink. 'He did not look at all like a soldier. (...) When Janek finally stopped and raised his weapon, he had the sudden feeling he was going to kill a simple sportsman.'[42] After the deed, his initial feelings of euphoria that he has now become a true patriot, capable of killing for freedom, are also short-lived.

This kind of scene, where the enemy cannot be superimposed upon the individuals who make up the foreign army, is a complete reversal of the distinction which *Le Silence de la mer* took such care to establish. Like the comparable scenes in *Mon Village à l'heure allemande* and *Le Royaume de l'homme*, it demonstrates the structural absence of the enemy as 'other', and the fact that the moment of recognition contains essentially a recognition of similarity. As such it also shows how far *La Peste* is comparable to other post-war novels of the Occupation, where the irremediable otherness of the enemy is superseded by an identity between the opposing forces.

Notes

1 Many of the characters in the novel belong to four main families: the Balansuns (le comte de Balansun, his wife and two children, Francis who is involved in the Resistance, and Hélène who works in Paris); the Delahayes (Cécile, a kindly if eccentric widow and a close friend of M. de Balansun, and her son Gérard, a childhood friend of Hélène who now also works in Paris as a journalist for *La Gerbe*. In the course of the novel he joins the Resistance); the Costellots (Mme Costellot and her son Jacques, plus his wife and father-in-law M. Lardenne); the Arréguys (Fernande, her husband and son Philippe who becomes involved with the 'Gestapo française').

2 P.199.
3 P.295.
4 P.475.
5 Virtually the only time in the novel the word is used, p.295.
6 In fact he is arrested and killed in Bordeaux by the 'Gestapo française'. Philippe tries to help him escape, and does get away himself.
7 Albert Camus, *Théâtre, Récits, Nouvelles*, Paris, Bibliothèque de la Pléiade, 1967, p.1972. Jean Pouillon wrote: 'Everyone knows from the very beginning of the book (...) that it is dealing (...) with the German Occupation of France.' 'Optimisme de Camus', *Les Temps modernes*, vol.1,

no.26, novembre 1947, p.923.
  8 *La Force des choses*, vol.1, p.182.
  9 'Réponse à Albert Camus', *Les Temps modernes*, vol.8, no.82, août 1952, p.349.
  10 *Du Témoignage*, p.105.
  11 'D'une conversion', no.2, décembre 1943, p.24.
  12 Paris, Librairie José Corti, 1947, p.30. He is here playing on the two senses of 'microbe' and 'germination'. (The book is a collection of four speeches given from 1945–47. The quotation comes from a 1945 speech.)
  13 Though it should be noted that Robert Desnos wrote a *contrebande* poem in 1944 entitled *La Peste*.
  14 *J'étais aumônier à Fresnes*, Paris, 1965, p.49.
  15 *La Peste*, in *Théâtre, Récits, Nouvelles*, p. 1219.
  16 An earlier draft of this opening sentence makes this plain: 'The curious events which are the subject of this chronicle took place in 1941 *during the Second World War, in our small town of Oran*', p.1975.
  17 Of course, Oran itself is playing a dual role as plague town and France. However, this is a second order substitution which emerges gradually.
  18 'Les Exilés dans la peste' (*Domaine français*, pp.37–47), pp.1959–67, *Pléiade*.
  19 P.1957 Pléiade.
  20 P.1247.
  21 P.1328.
  22 'L'Optimisme de Camus', p.925.
  23 See Etiemble, 'Peste, ou péché?', *Les Temps modernes*, vol.3, no.26, novembre 1947, p.916, and Cruickshank, *Albert Camus and the Literature of Revolt*, Oxford, 1959, pp.176–7.
  24 P.1473.
  25 I concentrate particularly here on the metaphysical aspect of the plague. The kind of resemblances between the plague and its opponents operating at other levels of the narrative are discussed in relation to the structures of aggression.
  26 P.1247.
  27 *Ibid.*
  28 P.1323.
  29 *Ibid.* Emphasis added.
  30 P.1419.
  31 After a sudden surge it begins to lose momentum at the end of the following section. A few pages later we read: 'Only one had the impression that the disease had exhausted itself or perhaps that it was withdrawing after having achieved all its aims'(p.1441), an unwittingly accurate statement on the narrative function of the specific medical plague.
  32 P.1425. Emphasis added.
  33 This disastrous power of the contaminatory effect of evil can also be found in another novel of moral reflection, Vercors's *Les Armes de la nuit*, Paris, 1946, which presents the drama of a prisoner returned from a

concentration camp who cannot come to terms with his own actions under conditions of extreme degradation.

34 I am referring to the characters specifically as *combattants* here; I discuss later the final scenes of the novel where the plague is presented as the sole enemy, and the fundamental change away from the notion of resistance which accompanies this.

35 Pp.355–6.

36 P.263.

37 Paris, 1948. Vol. V. of *Les Vies secrètes*.

38 P.230.

39 Paris, 1945; Londres, 1946. There are fairly substantial aditions to the 'édition définitive' (Paris, 1956; Livre de poche, 1962), all of which, like the scene considered here, expand on the elements constituting the structure of ambiguity. To avoid confusion, the date of the edition will be added after the page references.

40 P.237 (1962).

41 P.233(1962).

42 P.235 (1962).

Chapter two

Changing narrative structures: the figure of the individual

One of the major reasons for the disappearance of a Resistance group elaborated within a national opposition to the Germans is the choice of setting. Blémont in *Uranus*, Saint-Clar in *Les Forêts de la nuit*, Jumainville in *Mon Village à l'heure allemande*, the Parisian suburb in *Banlieue sud-est*, provide a socially and politically diverse cast of characters whose narrative coherence is furnished by the town itself. We are thus given a human fresco, French society in microcosm, where the links between individual characters are not forged by their actions but by quite contingent factors. Furthermore, the project of totality[1] which underlies this recurrent scenario means that it is the diversity of social position, of attitudes to the war, of individual psychology, of age, which is stressed. This finds its clearest expression at the level of form in *Mon Village à l'heure allemande*, where traditional third-person narration is interspersed with dramatic first-person monologues, the character speaking being indicated by a subheading. All the main characters speak directly in this way (as do the town itself, the dog Comme-Vous and La Statuette de l'Archange Gabriel), revealing the absence of a privileged narrative viewpoint at the level of the characters, with a concomitant valorisation of the implicit narrator. In all these novels the multiplicity of viewpoints, and the formal parity between them, precludes all possibility of the Resistance activists among them standing for and appealing to a *national* unity, especially since, as we have seen, the German soldiers are themselves integrated into the social structures of the town.

This kind of structure equally serves to block the forging of a political unity, given the variety of motivations and political positions displayed within the Resistance. In *Les Forêts de la nuit*, the characters who could be said to comprise the Resistance are extremely disparate (including networks in France, the Free French forces in London, airmen parachuted into France, the young men of the *maquis* who arrive in the town at the Liberation), with little connection on the level of the plotting between them as Resisters.[2] The contacts between them are never used as a basis for forging a collective Resistance identity; they are incidental to other major narrative events,[3] and to furthering the progression of the narrative.[4] Furthermore, there is no suggestion that they are representative of a wider group, a totality which, as in the Resistance fiction, would give a collective identity to the anti-German forces. Francis does indeed present to his father a grandiose picture of the development of Resistance activities in France and of the military might of the Allies. But this is partly qualified by the fact that it is being described to a man who can only think in clichés, and more importantly there is never any reference to this wider vision at the level of detailed accounts of individual Resistance activities, which themselves are remarkably infrequent. It is rather the supporters of Pétain who have the representative value in this novel: 'The Count had spontaneously and without argument supported the programme for a new France; and with him, thousands and thousands of good decent people throughout France.'[5]

But perhaps the most significant factor in the portrayal of the Resistance as a fragmented rather than a unitary force is the emphasis placed on the provisional nature of the unity of opposition. There is little which unites the idealistic, patriotic Francis de Balansun of the impoverished aristocracy and Le Mohican from the Parisian slums: 'In normal times I would have considered you as an enemy', says the latter, 'and perhaps a time will come when I will once more have to consider you as an enemy',[6] although they do establish a personal liking for each other. And neither has anything in common with the careerist Darricade. The Resistance is therefore unable to carry through its vision into the post-Liberation period, to overcome the kinds of conflicts and rivalries which the novel presents as characteristic of most of France during the Occupation, and to prevent its name being taken over by those interested in the purely selfish furtherance of their own career.

The very nature of choice and commitment in the post-war novels is also a divisive rather than a unifying factor. In Resistance fiction, commitment takes one of two forms: either it is a given, needing no elaborate explanation, or it constitutes a narrative dilemma to be solved. The latter pattern of hesitation concerning Resistance action being overcome by a decisive moment is very rare in the post-war novel, but it does occur. For example, Gérard Delahaye spends a long time before deciding to respond to a suggestion from a friend Pierre that he become involved in Resistance work. But the moment of choice occurs during a conversation with Jacques Costellot when Gérard rejects Jacques's stance of lack of commitment; here as elsewhere, major distinctions are being established between the French. And once he has made up his mind, Gérard virtually disappears from the story until the Liberation, his decision having no effect beyond this individual character. It therefore has no major structural function, but is just one of a whole range of attitudes and choices – pro-Resistance, pro-Vichy, pro-German, indifference – for, in the absence of a wider group to confer exemplary status on any particular individual choice, none can fulfil the totalising function so important to the novels of unity. The structural function of individual choice in the novel of ambiguity resides in the clashes between the various positions and the tragic, tragi-comic or purely farcical results which ensue, and is overdetermined by the ethical ambiguity, even absurdity which governs the development of these narratives.

The most striking aspect of the questions of personal responsibility and choice in these novels is the extent to which they no longer articulate relations between the individual and a wider group, but are seen in purely personal terms. As Mme Costellot explains to her cynical son Jacques:

You have to choose; these days you have to be in one camp or the other one. It's not a moral question any more – although my own choice and I would hope that of M. Lardenne are due first and foremost to a moral position. But it's above all a question of personal salvation, of life and death, or more or less.[7]

In a similar fashion, Darricade, who co-ordinates local Resistance activities, is motivated entirely by personal ambition and is very careful to remain on the right side of all in order to be ready for future shifts in the political climate.

The importance given to individual psychological factors also plays its part in reducing the *value* of ethical or political attitudes or decisions. In all the novels set in a small town or village much is made of the petty jealousies and rivalries which are exacerbated under the Occupation. *Mon Village à l'heure allemande* is an excellent example, where family quarrels, and the conspiracies and arguments of various factions form much of the narrative, generated by the insistent questions 'who is in command?' and 'who is the master?', which appear in several contexts. When Auguste, a fairly unsavoury character, returns to the village as member of the *milice*, shooting the *instituteur* and his dog, and arresting Pierre who is hiding from the STO and for whom he has a long-standing hatred, he is obviously motivated as much by personal satisfaction, power and a penchant for brutality as by any political commitment. Similarly, Léon, a member of the local *maquis*, daubs the shop of the collaborator Lécheur at night. He is finally shot by the Resistance for stealing from another villager. It is made perfectly clear that in both these actions the Resistance provides a chance to get his own back for personal grievances, in the same way that Lécheur dreams of destroying the village and killing all its inhabitants as a German *Gauleiter*, or with an SS regiment.

Political choices are therefore difficult to disentangle from personal factors. Furthermore, the nature of commitment is often due to innate psychological characteristics rather than to conscious decision. Characterisation in several post-war novels relies heavily on a psychological typology cutting across the dividing lines of different political allegiances.[8] This typology meshes with the importance given to age and generation, establishing different kinds of reaction to the particular circumstances of the Occupation, and this again can cut across political boundaries. The resultant concordance between a behavioural model of society, with the Occupation constituting the social and physical habitat, and an essentialist psychology, goes a long way to explain why commitment is not a process, but seen primarily as a static phenomenon.[9] The question of psychological truth is a major theme in *Les Forêts de la nuit*, where the war is said to be a catalyst revealing the inner truth of each individual.[10] Gérard returns frequently to the differences in age between his age group (late twenties) and those ten years younger, and reflects particularly on

Francis's spontaneous revolt against Vichy: 'He is of a different race, which knows nothing of problems,which is not bogged down in egotistical soliloquies. The boys of his age are all from this race. In good and in evil, they ring true.'[11] More importantly, as Jacques Tournier pointed out, his comment applies as much to Philippe Arréguy who becomes involved with the 'Gestapo française' as to Francis the Resister.[12] For the oldest of three generations, the problem is even more acute, as M. de Balansun comes to realise: 'We are very old, Cécile, very old indeed: we have understood nothing of these times.'[13] This is not the only novel to place great emphasis on the question of youth.[14] The kind of history lived by the protagonists of *Le Sang des autres*, 'Le Tilleul' or *Drôle de jeu*, which established a clear continuity between the Resistance and the recent past, is eliminated in favour of reactions to the specific circumstances of the Occupation. The absence of a political memory within the Resistance is a further reason for the absence of a political opposition to Nazism.

Personal eccentricities and the typology of generations and class mean that characterisation plays its part in the ironic structure of *Les Forêts de la nuit*, but on the whole the psychological dramas of the main characters are developed to a degree of intensity which involves them being drawn as individuals rather than just types, with Berthe the maid as a notable exception. *Mon Village à l'heure allemande* is very different, for it assiduously cultivates the quaint and the picturesque at all levels. It assembles the stock characters of village literature, the instituteur, the pompous *curé*, the anxious mayor, the repressed spinster, the village whore, etc.; the frequent recourse to direct speech only heightens the effect, as does the use of nicknames – la Germaine, le père Boudet, le Bien-Nommé (Lécheur), Tête-Brûlée (Léon). Taken together, these two novels show that, whether the characters are individualised or types, the psychology is essentialist and grounded in natural, not ethical factors.

Uranus by Marcel Aymé has also been seen as using a burlesque tradition.[15] It is set in the aftermath of the Liberation as the dramas and conflicts of the Occupation are finally played out, with the FFI patrolling the streets, and the Resistance, especially the Communist Party, in a position of such moral and political ascendancy as to be terrorising. As with *Les Forêts de la nuit* and *Mon Village à l'heure allemande*, much of *Uranus* deals with the intertwining of personal and political intrigues, and with the clash of various attitudes and positions, from the politically uncommitted to collaborators and Communist Party activists, and including black market profiteers like Monglat who is now using his wealth to finance the Communist Party and buy protection. A psychological typology plays a major role here. Clashes between the two Communists Gaigneux and Jourdan arise because of the dislike which the former, who is not only working-class but also generally suspicious of following the blind dictates of the Party, has for the intellectual Jourdan who has no time for the complexities of human behaviour, and in fact the latter has much more in common with the fascist Maxime Loin. They are shown to be similar types seeking compensation for personal inadequacies in a set of political certainties which also confer upon them a power they would never personally merit.

All these procedures which qualify choices and behaviour on psychological grounds, or which evacuate the political and moral content from a particular course of action, have the effect of re-posing the very question of personal responsibility, for the attribution of blame or merit becomes singularly difficult once it is shown that individuals are driven by more than purely conscious factors, or that they are not in control of the totality of the situation. One of the main functions of the use of psychology in the post-war novel is thus to blur the clear-cut distinctions between those of the Resistance and their opponents, and to underline the judgements of the Liberation and *épuration* as simplistic.

In *Les Forêts de la nuit, Uranus* and *Mon Village à l'heure allemande*, the very juxtaposition of a range of choices breaks with the structure of the novels of unity where a set of (pro-Resistance) choices are placed in a position of narrative dominance by being confirmed as knowledgeable. *Les Epées* by Roger Nimier, *La Culbute* by Henri Queffélec, and to a certain extent *Banlieue sud-est* by René Fallet present an equivalence between differing actions and attitudes through the absolute amoralism rigorously pursued by the central characters.

Banlieue sud-est concentrates on a particular social group, the younger generation who feel they have known little else but the war and who are particularly marked by it: 'Tormented ideals, fashions, loves and youth belong to tormented times. This sudden gulf between the generations who could not understand each other would not be effaced with the mere wipe of a sponge.'[16] All their energies go into their own amusements and pleasures, and wheeling and dealing in order to survive, since, being too young to have fought in 1940, they consider they bear no responsibility for the defeat. Facilitated by the contradictory, chaotic nature of the times, their cynicism translates a constant revolt against the values of their parents and the forces of order, both the Germans and Vichy, though the moralising discourse of the latter, and especially Pétain, is particularly singled out for attack throughout the novel. One of the main group of characters, Bernard, does become involved with the Resistance, and is initially dazzled to discover this secret, violent world behind that of boring everyday normality: 'He had been on the lookout for an Adventure (a woman or a revelation, fortune or movement) and now it had unexpectedly fallen on top of him, at a bend in the road, brutal, rough and already captivating.'[17] He is also very impressed by the young men he meets, to the extent of questioning his own attitudes: 'Does France have for them a face unknown to him?'[18] But he does not pursue the matter, and soon returns to his celebration of a life lived to the full: 'This is why he was devoting himself mind and body to this Resistance which he had fallen into like into a trap, which he did not believe in, did not understand, and in which he saw, for the time being, only a source of cigarettes and – why not – strong emotions.'[19]

If the narrator of *Banlieue sud-est* suggests his central characters are variations on a single theme,[20] the multiple identities of the main protagonist, in conjunction with a cynical espousal of various roles which deliberately avoid any hint of commitment, is the hallmark of *La Culbute* and *Les Epées*. Both aim to demonstrate the total vacuity of the moral claims made on behalf of the opposing factions of the period, and the simple division between the heroes of the Resistance and their abject enemies is on the one hand cruelly satirised, yet on the other essential to the whole schema of these novels in order that the *vision noire* of their own flowers of evil may be sustained as transgression.[21] As in *Banlieue sud-est*, the grandiose moral discourses of Vichy also provide a rich source for sarcastic commentary and parody.[22] In both the quintessential figure of the whole thematic structure is that of the traitor, who binds together the shifting network of political options, the double – or even multiple – identities of the hero-narrator, and transgression. Sanders is sent as a member of a Resistance group to join the *milice* and kill Darnand, and remains in the *milice* hunting down *maquisards*. Renaut is constantly composing letters of denunciation and inciting others to denounce. He also has to resist pressure to join the Resistance, the *Légion des Volontaires Français* and the *Parti Populaire Français*. Needless to say the only actions which have any value are their own, whereas the adherents of the Resistance or of Vichy are shown to be living in so many *images d'Epinal* which they are too naive to see through.

These three novels which in different ways place cynicism to the fore by ridiculing all commitment to a cause also generalise this attitude beyond the main character. Renaut delights in any image which accentuates the proliferation of contemporary discourses, as for example the slogans of various political parties and movements seen on a wall: 'Clever wall. It bears all languages and does not choose. It is a thousand times right.'[23] *Banlieue sud-est* and *Les Epées* which continue after the Allied landings lay great stress on the sudden shift of public opinion with the inevitability of the Allied victory: 'Unanimity is no longer just a word',[24] or even beyond: 'For three years [the French] had put up photos of the Maréchal; a saucy action, but not a dirty one. After the Liberation, the newspapers and cinema had forged a solid Resistance conscience for them. A year later, the Resistance scandalised them.'[25] Although the logic behind these novels is very different, in accentuating above all the diversity of political options they achieve the same effect as novels such as *Les Forêts de la nuit*, for this shifting kaleidoscope prevents any of them emerging as positive.

Structures of aggression

The discussion of the key moments and scenes of the recognition of the enemy has shown the extent to which relations of hostility and aggression are still operating in the post-war novel, as so many of them are centred on the questions of killing and being killed. In these novels, such relations are sustained to the very end, partly overdetermined by the fact that the divisions and conflicts of the *épuration* constitute the ending towards which all the narrative tends, partly because of the very absence of the enemy as other to whom these relations of aggression could be transferred. In other words, the structure of 'us *versus* them' is entirely missing, and what is found in these novels is a series of fragmented oppositions, of for example a small Resistance group against a German group, or of one individual against the rest of the world.

It has already been noted that the conflicts in *Mon Village à l'heure allemande* are generated by struggles for power and mastery within the village. The various intrigues often involve people spying on each other and there is a whole network of vocabulary around the 'look' which is itself extremely aggressive. Mlle Vrin, keeping watch at night to find out who is daubing 'Graine de Mort' on Lécheur's shutters, happens to be arrested by the Germans. On her release she compares the way she is stared at to a firing squad.[26] Lécheur recalls Elisée in 'Les Jeunes Gens' with his dreams of destruction and murder: 'Let the Occupation authorities appoint me Gauleiter of Jumainville. The lieutenant is too gentle. I'll arrest everyone, torture, tear out nails, cut out tongues, cut off breasts, ears (...); to finish, I'll shoot everybody, rram!'[27] The final straw in his battle with the town occurs when he is denounced on English radio,[28] which itself partakes of the general relations of hostility expressed through the visual vocabulary: '[The inhabitants of Jumainville] felt spied on. The cathodic eye of the radios seemed to possess the metaphysical power that abbé Varèmes reserves (...) for the radiant eye set in a triangle above the high altar.'[29] And Lécheur commits suicide. Suicide operating as a pendant to the individual's extremely egocentric hostility to the world is a feature of the structures of hostility determining the main character in both *La Marque de l'homme* and *Le Sang des autres*, so it is not surprising that the same mechanism is found here, affording a purely individual resolution which, like Gérard joining the Resistance in *Les Forêts de la nuit*, has no pivotal effect on the action.[30]

Although such structures are playing their part in many novels of ambiguity,[31] the clearest expression of this structure of hostility between the individual and the world is to be found in the novels of irresponsibility which use the first-person narrative form, *La Culbute* and *Les Epées*.

Georges Renaut de la Motte in *La Culbute* is constantly

oscillating between suicide and murder, the former an expression of his search for total oblivion, one of the few certainties in the fleeting, fragmented nature of existence, the latter part of his cultivation of filth, vice and otherness. He is driven by scorn, hatred, the desire to be a *salaud* and not a dupe,[32] by rage against anything, be it a song, an emotion or a person, which provokes a naive, unthinking response and thereby controls him. The novel is a sophisticated exploration of the limits of freedom and contingency, within which the notion of death as complete annihilation has a particular importance. On the other hand, the pursuit of crime as an embodiment of his difference is also sustained by the hatred directed to the world in general which is essential to his perception of himself as 'other', and this is expressed through his insistence on death and murder, which becomes increasingly focused on a woman, Simone, whom he often dreams of torturing or killing. However, death as access to oblivion, or even suicide as internalised aggression are not to be equated with the risk of dying for a political cause of whatever complexion: 'The general hostility to the Germans causes me to look on them favourably. Truth cannot choose banally the majority. Moreover, truth or not, I don't care. Let's try and save our charming little self, our lovely big job and, for the rest, let's try and do harm, enriching, it goes without saying, our mind and our wallet.'[33] Self-preservation is at one and the same time part of his cynicism, and intimately linked to the relations of hostility to the world. But any reproach of selfishness and hate is swept away in the name of the war he is waging on the 'monstrous stupidity of the world',[34] a personal echo of the relations governing the world:

I was not behaving better or worse than other people. Over the world there was nothing but blood and massacres, corpses, barbed wire, dead kids, tortures, famines, plundering, the horror of battles in the night and the rain, mud, shit, formol, crashed lorries, limbs torn off, weariness and a taste for annihilation, weariness and injustice, weariness and cruelty, weariness, weariness, weariness. (...) Bodies and minds could take no more. 'Enough', they asked. The leaders had a good snigger and replied: '*I am waging war.*' (...) That shut the sceptics up. Those corpses rotting where they lay – I am waging war! Kids dying of hunger – I am waging war!
Well me too, dammit, I was waging war.[35].

These relations of aggression, both directed outwards and internalised, also structure the character of François Sanders in

Les Epées.[36] The Occupation forms the major part of the novel which takes Sanders from his pre-war childhood to about 1946. The aggression is overtly double-edged here (one of the first scenes is his suicide attempt, aged fifteen), and should be seen in conjunction with the particular function of treachery and betrayal, both personal and political, in articulating relations between Sanders and others. It can partly be explained by his cultivation of his own difference in pursuit of *le malheur*, a paradoxical stance which is also a battle against the world: 'I always take the side of my enemies. Then if they lose, it means I really am the strongest',[37] and also by his relationship with his sister Claude whom he wishes to draw into his own exile and of whom he says: 'she might betray me, become normal, a stranger'.[38] Under the Occupation it is through betrayal that he maintains his superiority over the various warring factions. He is no more concerned with simple immorality than Renaut is, treating it with the same scorn, but is pursuing what could be described as 'an asceticism of evil'.

Both these novels close with the fight to the death underpinning the relations of Renaut and Simone, and Sanders and Claude, being played out. *Les Epées* ends on the brutal revelation of Claude's death. Renaut's attempt to pervert and control Simone, to bind them together by their mutual detestation, fails. Her hatred has become equally murderous. The last entry in his diary suggests a meeting she has arranged is a trap and he may not return. By implication he is right.

While the novels characterised by a fragmentation of the structure opposing the Resistance and the enemy, and which emphasise the multiplicity of warring factions under the Occupation, may be expected to display structures of unresolved aggression, it may be surprising to find *La Peste* in the same category, since it opposes a coherent group to one definite enemy, the plague, and the ambiguity characteristic of the symbolic plague does not at first sight impinge on the narrative account of the struggle against the disease, nor the historical struggle against Nazism. But a closer examination will demonstrate the structural coherence of the three levels of the narrative which permit the symbolic plague to develop as it does.

Tarrou's lesson that all men are 'plague-bearing' places all within a perpetual cycle of violence. His wish to be an 'innocent murderer' can only eliminate the *intention* of killing, not the aggression itself, which is inescapable, since the world is divided into 'executioners and victims', the latter distinguished from the former mainly by their ignorance, as an early draft makes clear: 'I tell you that there are first of all people who want to condemn, people whose job is to condemn and have killed, and that there are then people who do not want to kill, who kill rarely or not at all and always without knowing it. The first are executioners, the others victims.'[39] The definitive version accentuates the role of the plague and diminishes the aggressive potential of the victims,[40] and the ill and dying who fall prey to the plague do appear to be absolute victims in the conventional sense, while the medical teams wage war on their behalf. In other words, while the symbolic plague effects a simple distinction between 'executioners' and 'victims', the medical/historical plague relies on a tripartite system involving the external force of the disease, condemning the inhabitants to death and suffering, the victims themselves and the 'Resisters'.

There is no doubt that the plague itself is pure aggression. In the two death-bed scenes described in great detail, of Othon's son and Tarrou, it is clear that what is being inflicted is death by torture, and also that the victims are not submitting passively to it. The power of the plague can be ascribed to the fact that it partakes of the two major elements which structure all aspects of the novel and which can be summarised as 'personalisation' (imagination, violence and surprise) opposed to 'depersonalisation' (habit, banality), the former displayed in its capricious wilfulness, its capacity to surprise and its violence, the latter in the bureaucratic order which, as abstraction[41] it installs. An examination of these elements will show that while ostensibly pitting a group of men against an inhuman force, *La Peste* is essentially a story of like fighting like.

It is difficult not to see the inhabitants of Oran as, to say the least, something of a prime target. Its singularity lies in its very banality,[42] the importance of habit, the dominance of impersonal commercial relations. This is what attracts Tarrou, the epitome of what constitutes the personal in the novel, to the place, together with the eternal repetition born of habit and boredom found in the cast of idiosyncratic minor characters.[43] Personal relations in Oran are also placed under the sign of habit or, significantly, of violence: 'The men and women either devour each other rapidly in what one calls the act of love, or enter into a long habit for two ('une longue habitude à deux')'.[44] The only real individual feature of the town is the difficulty of dying, the solitude of the ill,[45] which has an obvious ironic function, not only through their soon to be discovered ability to die *en masse*, but also that this, the one aspect of life in Oran not subordinated to the order of routine and impersonal commercial exchange, is going to be the special domain of the plague with the panoply of statistics and index cards it brings in its wake. The plague is described as 'a prudent and impeccable administration, which works very smoothly',[46] and as such will affect all areas of life. After the initial trauma of separation from loved ones on the closing of the town which is a major and unusual emotional crisis in personal relationships, these too are drawn into the same process of abstraction and 'the order of the plague'.[47] However, if the victims have become a mirror image of one aspect of the plague, they are also remaining true to themselves: the pattern of separation has now become the same as that of love itself, being lived either in the devouring violence of death by the plague, or as a universal habit: 'Everybody was modest. For the first time, those who had been separated did not flinch from speaking of the absent one, from adopting the language of all, from examining their separation from the same angle as the statistics of the epidemic.'[48] Both in their modesty and their inability to find a *personal* language to express their feelings, everyone has in fact started to resemble Grand who, in opposition to Tarrou, is the figurehead, the diegetic embodiment of the impersonal in the novel (and whose true virtue lies in his attempts to break out of it and the suffering it causes him). As a good civil servant, he corresponds exactly to the plague whose accountant he is. It is not surprising that he is the first character to survive, for, as will be seen, the violent aggression which characterises the disease is governed primarily by the personal structures of the text.[49]

If the victims can thus be seen to resemble in many essential features the force which is attacking them, the same is true of the medical teams. The inadequacy of science, and especially of medical science, is one of the leitmotifs of the novel, in order to demonstrate that these human weapons cannot hope to encompass the plague which is properly inhuman, and not a purely medical phenomenon either. The medical code takes its place beside the bureaucratic and mathematical codes which order discourses on the plague; but none of them can destroy it, because they share its negative administrative qualities.[50] Irony is often directed at the municipality's attempts to 'administer' the plague,[51] but the Resisters are also part of the same process of depersonalisation. 'To struggle against abstraction, it is necessary to resemble it to a certain extent', reflects Rieux.[52] Even the 'sanitary teams' which were established under the sign of 'imagination' rather than 'administration',[53] become too exhausted to maintain elementary precautions against the disease: 'It was the struggle itself which made them then the most vulnerable to the plague.'[54] Only Cottard is explicitly described as a *complice* of the plague, but all the factors discussed above could be said to be governed by a structural complicity with it, due either to a similarity preceding the arrival of the plague in the town, or imposed by it. The case of Rambert illustrates clearly that to fight against the plague is to enter a different order, perhaps definitively. Choosing solidarity over individual happiness he joins the fight against abstraction.[55] But his reunion with the woman he loves at the end is a virtual dramatisation of Tarrou's warning: 'one has to watch oneself constantly to avoid being led in a moment of distraction to breathing in the face of another and giving them the infection'.[56] As Rambert waits at the station we are told that he has been changed by the disease: 'the plague had placed a distraction in him which he tried with all his strength to deny, and which nonetheless persisted like a dull anxiety.'[57] The emphasis placed on the fact that he does not see her face at all as she rushes towards him has an obvious psychological and narrative value, deferring the moment of knowing whether their relationship will continue, but equally, in the light of Tarrou's warning, deferring the moment of the possible transmission of the plague – which is another way of saying that their relationship will have been drawn into the structures of aggression.

This can be clarified by considering the emotional structures of the text, and especially the profoundly ambiguous figure of Rieux.

Alain Costes's major psychoanalytical study of Camus's work, *Albert Camus ou la parole manquante*,[58] brings out very clearly the aggressive nature of the plague. He elucidates the violence involved in incestuous desires, fear of castration and guilt, and assimilates disease to the imago of the phallic mother: 'Like her, the disease isolates, subjugates, enslaves, hobbles, castrates, violates the inner being of the subject, in a word: devours him.'[59] The long physical descriptions of the effets of the plague, which devours, burns, stabs, drowns, can only confirm this judgment, and many of the descriptions of the physical effects of the plague are clearly sexualised.[60] But for Costes, *La Peste* reaches a positive conclusion, arguing that the objectivisation of the terrorising phallic mother in the epidemic means it can be resisted without danger for Rieux who can finally overcome silence[61] by speaking through his chronicle. While Costes's analysis of the structures of violence are extremely useful, his judgement of Rieux is less persuasive. Rieux is implicated as both aggressor and aggressed in the battle against the plague; and the ambiguity of his position within the battle is matched by the ambiguity of its aftermath, where the nature of Rieux's victory is less straightforward than it may seem.

Costes draws attention to the scene in *L'Envers et l'endroit* where the young boy stays the night next to his mother, who has been attacked; Costes argues he is both identifying with the aggressor and terrified of the devouring mother, and concludes: 'Taking on himself the guilt of the aggressor, not only does the child expose himself to castration, (...) but also he fractures his ego/self ('Moi') *because he "becomes" the aggressor at the same time as he is the nurse (garde-malade) of the – of his – victim.*'[62] Even without the term *garde-malade*, one can hardly fail to be struck by the resemblance between this scene and the essential scenario of *La Peste*: those stricken by the plague with Rieux the doctor at their bedside. Indeed, the child decides 'on the doctor's advice' to stay with his mother. The incestuous desires and the aggression of the child are projected on to two anonymous adult figures; in this way the mother and child, both sources of aggression, both appear as victims. In *La Peste* too, aggression is quite unstable, and is certainly not restricted to the plague alone. It is not possible to accept at face value this scenario of suffering victim attacked by an external force, with the doctor at the bedside, either.

Rieux's constant revolt against the order of the world and specifically against death undergoes a curious reversal during the plague. 'For a period whose end he was unable to see, his role *was no longer to cure.* His role was to diagnose. Discover, see, describe, record, then *condemn*, this was his task.'[63] It is striking how far he resembles in this Tarrou's description of his father the judge: 'He merely said, it is true, "this head must roll" (...) Only it was not he who did the work. (...) He had nonetheless, according to tradition, to attend what were politely called the last moments and which must properly be called the most abject of assassinations.'[64] Pronounce the sentence, and be present at the death, for which he is not physically but still directly responsible; only the last phrase seems out of place applied to Rieux, but this is certainly how he is perceived at the height of the plague, occupying the same position as Tarrou's father, and as Paneloux delivering God's verdict, namely that of the administrator of 'hideous and derisory justice'. To use Cottard's comment on Othon, he has become 'the enemy number one': 'And the others, those condemned, were well aware of it too. Before the plague he was welcomed as a saviour, (...) now, on the contrary, he arrived with soldiers, and they had to bang on the door with their rifle butts before the family could be persuaded to open. They would have liked to drag him and the whole of humanity with them into death.'[65] The dissociation effected by the basic scenario of victims, disease and doctor, centring aggression on the plague, all but disappears in this passage, in which it can be compared to the scene of the death agonies of Othon's son, where crucial questions of responsibility are again raised. It is because Rieux considers that the child is 'vaincu d'avance' ('already beaten' – that is, he pronounces the sentence of death) that he decides to use the serum which causes his long suffering. It is the question of who is responsible for the suffering of the child which provokes the clash between Rieux and Paneloux in a scene which is asking whether the child is the victim of the doctor–Resister in revolt or of the plague–God?[66] Moreover, it is worth noting that in the first two cases of recovery, against all expectations, from the plague, Rieux is not able to spend the night at the bedside.

If Rieux is drawn into being the executioner's assistant in his active fight against the disease, there are also signs of another, emotional assimilation being effected. Love in Oran, it will be recalled, takes two forms: overt violence or the depersonalisation of habit marked by the virtual death of silence, and the absence of a personal, emotional dialogue.[67] And the kind of emotional drama which the violence of the struggle entails for Rieux is also described in terms of the plague and the symptoms it inflicts: 'His emotional life (sensibilité) was escaping from him. Knotted most of the time, hardened and dried up, it would burst now and then and abandon him to emotions he no longer controlled. His only defence was to take refuge in this hardening and to tighten the knot which had formed in him.'[68] It is as though the overt fight against the plague, where he is also profoundly implicated as aggressor, is producing a break with the lack of emotionality and personal feeling implied in the 'long habit for two' characterised by the relations of Rieux and his wife, their absence of dialogue. Although Tarrou tries to tell Rieux that the violence of the plague is specifically an interpersonal violence, as the epidemic recedes Rieux begins to hope:

Although his days were then as exhausting as when the plague was at its peak, the expectation of definitive liberation had dissipated all his tiredness. He was hoping now, and he rejoiced at this. One cannot always tense one's will and hold oneself stiff, and it is a joy to release at last, in an outpouring, the sheaf of forces standing upright (dressées) for the struggle. If the telegram he was waiting for was also favourable, Rieux could start again.[69]

The sexual symbolism makes it clear that the shift from 'habit' is a shift from impotence to desire and potency. And it is the function of Tarrou's death to teach Rieux that there is no third term, no alternative to 'devour' as opposed to 'habit', and that the personal implies overwhelmingly terrifying violence. Instead of a 'definitive liberation', Rieux now knows 'definitive defeat',[70] and sheds 'tears of impotence'.[71] It is only as a spectator that he will witness the explosions of joy in the town, with the multicoloured 'sheaves' of the fireworks rising in the sky, and decide to write his chronicle.[72]

The definitive defeat at the hand of the plague seems difficult to reconcile with the positive ending Costes perceives as Rieux decides to speak for all, or with *La Peste* as Resistance novel. The final sections certainly seem to leave the idea of defeat behind, as Rieux walks through the joyful crowd. But that Rieux is a spectator and not a participant means that in personal terms the words 'definitive defeat' must be given their full literal weight. Rieux has been returned to the structures of depersonalisation. Costes lays great emphasis on the structure of the 'duplication of the self'[73] in

Le Mythe de Sisyphe and *L'Etranger*, and quotes with approval Quilliot's judgement of the latter: 'The "I" registers impersonally what the "me/self" (moi) has lived.'[74] One could be forgiven for thinking it was in fact describing the narrative structure of *La Peste*, this deliberately unemotional chronicle with its curiously depressed tone, in which the narrator remains rigorously depersonalised; even having identified himself, he continues with the third-person narration. The whole project of writing, in its tautological exclusion of any originality, is, revealingly, an actualisation of his task during the plague, 'discover, see, describe, record, then condemn (to death)': 'His task [of a chronicler] is only to say: "This happened", when he knows that this, indeed, happened.'[75] Having discovered and named the plague, and seen its effects, he can describe and take note, and also condemn, as the essential lesson the writing will reveal is that all are condemned to death. Unlike Tarrou, who wages his personal battle against the plague to the end, whose notebooks are full of idiosyncratic details, who has a past, a present and a future (his quest for sainthood), Rieux is locked in the stasis of eternal repetition inherent to the narrative's circular structure: at the end of the novel his future lies in the writing of the novel. From the plague he has gained knowledge and memory,[76] both of which govern his decision to write against the town's forgetfulness. 'I no longer know whether I am living or if I am remembering', comments the narrator of *L'Envers et l'endroit*.[77] Rieux is caught in the same dilemma.

It is in this context that the final unity between Rieux and all those he speaks for (which Costes sees as a reuniting of the fragmented self), a unity based on their shared experience of the plague, must be seen. Rieux's decision to write 'in order not to be one of those who remain silent'[78] could indeed be a progress beyond the paralysing ambivalence of silence, but if so it is a profoundly double-edged one. For the inhabitants of Oran, once they had passed through the violence of separation and entered the routine of the plague and the structures of depersonalisation, also started to speak of their loved ones; but they spoke in 'the language of all'. That Rieux takes up the position of everyman, speaking for all because he has known the anguish of all, brings him no nearer to the possibility of a personal, non-threatening dialogue and is a further sign of the irrevocability of his defeat and depersonalisation.[79] The final unity of all at the end of the plague is a realignment rather than a continuation. The narration of the plague itself quite explicitly involved a wide variety of attitudes and conflicts, as well as what I have called a structural complicity between the victims and the plague on the one hand, the Resisters and the plague on the other. In Rieux's final reflection, all this complexity is swept away in favour of a simple dichotomy between the plague and the people,[80] which is not realigning the structures of aggression, as in the novels of unity, in order to produce a united people confronting the external aggressor. Here Pascal's famous metaphor of the human condition is used to generalise Rieux's defeat and eliminate all hint of 'resistance' as he watches the joyfully reunited couples: 'And they were denying that we had been that stunned people of which every day one part, crammed into the mouth of an oven, evaporated in greasy smoke, while the other, *weighed down with the chains of impotence and fear*, awaited its turn.'[81] Furthermore, all the guilt and anxiety linked to the structures of violence are finally concentrated on Cottard from whom Rieux, having named himself as narrator, dissociates himself.[82] By individualising the violence and producing one guilty man it is possible, as the Camus of *La Chute* will demonstrate only too convincingly, to give the rest a good conscience.

Although Rieux's original tactics against the plague are to 'adjust to it first in order to beat it later',[83] it is striking that the final joyous scenes are those of deliverance, not victory, however much the historical connotation of the Liberation lead them to be read as such. For the plague is invincible, it will reappear, and what it imparts is Tarrou's moral knowledge, that human relations are predicated on the violence of murder, or separation and exile, which is just the other side of the same coin. In this aspect, *La Peste* is similar to *Le Sang des autres* where structures of violence and the isolation of the individual articulate the crucial questions of desire and responsibility. The shift the novels of unity are able to effect, to an identifiable enemy and a group identity, relies on the relations of hostility which have governed the narrative development. What is not possible – and here *La Peste* is typical of the other novels of ambiguity – is to move from the relations of violence to peace, as Rieux's reaction to Tarrou's death makes clear:

Rieux was well aware that this time this was the definitive defeat, which ends wars and makes of peace itself an incurable suffering. The doctor did not know if, at the end, Tarrou had regained peace but in this moment at least, it was his belief that there would never be any peace possible for himself, no more than there is an armistice for the mother amputated of her son or for the man who buries his friend.[84]

Nor is there any peace possible for a world where the plague is just biding its time until its next manifestation.

The double fragmentation, then, of the enemy and the Resistance group by a variety of narrative procedures and the concomitant importance of the factors positing, explicitly or implicitly, an identity between them, is also structuring the kinds of conclusion (in both senses of the term: narrative ending and conclusion to be drawn) which these novels of ambiguity reach. The Occupation may have ended, but the conflicts which have generated the narration of it persist beyond it. *Mon Village à l'heure allemande* seeks to end on an optimistic note. One of the young men, Marcel, has decided to leave the village to join the Resistance and fight, coincidentally on the same day as the Allied invasion, and the novel ends with an image of his youth and strength overcoming the momentary expression of doubt, the nature of which is however significant: ' "What dawn are we heading towards?" Marcel asked aloud. He was looking at the village. Elise snuggled up to him. – Pierre would have said: hope, she replied.'[85] On his arrest by Auguste, Pierre had overcome his own doubts about the Resistance and sent a message that the time had come to act, so this exchange is recalling his example and more importantly the doubts he had, for they also concerned the future. He had long arguments with the *instituteur* Tattingies about the kind of world which would be produced by a fight based on illegality, hatred and murder. His own arrest and the news of Tattingies's death constitute the classic scene of recognition which allows him to recommend action, but his moral doubts are put aside rather than overcome: 'Now is not the time to listen to the voice of conscience, or of books. (...) Now the time has come to act',[86] incidentally affording a fine illustration of the shift from the structures of Resistance fiction, where the voice of conscience and action coincide absolutely; it is difficult to avoid the conclusion that the pessimism about the future which both Pierre and

Tattingies shared persists in Marcel's question, in spite of Elise's optimistic comment.

Les Forêts de la nuit and *Les Epées* both continue into the post-war period, and both are marked by a continuation of violence: the fear of another major war in *Les Forêts de la nuit*; the war in Indochina in *Les Epées* where Claude's husband Bernard, whom François hates, is killed,[87] and also an apocalyptic vision of the future: 'The voluptuous enjoyment which I happen to experience in betrayals must not be confused with weakness. It is just that I adore the end of the world. Betrayals, scandal, and cowardice occasionally, help us to think that the end of the world will come. That all goes very well together.'[88] One can see the structural coherence between the confusions and divisions of the Liberation and its aftermath, and the conflicts depicted in the course of the novels which prepare and give a basis to the narrative and historical denouements. In other words, the fragmentation of the structures of the individual and the enemy, and the insoluble conflicts that that entails, are overdetermined by the kind of ending which the narration of the Occupation, a historically dated phenomenon belonging to the time of the *énoncé*, is aiming to produce. This has important implications for the value of the Occupation in these novels which will be elucidated in relation to the position of the narrator, to which we must now turn.

Notes

1 And see below, 'A World in Chaos' in the next chapter.

2 For example in the opening scenes of the novel Francis takes Le Mohican, who has been sent to the town by someone else, across the demarcation line. Le Mohican agrees to take a message to Jean de Lavoncourt, Hélène's fiancé, who is thought to be in London. He returns much later, after Francis's death, to bring the news of Lavoncourt's suicide.

3 In the example quoted here it is the psychological drama of Hélène and her relations with Lavoncourt which provide the links.

4 Francis asks Philippe Arréguy to take a message to Hélène in Paris, to let her know contact with Jean might have been established, and so triggers a sequence of events which will indirectly play an important part in his own death, as Philippe gets involved with the 'Gestapo française', and develops a relationship with Hélène, thus giving a reason for Merkel to take the group to Bordeaux to interview Francis.

5 P.66.

6 P.32.

7 *Les Forêts*, p.52.

8 It is worth stressing at this point how different in this respect are the novels of unity, where no general typology independent of political or national positions emerges, since the figures of the enemy and of the individual constitute the structures generating the characters.

9 Where the psychological attribute of self-preservation dominates, choices are dictated by the power of prevailing public opinion. *Les Forêts, Uranus, Banlieue sud-est, Les Epées* all stress the sudden change of heart when it is clear that the Germans are losing, and this again can be contrasted with the depiction of commitment as the definitive culmination of a process in the novels of unity.

10 See particularly pp.307–8.

11 P.291. It is interesting to recall *Drôle de jeu* in this context, where Rodrigue goes straight from school into the Resistance and thereby received the political education of the militant, for the comparison highlights the different narrative function of age differences in these two kinds of novel.

12 Jacques Tournier, 'Jean-Louis Curtis: *Les Forêts de la nuit*', *La Table ronde*, no.1, janvier 1948, pp.130–1.

13 *Les Forêts*, p.479.

14 See especially *Les Forêts de la nuit, Mon Village à l'heure allemande, L'Education européenne*, and *Banlieue sud-est* (e.g. 'We are the youth of the Occupation. We were twelve, thirteen, fourteen years old in 40 (...) We have grown used to their swastikas, their pipes, their newspapers. For us the memory of "before the war" is quite faded (décoloré)', *Banlieue sud-est*, p.109).

15 Cf. Jean Cathelin, *Marcel Aymé ou le paysan de Paris*, Paris, 1958, p.125; Pol Vandromme, *Aymé*, Paris, 1960, p.55.

16 P.74.

17 Pp.313–4.

18 P.316.

19 P.326.

20 'Cous, Bernard, Claude, Alix, vous n'étiez qu'un seul type, gouailleur, menteur, cynique, vous étiez de l'année'.(p.62).

21 The reference to *Les Fleurs du mal* is explicitly made in *La Culbute*.

22 Georges Renaut de la Motte (*La Culbute*) works for 'La Jeunesse' in Paris. François Sanders (*Les Epées*) joins the milice.

23 P.31.

24 *Banlieue sud-est*, p.339.

25 *Les Epées*, p.138. To the extent that Sanders after the war regrets his time in the *milice*, since 'it is going to come slowly back in fashion' (p.185), hence losing its power of transgression.

26 P.63.

27 P.94.

28 Lécheur has already used the radio as an offensive weapon, deafening the town with Goebbels and Radio-Paris, accompanied again by dreams of murder.

29 P.221.

30 On the contrary, Elisée is executed as a *dénonciateur* by the Resistance at the end of the story, which *is* structurally important.

31 They can be traced in Bernard killing Zézette in *Banlieue sud-est*, the interpersonal violence in *Mon Village*, and the chains of psychological cause and effect leading to Francis's death in *Les Forêts*. Constant, the main character of Drieu's *Les Chiens de paille*, is constantly stressing he is waging war on the whole world, which culminates in his wishing to blow up himself and others in the ultimate sacrifice of suicide and murder at the end of the novel.

32 *La Culbute* is the sequel to *Journal d'un salaud*.

33 P.237.

34 P.195.

35 Pp.195–6.

36 Cf. p.161, 'Another dream placed a shining new sword in my hand. I sliced through the air, more and more blood appeared on the blade. Suddenly I recognised my blood. In striking strangers, I had wounded myself.'

37 P.26.

38 *Ibid.*

39 P.2000. This has been entirely replaced in the definitive version.

40 Rieux does return to this later: 'Tarrou knew nonetheless that no one can stop themselves condemning – even victims would find themselves being executioners sometimes'(p.1459).

41 'Abstraction' is a key term for Camus, denoting the non-human force (e.g. of history, or ideology) in the name of which men are treated as means, not ends, and frequently condemned to death, and also the stifling impossibility of dialogue.

42 'On s'y ennuie et on s'efforce de prendre des habitudes', p.1219.

43 Pp.1237–8.

44 P.1220.

45 Pp.1220–1.

46 P.1664.

47 P.1366, and see p.1365, where the inhabitants are described as suffering from 'décharnement'.

48 P.1366.

49 Lawrence Porter argues that 'symbolically speaking, his request that his manuscript be burned is what saves him from the pneumonic plague', and notes that, having removed the adjectives (which Porter describes as 'the misdirected emotionality') from his sentence, he is able for the first time to write to his wife ('From Chronicle to Novel: Artistic Elaboration in Camus' *La Peste*, *Modern Fiction Studies*, vol.28, no.4, winter 1982–83, p.595). This also concords with the structures of personalisation/depersonalisaion. In burning his manuscript, and turning away from the attempt to find a personal language, Grand is totally assimilated to 'depersonalisation', and this, together with Rieux's absence from his bedside, is indeed what saves him. That he is able to write to his wife, having removed the 'emotionality' from his sentence, prefigures the kind of salvation Rieux will find, which again, as will be seen, is a retreat from the hope of a personal language.

50   On the other hand, in a reversal similar to that operating with Grand, the dogged persistence with these limited human possibilities is itself a virtue, in so far as it constitutes a refusal to accept the concrete manifestations of the inhuman order, and the eternal repetition of the search for a serum, the interminable gathering of statistics, is a concentration on the task in hand. As the plague is revelatory of the order of the world, so the search for a cure expresses the philosophical attitude of revolt. Anything else would be a distraction, and, as is often stated throughout the novel, distraction is the plague's strongest weapon. That said, it must still be realised that the medical teams themselves are reduced to resembling their enemy.

51   Cf. p.1361, Rieux's comment on the arrangements for the disposal of bodies.

52   P.1293.

53   Rieux points out to Tarrou that unsuccessful attempts have already been made to recruit volunteers: 'It was done through official channels, without much conviction,' replies Tarrou, 'what they lack is imagination. They are never on the scale of scourges' (p.1323).

54   P.1377.

55   The priority he accorded to happiness was a refusal, not of group action, but of abstraction, as conversations with Rieux make clear.

56   P.1426.

57   P.1462.

58   Paris, 1973.

59   p.40. For the arguments concerning the projection and introjection of the imagos of the good mother and the bad mother, see pp.37–45: 'Histoire des imagos maternelles'.

60   Cf. p.1292. Furthermore, if one brings together the two scenes Costes discusses in *L'Envers et l'endroit* (where the child spends the night next to his mother after she has been attacked by an unknown aggressor, and of the kitten found half-eaten by its mother) with the scene in *L'Etranger*, which Costes discusses as Meursault's real crime, when he agrees to help Raymond humiliate his mistress by spitting on her, the minor figure of the old man (whose clothes are of a 'coupe militaire' which Costes would link to Camus's father) who spits on cats could be seen as generated by the same metaphors of aggression.

61   Costes also brings out the ambivalence of the silent women found in so many of Camus's novels, including *La Peste*.

62   P.88. Original emphasis.

63   P.1375. Emphasis added. The negative weight of the term 'condamner' within Camus's thematic structure around the death penalty cannot be over-emphasised; and in this novel he can also play on the medical sense of 'condamné' as 'doomed', ie 'condemned to death'.

64   P.1422.

65   P.1376.

66   It therefore reveals a strong similarity to *La Marque de l'homme* and

Le Sang des autres where the question of responsibility is raised in relation to the innocent hostages (are they victims of the Resistance or of the Germans?). And in each case it is interpersonal relations of aggression which are structuring the terms of the oppositions and providing the affect of trauma. I would therefore not agree that 'The plague offers many circumstantial similarities to the Occupation, but it is powerless to convey a sense of its human agency and moral ambiguity.' (Cruickshank, *Albert Camus and the Literature of Revolt*, p.177).

67   This is also the dichotomy found in relation to God, who is in 'that sky where he says nothing' (p.1313) and also the torturer of children whom Paneloux says should be loved (p.1397).

68   P.1375. This relationship between the plague and emotionality-desire can also be seen in the episode when Rieux surprises himself talking about his wife to Grand (pp.1374–5). And the first sign that Tarrou has the plague is that his notebooks start talking about personal matters and specifically his mother 'whom I have always wanted to go to (rejoindre)', p.1446.

69   P.1451.

70   P.1458.

71   P.1457.

72   P.1473.

73   *La Parole manquante*, p.54.

74   *La Parole manquante*, p.82. Quilliot, *La Mer et les prisons*, Paris, Gallimard, 1970, p.102. See also Quilliot, p.180.

75   P.1221.

76   P.1459.

77   Paris, Gallimard, 1958, p.71.

78   P.1473.

79   And this can be seen as another reason for the choice of the form of the chronicle which virtually eliminates the subject of the narration.

80   This is the dichotomy of the symbolic plague, between 'executioners' and 'victims', and the violence of the latter is discreetly recalled in this final section, as was mentioned in n.47.

81   P.1465. Emphasis added. (The relevant *Pensée* of Pascal is no. 434 (Brunschvicg edition no. 199): 'Qu'on s'imagine un nombre d'hommes dans les chaînes, et tous condamnés à la mort, dont les uns étant chaque jour égorgés à la vue des autres, ceux qui restent voient leur propre condition dans celle de leurs semblables, et, se regardant les uns et les autres avec douleur et sans espérance, attendent à leur tour. C'est l'image de la condition des hommes.')

82   P.1469.

83   P.1474.

84   P.1458.

85   P.373.

86   Pp.366–7.

87   And affords a further example of aggression both internalised and directed outwards in this novel: 'I am the one who is hit by that bullet and has that exemplary death struggle of which I've been told', p.184.

88   P.183.

Chapter three

Structures of irony

'The game of war and chance'[1]

In *L'Univers concentrationnaire* (The Concentration Camp World), David Rousset places the concentration camps under the patronage of the modern masters of the grotesque, Jarry's Ubu, Kafka and Céline,[2] to present the incongruous juxtaposition of terror and bureaucratic order; but the discovery of the grotesque absurdity of this closed world is a key to survival, a sign of human resilience defying inhuman degradation. The post-war novel of the Occupation is paradoxically both less bleak and more pessimistic, burlesque or grotesque rather than tragic, as the incongruities of the human tragi-comedy are ironically highlighted by the narrator or by the structure of the narrative. All the novels of ambiguity accentuate to a greater or lesser extent the incoherence of the times, its failure to be accommodated within clear moral categories. The kaleidoscope of opinions and actions in *Les Epées* and *La Culbute* are reduced to appearing no more than absurd posturings as the main characters at the centre move between pro-Resistance, pro-Vichy and pro-German groups, cynically playing their part in each and being enthusiastically welcomed by all. In *Uranus* and *Mon Village à l'heure allemande* the presence in the narrative of a multiplicity of positions and attitudes inextricably linking political differences and personality clashes has a major role here, and combines with the episodic structure to create a disjointed effect, emphasising contingency at the expense of causality.

In *Les Forêts de la nuit* the role of the contingent is particularly important, taking the form of a primary disparity between intention and result which is the major theme of the Liberation scenes, but also structures minor episodes in the course of the

novel. The fate of the letters Hélène de Balansun writes to Jean
de Lavoncourt is a case in point. They all pass through many
hands and most of them, for a variety of reasons ranging from
fear of arrest to perverse bad temper, are destroyed. Two actually
reach Spain, but Jean has already left for London when the
second arrives and the man who has agreed to forward letters is
arrested. So the letter not only fails to reach Jean, but ends up in
the hands of a local concierge 'who had it translated by her
daughter's lover, a journalist, and kept it carefully as a model of
love literature'.[3] The irony of this passage is operating at several
levels and can be categorised according to Robert Scholes's useful
definitions of the diachronic and synchronic modes of narrative
irony.[4] The diachronic mode, the disappointment of the protagonist's expectations, underlies the intentionally humorous manner
in which the various letters fall by the wayside and frustrate
Hélène's hope of communicating with Jean.[5] The fate of the final
letter illustrates the synchronic mode, the disparity between the
two codes; a letter inscribed within the code of interpersonal
communication (involving both an intimate relationship and
separation)[6] is reinscribed as an anthology piece within a literary
code. As such it is a paradigm for the content of synchronic irony
in the post-war novel, particularly, as will be seen, in relation to
the Resistance: divorced from its original intention and context, it
is turned into pure spectacle.

On the great day of the Liberation in Paris and Saint-Clar,
expectations and intentions also fail to be realised, for its import
lay in 'the gap between what should have been and what in fact
was'.[7] The conflicts and moral confusions of the Occupation years
concord to turn what should have been the culmination of the
fight against the Germans and the beginning of a new era into an
empty spectacle, the parochialism of which is particularly underlined in Saint-Clar: 'After the monstrous constraints of the
Occupation years, after being plunged for so long in mud, blood
and stupidity, one was entitled to expect a magnificent leap,
exemplary punishments, ritual murder of the real culprits, the
undamming of the lustral waters of joy and hope.' Instead they
were treated to 'a speech in the good old electoral tradition and
the farce of the head shaving'.[8] All that counts is the *appearance* of
solidarity, in mass demonstrations of righteousness, and the narrative accumulates the incongruities which prove the point.

Anyone who is prepared to fight is welcomed on the Parisian barricades and Philippe Arréguy, who has been hiding from the 'Gestapo française' since Francis's murder, reappears and joins the FFI for the love of a battle. In Saint-Clar too, the demonstrations of patriotic fervour at the public humiliation of its sacrificial victims like Cécile Delahaye have very shallow roots: 'Stupidity and hatred surged through this well fed, happy crowd of Saint Clar who had never suffered, for whom the war had been a Golconda and the Germans a blessing.'[9] The irony of these scenes belonging to the synchronic mode resides in the disparity between two moral codes; on the one hand the mass demonstrations of pro-Resistance anti-German feeling, on the other that constituted by the denunciations of the observers – Gérard Delahaye in Paris, Jacques Costellot in Saint-Clar, and the narrator – which underline it as a spectacular morality play for the benefit of the participants' consciences and manipulated by those orchestrating it. For Gérard, an *abbé* on a barricade is an actor overplaying his part of the 'curé combattant',[10] while the 'lynching' of a German corpse demonstrates that the darker aspects of the forests of the night are uncomfortably close. Jacques feels similar revulsion and disgust at the scenes in Saint-Clar. It falls to the narrator to highlight the absurdities arising from the public expression of Resistance fraternity on the part of those jockeying for political power, and especially Darricade, trying to outmanoeuvre the Socialists and Communists and remain on the right side of public opinion; avoiding any mention of the dead Francis because of the compromising expression of alliance with the bourgeoisie that might imply; publicly embracing *le capitaine* Figeac, the head of the local *maquis*,[11] whose prestige he sees as a personal threat. Figeac himself looks forward to the reimposition of a proper military hierarchy; he did not enjoy his subordinate role in the *maquis*, in a brigade commanded by a twenty-year-old Spaniard, nor the deplorable Resistance habit of being addressed in the intimate 'tu' form. One could multiply the examples, from the burlesque episodes of Fernande's public denunciations of Darricade's amoral behaviour during the Occupation, or M. de Balansun's discomfiture on realising the parade of young men he is smartly saluting is led by a well-known local tearaway, to his tragic intuitive realisation of the truth of Francis's death and its futility. As he oscillates between despair at this certainty and hope he may be wrong, his recurring phrase 'Francis has died for nothing' encapsulates the major theme of the novel, that the upheaval of the war has also been pointless, a temporary disturbance within the senseless human order.

A world in chaos

The conclusions drawn by *Les Forêts de la nuit* go far beyond the confines of one small town in south-west France. It is explicitly stated that the Occupation has drawn Saint-Clar into the wider conflict: 'The town was directly involved in History (...) Its destiny was linked to that of the entire planet, and it was vaguely (obscurément) aware of the fact.'[12] That the novel is seeking to elucidate a truth about the Occupation which is not a purely local truth is, however, primarily borne by the structuration of the characters, which is dependent on producing the gamut of possible figures – collaboration, Resistance, indifference, profiteer, support for Vichy and le Maréchal, occupying forces (pro-Nazi and anti-Nazi). In other words, the novel presents a political and social cross-section which enables Saint-Clar to be both a particular town in the south-west close to the demarcation line and typical of France as a whole.[13] This exemplary typicality which is the basis for the generalising comments in the text also surfaces at the time of the Liberation, in relation to the disappointing return to the status quo which characterised the celebrations: 'But was Saint-Clar perhaps an exceptional town in France? Would we perhaps, also, soon learn that the greatness and sacrifice of a handful of the French had easily redeemed the spineless behaviour of the pallid, weary mass? Would it perhaps be fitting to wait for a few days, a few months, to see the true face of the country form and shine forth once more?'[14] But nothing in the post-war section of the *Epilogues* either contradicts the pessimistic judgements made, or restricts them to the particular circumstances and conditions prevailing in Saint-Clar.

A similar political and social cross-section conferring typicality on the events and conflicts of the novel is found in *Mon Village à l'heure allemande* and *Uranus*. Jumainville is described as 'just a typical French village, no more, no less'.[15] Georges Brassens comments in his 1965 preface to *Banlieue sud-est*: 'Most French towns were in the same boat at the time, and the book became universal. It was a tourist guide through our adolescence for all of us',[16] which is fully confirmed by the range of characters and events and by the frequent general descriptions of 'the youth of the Occupation'. Even the extremely small cast of main characters in *Les Chiens de paille* which is, furthermore, set in an isolated part of the north-western coast of France, includes a Communist, a Gaullist, a collaborator and a black marketeer, fulfilling the function of metonymically representing France and thus supporting the general comments of the detached observer Constant. *La Culbute* and *Les Epées* also ensure that the attitudes and actions of the main protagonist-narrator are not read as purely personal idiosyncracies by relating his vision of the world to the general state of France.[17] The tripartite structure most clearly in evidence in *La Peste* – the particular setting and events constituting the 'narrative real', which metonymically relates to the general situation of France under the Occupation, and in turn supports wider considerations of the nature of existence in the world – is in fact a characteristic feature of the novel of ambiguity.

The social and political chaos of the Occupation and its aftermath is often echoing that of the world, or is shown to have universal implications for the nature of human endeavour, and this ensures the *thematic* coherence of the different levels. The impossiblity of effecting a transition to peace after the war is also frequently emphasised. The planet Uranus of whose bleak desolation Watrin dreams, corresponding to the devastation of Blémont after the bombing, articulates the descriptions of the town with wider, quasi-metaphysical considerations. In *La Culbute* and *Les Epées* it is the absurdity of life which is exemplified in the grotesque farce of the Occupation, and particularly in any attitude of moral seriousness, whereas *La Peste* and *L'Education européenne*, equally concerned to demonstrate the limitations of human endeavour in the face of the absurd, highlight the moral qualities of that endeavour as the true source of human dignity. What is emerging from all these novels is not a local but a universal truth.[18]

Both the novels of unity and the novels of ambiguity operate within a moral framework, but the relation of the ethical to the narrative event is very different in each. In Resistance fiction the relation is one of continuity: the perception of the war as a cultural event means that the transcendent values of humanism which are being defended form both the context and the purpose of the events of the narrative, whereas in the post-war novel, although the values of justice, fraternity, reason, and of right and wrong are still present, the narrative event is in contradiction with the ethical, which is variously encoded by these very events as unrealisable, inappropriate, or belonging to the past. But if it is not the event which produces the ethical reading of the world, then the major question is where the latter comes from. In the novels of irresponsibility (*La Culbute*, *Les Epées* and to a certain extent *Banlieue sud-est*), deliberate transgression constitutes the identity of the main characters, and this sustains the presence of the ethical. The knowledge that the world is flouting what are presented as previously acceptable moral categories is borne in *Uranus* by the educators (Archambaud, one of the main characters, in his role as father, Didier a local teacher) who have to prepare the younger generation for contemporary reality, though their observations are subordinated to those of the 'super-educator' of the text, *le professeur* Watrin. For *Mon Village à l'heure allemande* the relation between ethics and the world is hypothetical, unresolved, consisting in the interrogations of what the future will bring – 'a human jungle or a return to beauty, truth and all the tralala'.[19] *Les Forêts de la nuit* encodes justice and purity as unrealisable in the repeated use of the past conditional 'should have', which functions as an unfulfilled imperative. Janek of *L'Education européenne* and Rieux of *La Peste* both transmit what they have learnt through experience: the disparity between human aspirations to justice, meaning and truth and the reality of the human condition.

In every case, the structural disparity between the 'narrative real' and the extradiegetic commentary means that what will emerge as the knowledge to be transmitted is not inherent in individual actions or events, but is centred on the figure of the narrator or those who assume the narrator's function as observers or instructors. The novels of ambiguity are no less didactic than the novels of unity, but the fact that knowledge is structured hierarchically, belonging to the narrator and his surrogates rather than the characters, to the observer rather than the observed, means that the reader is now invited to share the narrator's view of the spectacle of the human comedy.

The narrator and the hidden God

Francis Jeanson devotes a section of his famous review of *L'Homme révolté*: 'Albert Camus ou l'âme révoltée' (Albert Camus or the soul in revolt) to *La Peste* which he describes as 'a transcendental chronicle': '*La Peste* related events seen from on high, by a subjectivity outside the situation which was not living them itself and was content to look on.'[20] Camus protested strongly at this interpretation, as the narrator Rieux is one of the main actors of the drama of the plague and the evolution from *L'Etranger* to *La Peste* 'was a movement towards solidarity and participation'.[21] But Jeanson is surely right to insist that the impersonal style of narration cannot be dismissed as being of no matter, and that the narrator and the doctor are different textual figures, situated at different levels of the narrative.[22] As extradiegetic narrator of the plague Rieux enjoys the omniscience characteristic of the subject of the *énonciation* in relation to the events and characters being narrated, stemming from his superior knowledge and moral authority, for the narration of the plague is governed by the message it is to produce, that the disease is only a symptom revealing a capricious creation hostile to men. And it is to this that Jeanson takes exception: 'For anyone looking on from on high, the agitation of people down on the earth's surface could well appear pretty meaningless.'[23] The all-encompassing vision inherent in Rieux's position as narrator is also embodied diegetically, when the character Rieux installs himself on the terrace, firstly with Tarrou, but finally alone, and it is from a position of dominance above the town that he decides to write his chronicle.

This 'view from above' is found in all the novels of ambiguity, establishing the *structural* coherence of the three levels of the narrative, for they all seek to deduce a moral lesson from the particular events of the Occupation which they narrate. Though the modalities vary, from a sombre realisation of the absurd contingency of existence, as in *La Peste*, to a now lighthearted, now vituperative presentation of the absurdities of life, the marriage of technique and metaphysics which Jeanson described as a 'resolutely absurdist stylistic procedure'[24] could apply to them all. The epilogue of *L'Education européenne* ends with Janek Twardowski rising to a position of absolute ascendancy over the events he has lived, by means of an image giving an unwittingly literal interpretation of 'agitation on the earth's surface'. He is now the sub-lieutenant Twardowski, revisiting the forest hideouts and recalling the past, and specifically the last moments of his friend Dobranski, when Janek promised, though convinced of its futility, to finish the novel Dobranski had wanted to write. Inserted into this dialogue is an image of columns of tiny, busy ants, each dragging a small blade of grass, each impelled by the great importance of their difficult task. As Janek was convinced that men would not heed the message of the book to mend their ways, so ants now crawl straight over the copy of *L'Education européenne* which lieutenant Twardowski has placed on the ground. The distance between Janek and the ants is then transformed into that between Janek-narrator and men in a final vision of creation itself: 'The world where men suffer and die is the same one where ants suffer and die: a cruel incomprehensible world, where the only thing that counts is to carry ever further an absurd twig (...) without ever stopping to rest or to ask why....'[25] The superior knowledge underpinning the authority of the narrator is revealed in both *La Peste* and *L'Education européenne* to lie in the recognition of the limitations of human endeavour, a truth which informs the narration of events and of which the majority of characters are ignorant. A similar disparity in knowledge lies at the heart of the irony in all the novels of ambiguity, which operates primarily with the narrator displaying his knowledge at the characters' expense. Of course in practice this cannot be separated from the content of that knowledge, that human actions are taking place in a world of lost or unattainable values; incapable of fulfilling their own expectations, they can only demonstrate the validity of the narrator's.

There are many variations on this common schema. I shall concentrate here on *Uranus, Les Chiens de paille* and *Les Forêts de la nuit*, which exemplify the absurdist implications of the 'view from above' within a traditionally realist form, before turning to the novels of irresponsiblity where the irony extends to the very mode of writing.

Watrin and Archambaud are the two major sources of moral commentary on the social and human experience of the Liberation period as it is presented in *Uranus*. Archambaud consistently underlines the manner in which all pay lip-service to the Resistance, whose prestige is backed up by the military terror of the FFI. The jockeying for power between the Communists and the Socialists, each trying to exploit their Resistance credentials, is shown to reinforce the simplistic equation between the Resistance and moral purity which overrides all other considerations. In this sense too, Blémont exemplifies France: 'Going beyond the town's limits, Archambaud considered the question at the level of the *département*, then at the level of the entire nation. The hypocrites now numbered millions. In all the provinces of France, in the villages, in the large towns and the small towns, he saw two-faced people proliferating.'[26] The end of the Occupation has produced a complete about-turn which is aiming to efface the past, and specifically the support for Vichy and the Maréchal, in line with the new morality. Preparing for the celebrations to welcome home the town's prisoners, Archambaud recalls the Maréchal's visit to Blémont. The same crowd is now going to applaud the insults which he expects the speakers to heap on Pétain; but there is no suggestion that the 'grande clameur de tendresse (great noise of affection)'[27] which had greeted Pétain was itself in any way forced: there is nothing inherently hypo-critical about public manifestations or political opinions. Archambaud is articulating the socio-political thesis of the book, that the criminalisation of support for Vichy by the politicians [28] has installed a general fear dictating public obeisance of the new morality, precisely because support for the Maréchal was universal and sincere. (And it is worth opening a lengthy parenthesis here to note how common, not to say banal, is the scenario of 'the crowds welcoming de Gaulle after having welcomed Pétain', from the post-war novel to *Le Chagrin et la pitié* and beyond, in critical and imaginative writing. As with *Uranus*, there is always an anti-'résistantialisme' – or even, it might occasionally be recognised, anti-Resistance – axe to grind, which has a certain ironic charm, given the frequency of the statements on collaborationist turncoats and sudden espousal of less compromising causes as Germany's star wanes, in the clandestine Resistance press.)

Watrin completely agrees with Archambaud on his analysis of contemporary manners but puts a very different gloss on it; since the bombardment of Blémont he has been transported in dreams to the bleak horror of the planet Uranus where he experiences the anguish of the absence of all hope, and the Earth now appears to him in a different light. From these interplanetary heights the rich diversity of all forms of life is a source of poetry and wonder:

One cannot conceive of anything finer or gentler than men. No, Archambaud, don't say anything. I know. But their wars, their concentration camps, their works of justice, I see them as impishness and ebullient behaviour. Don't they have songs for suffering? Don't talk to me of selfishness or hypocrisy. The selfishness of man is as adorable as that of a butterfly or a squirrel.[29]

This zoological vision of the planet excludes a moral attitude to social, political and moral conflicts which are inscribed within the natural order of things.

The narrator espouses the points of view of both his surrogate observers. There is never any suggestion that Archambaud's analysis or reason for indignation are either unreliable or criticisable. The case of Watrin is more complex. He is a rather burlesque figure, both in his lyrically effusive manner and the somewhat ridiculous exaggeration that the human jungle is as much a source of wonder as any other, which is in direct contradiction to the Archambaud position and also refuted by some of the scenes of the novel. The identification of the ruins of Blémont and the planet Uranus is strong enough for the alternative reading of the Earth as source of despair and anguish to be sustained. Where Archambaud and Watrin agree is that men are far more complex creatures than political and intellectual systems of thought, which deal in moral abstractions, allow. Throughout the novel the Communist Jourdan is a particular butt for irony, in the caricaturally limited nature of the fixed ideas and stereotypes of good and evil he is shown to believe in.

Archambaud's perception of an absurd attempt to engineer a national *volte-face* also relies on a disparity between human experience and simplistic ideas imposed from elsewhere, and his interest leads directly into the substance of the narrative: 'He watched for the difficulties such a situation could create in everyday life, and the moral or psychological abnormalities which resulted.'[30] Concentrating on the social and personal aspects of daily life under the Liberation, the narrative ironies, conveying variously amusement or indignation, present life in Blémont as an ultimately meaningless variety of clashes and conflicts, or an unsustainable morality play imposed by a powerful few. The very choice of the central situation illustrates this. Because of the shortage of accommodation, the Archambaud family (father, mother and Marie-Anne their daughter) has to house Watrin and the Gaigneux family (parents and four children). Into this household comes Maxime Loin, whom Archambaud discovers one night hiding from the FFI and agrees to shelter. All the possibilities afforded by such a situation are exploited – arguments in the kitchen between the two wives; amorous intrigues involving Loin, Gaigneux, Marie-Anne and Mme Archambaud; the need to keep Loin's presence from Gaigneux and Jourdan, a frequent visitor. And there are innumerable examples of particular remarks, or episodes which, displaying all the extravagances of a farce to amuse rather than engage the emotions, exemplify Watrin's indulgence towards the endearing habits and the resilience of the human animal whom it is impossible to take seriously however seriously he takes himself. One example would be the characterisation of Léopold, the larger-than-life alcoholic café proprietor, who is the only true enthusiast for Racine in the classes which now have to be held in his café and who finally turns his hand to composing alexandrines, but in inappropriate contemporary slang. On the other hand, that Léopold is shot by *gendarmes* who come to arrest him acting on the orders of those protecting Monglat is not given the same tonality at all. Nor is the public beating-up of Gallien, a Maréchaliste ex-prisoner of war, at the welcoming ceremony at the station. Only Watrin goes forward to help him – Archambaud cannot find the courage to join him, and a doctor refuses to see to him. Watrin is finally escorted away by the police, leaving the wounded man on the ground as the speeches continue: ' "Delivered from its enemies, from all its enemies, a young, ardent France, led by an elite whose intelligence, vision and humanity are the admiration of the whole world..." proclaimed the speaker.'[31] If, as Jean Cathelin argues, Aymé is concerned to present 'part of the recent history of France which greatly resembles the Shakespearian definition of life: "A tale told by an idiot, full of sound and fury" ',[32] he achieves it as much as anything through the distancing effect of this farcical juxtaposition of characters and incidents.

None of the characters is in overall control in *Uranus*. The Communists think they are, politically, but in fact they are manipulated by Monglat as he uses his powerful friends in Paris. Only the narrator and the reader are aware of the foibles and the private dramas of all the characters, of the true facts behind the sequence of events. The same is even more true of *Les Forêts de la nuit*. The ignorance of the characters, each of whom has only partial knowledge of the events of the novel and the motivations of those concerned, is a major factor sustaining the importance of contingency, one of the bases for the technique of incongruous juxtaposition which is fully exploited, both to underline their ignorance and make a mockery of their actions and hopes which are always necessarily off target. By the end of the novel little can be taken at face value. Mme Costellot's mention of the efforts she made to intervene on Francis's behalf with von Brackner and the German authorities, Darricade's rise to fame with the image of Francis the Resistance martyr in tow, have ironic depths by virtue of the reader's superior knowledge. In all this the narrator is very evident – in the generalising scenes looking down on the town and its inhabitants, in the characterisation which, as in *Uranus*, is constituted by the thoughts of the characters and the narrator's judgements, and particularly in the Liberation scenes, where the disappointment that the events do not match what should have been is to be located in the extradiegetic discourse of the *énonciation*.

The narration of the Occupation years in *Les Forêts de la nuit* is constituted to a great extent by political and personal clashes between the French and within the Resistance, and therefore the hopes expressed on the great Liberation day, for a 'purifying wind (souffle)', a 'magnificent leap' which would change the face of France, appear virtually from nowhere, just as the working-class masses, the *maquisards* and the FFI do. The only Resistance character committed to the fight against social injustice was *le Mohican*, but he equally underlined the class differences opposing him to Francis, and the provisional nature of their common cause, and predicted, after an extremely sarcastic description of the defeat of the Germans and the nation in unison celebrating its victory with freedom restored: 'It will all just be starting.'[33] His judgement is fully confirmed – indeed, operates as a virtual *annonce* – by the Liberation scenes where the mass celebrations are at the same time the proof that nothing has changed. For the voice enunciating the judgement on these scenes, the possibility of change is already past, they are excluding what *should have* happened. But in the past of the novel which has been enunciated, everything tends to precisely the cynical victory being described. In other words, this is one of the 'moments de décrochage' (literally 'unhooking'), in Claude Duchet's terms, revealing the *hors-texte*, by which he means the implicit knowledge and codes of the text [34] which is constituted here by the Resistance discourse of heroism, grandeur and social renewal. With a mechanism recalling *Drôle de jeu*, this discourse is deliberately set aside in the *Avertissement*: 'Many books, since the end of the war, have shown and celebrated those whose fight saved honour and contributed to victory. I would have added nothing to these works', and the diegetic development specifically disproves it. This reveals the historical gap between the *énonciation*, which is post-Occupation, and the *énoncé*, for in all novels where the final battles for Liberation and the immediate post-Liberation period form the conclusion to the narrative,[35] the Occupation is thereby produced as an historically dated phenomenon, belonging to the time of the *énoncé*. From the point of view of the analysis of the temporal structures of the narrative levels, Resistance and Occupation could be said to occupy a similar position to that of the pre-war history in the Resistance novels, where questions or predictions concerning the future can also be classed as ignorant or knowledgeable in relation to later narrative developments which constitute the historical present of the *énonciation*. In *Les Forêts de la nuit* irony is the major expression of the tension between the *énoncé* and the *énonciation*, proving that human and social reality will defeat the Resistance coding of it as potentially noble, and also operating at the expense of the town's inhabitants who collectively exemplify, in greater or lesser degrees of stupidity and selfishness, the limitations of human endeavour.

Drieu la Rochelle composed *Les Chiens de paille* about the same time as his article 'Bilan', summing up his achievements and failures at the *NRF*,[36] and the political thesis of the novel is very similar to the arguments set out there, that the world is entering a new phase in its history in the battle between the two empires of America and Russia, and France is prevented by its own decadence, which Vichy has proved incapable of countering, from saving itself from foreign occupation. The political activists in the country are all hitched to the bandwagon of one or another foreign power. In the article, however, Drieu comes down firmly

on the side of Hitler as the only man in a position to safeguard
Europe against foreign domination – England is seen as no more
than a puppet of the United States – and specifically against
Russia which is identified as the greatest threat. In the novel Germany does not enjoy this prestige, and the collaborator Bardy
represents just one of several options alongside the Gaullist Pré-
ault, the Communist Salis, and Cormont, the believer in 'the
wretched and derisory myth of "France standing alone" '.[37] The
intrigues between these various characters, especially for the control of a secret arms depot, is narrated from Constant's point of
view, who is both character and commentator on the cast of characters. He is further set apart from the other characters both on
the level of characterisation – he is the adventurer with a truly
global knowledge of the cultures of the world and all possible
experiences, and who is now going beyond adventurism – and
through his metaphysical interest in Eastern, Christian and
Nietzchean philosophies which underlies the political perception
of the upheavals taking place in the world as constituting yet
another clash between decadence and barbarity to engender a
new world order. The figure of the traitor is again central here,
linking the metaphysical, the political and finally the diegetic as
Constant, deciding that Cormont on the one hand and the inter-
nationalists on the other are locked in a static battle beyond which
they cannot progress, takes on the role of Judas to sacrifice the
Christ-like figure of Cormont and accomplish the destiny of
France.

The distance between humanity and Constant, who variously
espouses the point of view of the gods, of God and of non-being
which is beyond any individual creator, is more pertinent than
the differences opposing the various factions. As in the other
novels of ambiguity, the 'view from above' accompanies the
absence of any figure of the enemy. Gaullists and collaborators,
for example, are marked by resemblance, not difference;[38] men
are creatures governed by passions which enslave them for they
fail to recognise the futile nature of their passions, of all existence, which would save them.[39] But if Constant if omniscient, he
is certainly not omnipotent and is himself at the mercy of the
extradiegetic narrator who is as elusive as any hidden God,
appearing primarily to deliver the thunderbolt of the final paragraph, in the shape of an English plane which drops a bomb on

the house where Constant is about to blow up Cormont, Susini the black marketeer and himself.[40] The historical gap between *énonciation* and *énoncé* is also revealed. Constant reflects that the divisions and conflicts opposing Gaullists and Communists, Gaullists and Gaullists, Gaullists, Communists and collaborators, form a kind of dance whose rules are understood and respected by all, but which would still erupt into violent explosions: 'which break with all half-measures. (...) But France, in 1942, had *not yet* reached that point; deaths by violence were *still only* counted in tens.'[41]

Jeanson accused Camus of writing a metaphysical novel which should have been called 'the human condition': 'The real scene is not this town, but the world; and the real characters were not those men and women of Oran but all humanity, not that disease but absolute Evil',[42] a statement which, allowing for the different metaphysical content, might have been made of any of the novels under consideration here. In *La Peste* evil in the world is both alien to man and elided with the human condition. In the other novels of ambiguity, it is the nature of man himself which explains the irrational absurd world which confronts the individual. Both perspectives reveal the ahistorical character of the 'view from above', of the heights from which the narrative subject, excentric to the world, can thereby seize it as a totality: the particular conditions under the Occupation are a manifestation of the infernal cycle of human action in the world,[43] which is thus intimately bound up with the essentialist view of human nature: 'Men were always the same',[44] reflects Rieux. The unbridgeable gap between the realities of the Occupation and straightforward moral judgements of right and wrong is underpinned by the absolute knowledge that value cannot be produced by action in the world. The common thread linking these novels is that the world is inauthentic.

If irony can generally be said to reside in a discrepancy between a statement and contextual information,[45] then the latter is revealed in the whole range of narrative ironies deployed at the expense of characters who rely on their actions being meaningful or on being able to behave in accordance with well-defined codes of behaviour. But this can be further refined. Robert Scholes isolates three kinds of irony in narrative, two of which[46] are extremely pertinent here: the irony that needs 'no authoritative discourse to focus it but draws upon simple principles of value and a clear social consensus',[47] and the irony that is 'controllable only at the price of introducing a highly coercive and manipulative discourse'.[48] Both kinds are to be found in the novels of ambiguity, the former presenting the spectacle of the Occupation and Liberation as an enactment of the well-known adage: 'Plus ça change, plus c'est la même chose' (the more things change, the more they stay the same), the latter directed at any discourse which asserts that value can be grounded in man's action in the world, and primarily at Resistance discourse whose central value is man himself. We have already see the manner in which this refutation operates in *Les Forêts de la nuit. Uranus* is concerned to demonstrate that any social renewal produced by a Communist– Socialist dominated Resistance is a moral sham, not least because the ideas which inspire it are insubstantial abstract doctrines bearing no relation to reality. *Les Chiens de paille* seeks to demonstrate the hollow nature of all transcendence in that it is always a sign of decadence. France is said to have entered a phase of decadence and is thus in this latest battle realigning the forces of civilisation and barbarity, re-enacting the destiny of the Jews overrun by foreign troops. Political and metaphysical theses converge at this point, for in spite of the general language, and its anti-semitism, it is Resistance discourse which is being pinpointed, and particularly its concern with the absolute and the universal:

The Jews were now only intellectuals and men of letters, not even men of letters, but kinds of priests, frenetic monks, vain, hideous, grotesque, and who, in the middle of Greek philosophers and athletes, of Roman aristocrats and soldiers, continued to make speeches about the supremacy of Jewish genius, naturally a 'purely intellectual', entirely spiritual supremacy! Having had their arses kicked and kicked again, they spoke of the supremacy of their arses over the boot that was doing the kicking.[49]

It is here that a connection can perhaps be established between the novels of ambiguity and the crisis of humanism which becomes so insistent by the end of the war, for what is denied by the overriding vision of the superior narrative viewpoint is the possibility of transcendence. Human actions in the world, caught in the realm of the contingent and the relative, cannot fulfil aspirations to the absolute, whereas in the Resistance fiction action in the world undeniably founds the values of humanism, and there is an unbroken continuity between the narrative event and the values it incarnates. The impossibility of transcendence takes two forms in the novels of ambiguity. The first could be called the tragic mode, registering the crisis of values but not completely rejecting them as such. Vercors and Camus both illustrate this. [50] The more usual form lies in the convergence between the knowledge of the meaninglessness of human existence, and the socio-political thesis on the nature of Resistance morality (or more accurately, of 'résistantialisme') which is accordingly seen as inappropriate. Both concord in the use of irony to demonstrate absurdity, and in the appeal to the hidden God.

Lucien Goldmann, whose work *Le Dieu caché*[51] is being explicitly recalled here, shows that the figure of the hidden God, both present and absent, is essential to the seventeenth-century 'tragic consciousness', the perception of the divorce between the absolute values of God and the impossibility of realising them in the world. Jeanson brings out the importance of the ever-absent, ever-present God in Camus's work: 'Camus is certainly not an atheist, but a passive antideist. He does not deny God's existence (because he accuses him of injustice), (...) all he wants is to challenge him',[52] and Sartre talks of man in Camus's world of eternal injustice, demanding meaning from a God who is eternally silent.[53] Camus himself has Rieux refer to God 'in that sky where he says nothing'.[54] In this, as in so many other ways, *La Peste* is typical of the post-war novel of the Occupation, for they all use references to God, a signal that human action is being judged in reference to a transcendent absolute. But rather than the impassive, silent interlocutor of Camus's man in revolt, God is merely a figure in the cosmology, an ironic or anguished observer mirroring the stance of the God-like narrator.[55]

In spite of the importance of this particular *vision du monde* for a realisation of the loss of value in human existence, to agree with Jeanson that *La Peste* – and by extension any of these novels – is *really* (and therefore only) a metaphysical novel would be tantamount to saying the 'narrative real' can be effaced from the text. On the contrary, the frequency of the mechanism of the character-turned-author should alert us to the very specific structures of these novels. Edwin Moses writes: 'To have an external narrator tell the story of an enclosed city which is a symbol of the whole world would be ridiculous on the face of it: it would make the narrator into God.'[56] However much the identification of Rieux as narrator fudges the presence of an implicit, non-individualised narrator, however much Rieux enjoys a God-like omniscience, Moses is making an essential point[57] that Rieux as narrator is structurally tied to the diegetic development of the plague. In these novels, action in the world – which *is* the diegetic development of the Occupation and Liberation periods – is constitutive of the knowledge of the text, that no action can found value, and it is the function of the narrator, who is both of this world and not of it, to *realise* the contradiction.[58]

'In the country of the Ironic, Omniscience itself appears absurd': thus Scholes sums up his third category of irony,[59] that of the self-conscious narrative consistently using the ironic mode to draw attention to its own artifices. It is perhaps not surprising that a constant juggling with the *énonciation* and the *énoncé* is most apparent in novels such as *La Culbute, Les Epées* and *Banlieue sud-est* which portray the Occupation years as a grandiose melodrama of contradictory scripts earnestly acted out by a large cast of ham actors,[60] where the narrator emerges primarily as script-writer *extraordinaire*. Gone is the absolute assurance of *La Peste* and *L'Education européenne*, where the seriousness of the account of the character–narrator is never questioned. In none of these novels is the perception of the absurdity of life, of which the Occupation is a particularly acute manifestation, at all in doubt; what is destroyed in *La Culbute, Les Epées* and *Banlieue sud-est* is the possibility of the narrative detachment from that realisation which sustains the 'view from above', and therefore the implicit assumption that the project of writing is not itself subordinated to the order of the absurd.

The suicide letter of the young François Sanders in the first chapter of *Les Epées* serves as a paradigm of the kind of shifts deployed to signal the literary status of the writing. After a portrait of himself and his family he continues: 'I think nothing has been forgotten. I have just reread what I have written. It is a very good piece of homework and I think I would get a high mark if the subject of the essay had been: what are your thoughts on the eve of your suicide? Express them in the most touching way you

can, in a letter to a stranger. Make a plan.'[61] All the irony resides
in the clash of two incompatible kinds of writing – part of a
narrative development marking the precocious cynicism and
authority of this fifteen-year-old fourth-former, or a no less cynical parody of essay writing and its bellelettristic pretentions – and
the concomitant doubt as to how the preceding pages should have
been read. Similarly, the Stendhalien footnotes,[62] the café Lafca-
dio situate the narration within a tradition of literary irony, and
also, by these ironic signals of the presence of the narrator, place
to the fore the irredeemably literary nature of the narrative event
and its relation to the narration.

Banlieue sud-est uses a whole range of devices to call attention to
the narrative: imitation of documents, ironic headlines used
particularly for the generalising images typical of the 'view from
above',[63] footnotes, descriptive passages striking a deliberately
false lyrical note and parodying the designation 'literature',[64] the
appearance of M. René Fallet, firstly as character,[65] and, in the
final pages, as author.[66] Moreover, the first chapter of the novel
has a most ambiguous status. Given that the second chapter
begins with the main character suddenly waking up, it could be
read as his extravagant dreams; narrated by a disembodied 'I',
each paragraph describes a different identity, 'I am the bloke who
possesses love', 'I am a large rock in the forest of Fontainebleau', 'I
am a woman.' But it would be more in keeping with a narrative
which refuses to take its own narration seriously to read it as an
amusing display of the omniscience and omnipotence of the
narrator who, outside diegetic time, is truly outside time: 'I am
the master of the universe. I am immortal',[67] for whom literally
anything is possible: 'I am the greatest cycling champion the
Earth has ever seen. Same as for the "Love-Me"; here, I say "I
win", and it's done'.[68] and who, in the very accumulation of
narrative identities, in fact has none.

If the ironic devices in *Banlieue sud-est* and *Les Epées* are concerned above all to recall that there is no transcendence of the
written, this is an even more central concern of *La Culbute*, which
sustains a constant tension between the will to omnipotence of the
self as narrator and his subordination to elements beyond his
control, between freedom and destiny.[69] Bearing particularly on
writing and signification, *La Culbute* can therefore be placed in a
long tradition of reflection, from *Jacques le Fataliste* to *Djinn*, on

the nature of narrative, its tendencies to absolute contingency and absolute necessity, and its relation to reality. Georges Renaut realises that, as far as writing is concerned, omnipotence is on the side of necessity: by adopting the handle 'de la Motte', having a card printed with his new name, he is his own creation.[70] The project of the diary is to subordinate the formlessness of existence to necessity, and it is in this light that one can understand his letters of denunciation, which are so many attempts to write other people into his narrative. M. Fouilloux in the flat upstairs is arrested, Renaut having denounced him for listening to English radio, and he hears the family acting out the scene he has written for them (Fouilloux's brave words as he is taken from his family, his wife's cries of 'My husband, my husband'); unbeknownst to them, others are players in the film he is directing. His superiority lies in his knowledge: 'I am acting in *My Life* (...) A realist film, made by destiny.'[71] But he is constantly in danger of falling into the void of absolute freedom: 'And I am also acting in a second story (...) a fantasy film. I do not know its title – I am looking in vain for the director's team and the producer.'[72] His drama does not lie in trying to choose the ordered laws of narrative over reality, but in a veritable crisis of signification. For the world of reality and objects is also ruled by the tyranny of signs:

It is not life which imitates life, just like that, gratuitously. Art is needed as an intermediary. Life imitates the imitation that art creates of life. We have heard the sound effects people on the radio substituting spoons for the sea too often (...) and we no longer know, always supposing they exist, what natural sounds are like. The bed and the lift are play-acting at imitating life, they are making theatre with life, they are sound effects. We can suspect them of being as cruel as men.[73]

It is also governed by their anarchic proliferation. There are so many images labelled 'Laval' circulating in the world that the question *'who is Laval?'* becomes particularly hard to answer: 'Is Laval the man smiling nicely at Hitler or the man saving France by the sweat of his brow?'[74] and, as with Pétain, Churchill or Hitler, the possibility of affixing value of unique truth to one image rather than another is undermined by the very indeterminacy of the sign which cannot be fixed to one original essence. From that point of view, however, they resist the order and logic of narrative: 'They have lost their being. Having acted so much they have produced too many individuals under their own skin and they are no more than a haunted stage. Mystery, nasty mystery. How then can history be written?'[75] A similar disparity underlies his reactions to the enigmatic phrases of the English radio; at first he celebrates their freedom and opacity, and then realises they might be obeying a logic, encoding his own death sentence. His project to impose his own script (although he is often tempted by the total freedom, and nihilation, of signification) is constantly threatened by the fear of being written into someone else's 'film'.

The insistence in *La Culbute* on the irremediable facticity of human existence can thus be said to echo the impossibility of transcendence characteristic of the other novels of ambiguity. Similarly the narrative games and strategies in *Banlieue sud-est, Les Epées* and *La Culbute* around the omniscience of the narrator-author also serve to construct this figure as both diegetic and extradiegetic, recalling *La Peste* and *L'Education européenne*, and it is here that one can elucidate the essential ambiguity at the heart of the structures of irony, an ambiguity which might be summed up as variations on the famous phrase 'loser takes all'. Georges Renaut, for example, goes to the rendezvous which he fears contains the hidden sentence of death, but his diary remains, permanently inscribing his disappearance within the order of the narrative: like the narrator of *Banlieue sud-est*, on the level of the *énonciation* Georges Renaut is indestructible. In all these novels, however painful the knowledge, however dramatic the defeat which recognition of the futility of action in the world entails, it is nonetheless the key to narrative survival.

Notes

1   'Le jeu de la guerre et du hasard', *La Culbute*, p.11.
2   Paris, 1971, pp.10–11, p.43.
3   *Les Forêts*, p. 151.
4   *Semiotics and Interpretation*, New Haven and London, p.75.
5   This passage is preparing for the episode when Hélène sends her last letter to Jean breaking off the relationship. 'That kind of letter always arrives', she reflects (p.230). And it does, provoking Jean's suicide. Given the difficulties of communication as proved by these earlier letters, one could say that her expectations are ironically *fulfilled*.
6   One of Hélène's other letters is given in full on pp.149–50 and serves as an illustration of the type.
7   P.475.
8   P.469.
9   *Ibid.*

10 P.450.

11 ' "Le baiser de Lamourette" était de rigueur ce jour-là', comments the narrator. p.456.

12 P.307.

13 It also relies on the classic Paris/province opposition of the provincial novel.

14 P.476.

15 P.18.

16 P.8.

17 See *La Culbute*, p.103, pp. 195–6 and *Les Epées*, p.100.

18 'Truth' here being used in the sense of what the narrative presents as true.

19 P.309.

20 *Les Temps modernes*, vol.7, no.79, mai 1952, p.2072.

21 'Lettre au directeur des *Temps modernes*', *Les Temps modernes*, vol.8, no.82, août 1952, p.321.

22 See in the same volume, 'Pour tout vous dire...', p.355.

23 'Albert Camus ou l'âme révoltée', pp.2073–4

24 'Albert Camus ou l'âme révoltée', p.2073. S.B. John also comments on the importance of the omniscient narrator in post-war fiction, in 'The Ambiguous Invader'.

25 P.175 (1946).

26 P.35.

27 P.319.

28 Antagonism to political parties being itself a Vichy theme, that Pétain appealed directly to the French, and not as a politician. There is no mention in *Uranus* of a similar guilt generated by support for Laval. Nor any hint that a pro-Vichy attitude might have conceivably been misplaced. On the contrary, the 'bouclier' theme is extended to include collaboration, when Archambaud debates whether to shelter Loin the fascist: 'He did not feel any sense of solidarity with this man and resented him having seen collaboration as a means of subjugating France, whereas for Archambaud himself it was a means of defence'(p.42).

29 P.236.

30 P.36.

31 P.340.

32 *Marcel Aymé ou la paysan de Paris*, p.119.

33 P.36. And his views are echoed, from the other side of the political fence, by the 'Resister' Darricade: 'For Darricade, the real fight had begun at dawn that day' (p.459).

34 'Le hors-texte reste plus ou moins perceptible tout au long de la chaîne narrative, notamment aux moments de décrochage entre discours et récit, entre énonciation et énoncé, entre le je et le on, entre la parole rapportée et son support textuel', 'Réflexions sur les rapports du roman et de la société', *Roman et société*, p.71.

35 A variation on this occurs in *Le Chemin des écoliers*, by Marcel Aymé, which does end during the Occupation, but where the post-war fates of many of the characters are given in footnotes. The time of the *énonciation* is again post-Occupation.

36 *NRF*, janvier–juin 1943, pp.103–11. In the Preface to *Les Chiens de paille*, he says the novel was written in the spring of 1943.

37 P.186.

38 P.39.

39 P.53.

40 Thus confirming the quotations placed as an epigraph, on the absolute indifference of creation towards men.

41 Pp.193–4 Emphasis added.

42 'Albert Camus ou l'âme révoltée', p.2073.

43 Cf. *Les Forêts*, the scenes of the crowd jeering at Balansun and Cécile 'were *exactly* the same as the hallucinating images of pogroms in Nazi Germany, which the French newspapers were publishing in 39–40' (p.469). Emphasis added.

44 P.1473.

45 Helmut Bonheim, *The Narrative Modes*, Cambridge, 1982, p.156.

46 The third will be discussed later in this chapter.

47 *Semiotics and Interpretation*, p.86.

48 *Ibid.*

49 Pp.149–150.

50 Vercors, for example, writes of the degradation imposed by the Nazis, and also, in *Les Lettres françaises*, denounces the failure of the *épuration* (i.e. the failure to reject those in Resistance eyes guilty of collaboration) as immoral ('La Gangrène', *LF*, no.39, 30 janvier 1945, p.1.

51 Paris, 1955.

52 Jeanson, 'Albert Camus ou l'âme révoltée', p.2085.

53 Sartre, 'Réponse à Albert Camus', p.346.

54 P.1323.

55 See particularly *Les Chiens de paille*, pp. 34–5; *Uranus*, p.195.

56 'Functional Complexity: the Narrative Techniques of *The Plague*', *Modern Fiction Studies*, vol.20, no.3, autumn 1974, p.423.

57 Although he does discuss Rieux as sole narrator, and is therefore confusing Rieux, extradiegetic narrator of the plague, and the extradiegetic narrator of the *text*, who is responsible for example for the substitution plague/Occupation (which Moses does not discuss at all).

58 A good example at the level of narrative description would be Watrin's reaction to Gaigneux's defence of the extremely unsavoury Rochard, who has landed Léopold in prison: 'The professor gave him a smile that was both discouraged and amused' (p.161), 'discouraged' in so far as Watrin is genuinely hoping Gaigneux will help obtain Léopold's release; 'amused' by yet another picturesque example of the human 'jungle'.

59 *Semiotics and Interpretation*, p.86.

60 Echoes of which occur in other novels. Cf. p.396 above, re the abbé on the barricades.

61 P.13.

62 P.104: 'C'est un milicien qui parle'; p.106: 'C'est une âme sans

idéal qui parle.'
63 'PANORAMIQUE' (p.340), 'FIN DU PANORAMIQUE' (p.341), 'REPRISE DU PANORAMIQUE' (p.347), 'RE-FIN DU PANORAMI-QUE' (p.351).
64 Pp.127–9.
65 Pp.284–5.
66 Pp.381–2.
67 P.12.
68 *Ibid.*
69 P.19.
70 P.15.
71 P.77.
72 *Ibid.*
73 P.19.
74 P.121. Jean Duffy makes a not dissimilar point in relation to Claude Simon's novel *La Corde raide*, in 'The Subversion of Historical Representation in Claude Simon', *French Studies*, Volume XVI No.4 October 1987, pp.422–3.
75 P.122.

Conclusion

Despite many differences of subject matter, style and approach, a clear set of constants emerges from this group of novels: a range of conflicting social and psychological types, political positions and attitudes under the Occupation are presented by a detached observer in such a way as to render untenable a straightforward pro-Resistance reading of those years, firstly in the impossibility of establishing any clear differentiation between the Resistance and the enemy, and secondly by situating the social and political dimensions within a general metaphysical framework. From the transcendent heights from which it is judged, the conflicts of the Occupation are no longer geared towards a specific set of historical circumstances, but rather the Occupation as a whole, governed by a static vision of the nature of things, becomes an exceptionally acute manifestation – or revelation – of the order of the world.

We have already seen that, through the events of the narrative, the novels of ambiguity encode the values of the Resistance as hopelessly simplistic or simply unrealisable, so it is not surprising to find the point is also made explicitly. Maxime Loin, the fascist fugitive in *Uranus*, has been lent a novel:

The novel was set in Lyon, in 1943, in Resistance circles and on every line there was cause for indignation. Everything annoyed him, the heroism, good humour, ingenuity, the noble hearts, and virile beauty of the Resisters, as also did the cowardice, greed, pride, unfathomable stupidity of the Vichy traitors. If he had had the power, he would have had the author clapped in jail. *With his beautiful light-coloured eyes, Patrice stared scornfully at the disgusting individual.* Patrice was a young Gaullist student, the disgusting individual a black marketeer who was passionately hoping for Germany's victory. Loin sniggered quietly. His revenge was the thought that the black marketeer had not lost out with the Gaullist victory.[1]

As a parody of the major opposition of Resistance fiction between the Resistance and the enemy, it bears, like all parody, a recognisable relation to its object of satire, but it is the particular nature of the exaggeration which reveals much concerning the status of the Resistance in the novel of ambiguity. The description of this novel presents it as a sermon in fictional form, an utterly simplistic confrontation between heroes and villains, the latter constituted here by the references to Vichy, support for Germany and profiteering. This is exactly the same kind of opposition as is found in contemporary Gaullist and Communist Party pronouncements where one national Resistance has triumphed over a collective enemy.[2] In other words, this representation of pro-Resistance fiction in *Uranus* is drawing on the public post-Liberation discourse to turn it back upon itself as a moralising literature unrelated to the complexities of the Occupation and, furthermore, the purveyor of a hypocritical moral stance given the realities of post-Liberation France. It is a demonstration in the fiction of the imbrication of the Resistance myth and the denunciation of 'résistantialisme', of how *necessary*, ironically enough, the former is to sustain such denunciations.

Interestingly, *Uranus* does not specify when its Resistance novel was written and thus manages to elide a post-Liberation commentary with Resistance literature itself. *Bête à vivre*, by Pierre Leforestier,[3] set entirely after the Occupation, has one character, Michel Bernier (who landed in Fresnes as a result of a letter of denunciation after the Occupation, but who is making an excellent living on the black market from the contacts he made there), explicitly denounce the one-sided approach in the press which was dividing all France into 'The Collaborators and the Resisters, that is the Traitors and the Incorruptibles'.[4] However, the main character Robert is more annoyed by 'how monstrously simplistic this classification is. (...) How can it be said that that describes the whole of France? What did one do with the huge gregarious mass who had applauded Pétain and then acclaimed de Gaulle?'[5] But it is specifically in the production of 'Resistance scenarios' that *Bête à vivre* joins *Uranus* in highlighting the crude conventions of narrative which are being cynically manipulated. Bernier has moved from the black market to literature to make his fortune, recycling his prison experiences – though with appropriate political changes to turn them into a Resistance story. He advises Robert to do likewise, drawing on his escape: 'Just a soldier, (not an officer), an ordinary bloke, do you see? The Stalag: the Jerries are cruel, the French are cunning. The return to France, great emotion on touching French soil once more.'[6] And so on, through a flashback to the emotional farewell to his fiancée at the general call-up, to the *maquis* and his heroism, the parades at the Liberation and the reunion with the fiancée. It is entirely governed by the connotation 'heroism of the French', one of many production-line melodramas which, like the grandiose speeches in *Les Forêts de la nuit*, turn the Occupation into pure spectacle, a morality play for public consumption.

It is difficult not to be reminded here of the approach of 'the mythologist' which Barthes elaborates in 'Le Mythe aujourd'hui' (Myth today),[7] analysing the way in which culturally and historically determined signs are produced as both natural and factual, especially in the light of Bernier's dismissal of Robert's objection that it was the wrong season for a 'First Kiss Under The Flowering May': 'You've *got* to have flowering may for a first kiss. Otherwise no one will understand anything.'[8] The novels of ambiguity consistently display these 'Resistance fictions'[9] as 'paroles mythiques',[10] discursive constructs invested by a naturalising myth equating Resistance with heroism and the French nation. The dramas and conflicts of the Occupation are reduced to an edifying storyline which in all these novels is deliberately presented as such, and strongly satirised as a one-dimensional *image d'Epinal*, a reenactment of Cowboys and Indians played by adults,[11] or a picture-book history of France.[12] Throughout *L'Education européenne*, Dobranski tells stories to his fellow partisans, fairy stories of heroism and resistance whose fanciful nature is particularly underlined by the partisans' isolation, precarious struggle for survival and unheroic existence.

Resistance as grandeur can only be lived as a myth, and it is the distance installed by this constant insertion of the Resistance into previously established codes of heroes and villains which enables the apparently spontaneous demonstrations and individual acts of commitment to be held up as fabricated – by extension false – and overdetermined by certain historical, national or literary stereotypes.[13] In ways not dissimilar to *La Culbute*, or Hélène's letter to Jean in *Les Forêts de la nuit,* they are re-situated in a context which displays them as pure signs with no access to meaning or truth.

The structure of ambiguity therefore bears witness to a complex ideological battle over the nature of the Occupation and the values of the Resistance. Like the novels of unity, then, these novels are seeking to transmit knowledge of what they are construing as the truth of the Occupation; they are equally dogmatic, didactic and partisan, and it would seem to me to be begging more questions than it solves to suggest that this essentialist, absurdist pessisism is in fact more true, more historically accurate, than the pro-Resistance fiction. What emerges from studying the novels of the Occupation and post-Liberation years is the fact that none of this fiction can be considered to be unproblematically faithful to the event. These novels are important elements in the complex battle for the meaning of these years and which, as the Barbie trial, as recent sales of novels by Deforges and Sagan, and of Ferro's biography of Pétain show, is far from over. They demonstrate that the 'truth' of an event is discursively constructed and inherently unstable, a minor example of which is that in the post-war period, and no doubt inevitably, Resistance literature becomes evidence of the nature of Resistance rather than arguments for it. The kind of reflexion borne by the structure of ambiguity is reinscribing the history of the Occupation within the context of the present, a process which the 'mode rétro' is in its own way continuing. The undervaluing of this body of literature has in fact obscured a major lesson to be learnt from it: the essential historicity of literature.

Notes

1 Pp.189–90. See also the portraits of the Resister and the collaborator in Cl. Jamet, *Le Rendez-vous manqué de 1944,* Paris, 1965, pp.27–8, quoted in Dominique Veillon, *La Collaboration,* Paris, 1984, pp.395–6.

2 Laval's phrase 'Je souhaite la victoire de l'Allemagne', significantly recalled in the quotation from *Uranus,* was important in articulating Vichy as a form of wilful collaboration. For the 'Maréchaliste' elaboration of a good Vichy (Pétain) as opposed to a bad Vichy (Laval), see Azéma, *De Munich à la Libération,* p.358.

3 Paris, 1946. The story of Robert who escapes from a prisoner of war camp to reach France in the immediate post-Liberation period, of his

elderly parents whose house in Saint-Lô was destroyed in the fighting and of his wife Micheline.

4   P.145. Cf. Rioux, *La France de la Quatrième République*: 'Only the press, symbol of Collaboration and decisive weapon for the Resistance, was very strictly controlled: spectacular trials of owners and editors, property confiscated. It was hit by all forms of the *épuration*, political, professional and economic'(p.59). This helps to explain the very public coverage of the Resistance message, and was itself a source of controversy. Some felt a free press should not be expressing just one point of view in this way; others that on the contrary the *épuration* of publishers had been very limited. See Luc Estang, 'A travers la presse littéraire', *Poésie 45*, no.28, février–mars 1945, pp.118–19, and Vercors, 'La Gangrène', *LF*, no.39, janvier 1945, p.1.

5   P.145.

6   P.211.

7   *Mythologies*, Paris, 1970.

8   P.211.

9   A term which must also embrace the public speeches, mass demonstrations.

10   'Le Mythe aujourd'hui', pp.193–5.

11   *Mon Village*, p.324; *Les Forêts*, p.63. There are obvious thematic links here with *Drôle de jeu* and Annie's accusations that the young men of the Resistance are children playing at war. The very different resolution of this argument in *Drôle de jeu* demonstrates yet again the importance of the overall narrative economy in which the themes are inscribed.

12   *Les Epées*, pp.110, 113; *Banlieue sud-est*, p.346.

13   There are even traces of this procedure in *La Peste*, when Rieux reflects on the language of the local newspapers and foreign radio: 'And each time the tone they took, of epics or prize day speeches, annoyed the doctor' (p.1331).

Select bibliography

Unless otherwise stated, the place of publication is Paris for French titles, London for English titles.

Fiction

(i) *Novels of unity*

Adam, George (under the pseudonym of Hainault), *A l'Appel de la liberté*, Editions de minuit, 1944, 1945.

— *L'Epée dans les reins*, Gallimard, 1947.

Aragon, Louis (under the pseudonym of Arnaud de Saint-Roman), *Les Bons Voisins*, Bibliothèque française, 1942; re-*La France libre* (Londres), vol.II, no.42, 15 avril 1944, pp.428–34; *Servitude et grandeur des Français* (see below); *Trois contes* (see below).

— (under the pseudonym of Arnaud de Saint-Roman), *Le Mouton, Almanach des Lettres françaises*, 1944; reprinted in *Servitude et grandeur des Français*.

— *Pénitent 43, Les Lettres françaises*, no.21, 16 septembre 1944, p.3; reprinted in *Servitude et grandeur des Français*; *Trois contes*.

— *Servitude et grandeur des Français : Scènes des années terribles*, La Bibliothèque française, 1945.

— *Trois contes*, Londres, Les Cahiers du silence, 1945.

Aveline, Claude (under the pseudonym of Minervois), *Le Temps mort*, Editions de minuit, 1944, 1945; Londres, Les Cahiers du silence, 1945.

— *Le Temps mort*, suivi d'autres récits et de quelques témoignages, Mercure de France, 1962.

Beauvoir, Simone de, *Le Sang des autres*, Gallimard, 1945; *The*

Blood of Others, Penguin.

Bost, Pierre (under the pseudonym of Vivarais), *La Haute Four-che*, Editions de minuit, 1945; Londres, Les Cahiers du silence, 1946.

Chamson, André (under the pseudonym of Lauter), *Le Puits des miracles*, in *Nouvelles Chroniques*, Editions de minuit, 1944, 1945.

— *Le Puits des miracles*, Gallimard, 1945.

Morgan, Claude (under the pseudonym of Mortagne), *La Marque de l'homme*, Editions de minuit, 1944, 1945.

— *La Marque de l'homme*, Editions de minuit, 1946.

Parrot, Louis, *Paille noire des étables*, Robert Laffont, 1946.

Thomas, Edith, *Contes d'Auxois*, Editions de minuit, 1943, 1945.

Triolet, Elsa (under the pseudonym of Laurent Daniel), *Les Amants d'Avignon*, Editions de minuit, 1943, 1945; reprinted in *Le Premier Accroc coûte deux cents francs* (see below).

— (under the pseudonym of Laurent Daniel), *Yvette*, La Bibliothèque française, 1944; reprinted in Jean Paulhan et Dominique Aury (eds.), *La Patrie se fait tous les jours*, Editions de minuit, 1947.

— *Le Premier Accroc coûte deux cents francs*, Editions Denoël, 1945; Folio, Gallimard, 1980, with Elsa Triolet, 'Préface à la clandesti-nité'.

Vailland, Roger, *Drôle de jeu*, Buchet-Chastel, 1945; Livre de poche, 1969.

Vercors, *Le Silence de la mer*, Editions de minuit, 1942, 1945; Londres, Les Cahiers du silence, 1944.

— (under the pseudonym of Santerre), *Désespoir est mort*, in *Chroniques interdites*, Editions de minuit, 1943, 1945; reprinted in *Le Silence de la mer et autres récits* (see below).

— *La Marche à l'étoile*, Editions de minuit, 1943, 1945; Londres, Les Cahiers du silence, 1945.

— *Le Nord*, *Poésie 44*, no.21, novembre–décembre 1944, pp.48–57.

— *Le Silence de la mer et autres récits*, édition définitive, Albin Michel, 1951; Livre de poche, 1960; Livre de poche, 1980 (includes *La Marche à l'étoile*).

— *Le Songe*, *Les Lettres françaises*, no.20, 9 septembre 1944, p.3; Editions de minuit, 1945; reprinted in *Le Silence de la mer et autres récits*.

— *Le Songe*, précédé de *Ce Jour-là* (reprinted in *Le Silence de la mer et autres récits*), Pierre Seghers, 1949.

— *Les Mots*, Collection 'Nouvelles originales', Editions de minuit, 1947; also in *Les Yeux et la lumière*, Se Trouve à Paris, 1948.

(ii) *Novels of ambiguity*

Aymé, Marcel, *Le Chemin des écoliers*, Gallimard, 1946.

— *Uranus*, Gallimard, 1948; Livre de poche, 1969.

Bory, Jean-Louis, *Mon Village à l'heure allemande*, Flammarion, 1945; J'ai lu, 1972.

Buchet, Edmond, *Les Vies secrètes*, Tome V: *Le Royaume de l'homme*, Corrêa, 1948.

Camus, Albert, *La Peste*, Gallimard, 1947; reprinted in *Théâtre, Récits, Nouvelles*, préface par Jean Grenier, textes établis et annotés par Roger Quilliot, Bibliothèque de la Pléiade, Gallimard, 1967.

Curtis, Jean-Louis, *Les Forêts de la nuit*, Julliard, 1947; Livre de poche, 1969.

Drieu la Rochelle, Pierre, *Les Chiens de paille*, Gallimard, 1964.

Fallet, René, *Banlieue sud-est*, Domat, 1947; Livre de poche, 1967.

Gary, Romain, *L'Education européenne*, Calmann-Lévy, 1945; Londres, Editions Penguin, 1946; édition définitive, Gallimard, 1956; Livre de poche, 1962.

Leforestier, Pierre, *Bête à vivre*, Editions du chêne, 1946.

Nimier, Roger, *Les Epées*, 1948; Livre de poche, 1967.

Quéffelec, Henri, *La Culbute*, Editions Stock, 1946; Livre de poche, 1973.

(iii) *Other fiction consulted on the war or the Occupation*

Aragon, Louis, *Les Communistes*, 5 vols., La Bibliothèque française, Les Editeurs français réunis, 1949–1951.

Auclair, Georges, *Un Amour allemand*, Gallimard, 1950.

Bastide, François-René, *Les Adieux*, Gallimard, 1956.

Bataille, Michel, *Patrick*, Robert Laffont, 1947.

Blondin, Antoine, *L'Europe buissonnière*, Editions Jean Froissart, 1949.

Boisdeffre, Pierre de, *Les Fins dernières*, Editions de la table ronde, 1952.

Bost, Jacques-Laurent, *Le Dernier des métiers*, Gallimard, 1946.

Boulle, Pierre, *Un Métier de seigneur*, Julliard, Sequana, 1960.

Boutron, Michel, *Hans*, Segep, 1950.

Céline, Louis-Ferdinand, *D'Un Château l'autre*, Gallimard, 1957.
— *Nord*, Gallimard, 1960.
— *Rigodon*, Gallimard, 1969.
Chabrol, Jean-Pierre, *Un Homme de trop*, Gallimard, 1958.
Chaix, Marie, *Les Lauriers du lac de Constance: chronique d'une collaboration*, Seuil, 1974.
Chamson, André, *Le Dernier Village*, Mercure de France, 1946.
Cogniot, Georges, *L'Evasion*, préface de Jean Fréville, Editions raisons d'être, 1946.
Curtis, Jean-Louis, *Gibier de potence*, Julliard, 1949.
— *Siegfried*, Julliard, 1946.
Debû-Bridel, Jacques, *Déroute*, Gallimard, 1945.
Deforges, Régine, *La Bicyclette bleue*, 3 vols., Ramsay, 1981–85.
Dutourd, Jean, *Au Bon Beurre*, Gallimard, 1952.
Ehrenbourg, Ilya, *The Fall of Paris*, translated from the Russian by Gerard Shelley, Hutchinson & Co (Publishers) Ltd, n.d. [1942].
Gary, Romain, *Le Grand Vestiaire*, Gallimard, 1948.
— *Tulipe*, Calmann-Lévy, 1946.
Gascar, Pierre, *Les Bêtes*, suivi de *Le Temps des morts*, Gallimard, 1953.
Joffo, Joseph, *Un Sac de billes*, Editions J.C. Lattès, 1973.
Kessel, Joseph, *L'Armée des ombres*, Londres, Editions Penguin, 1945.
Laborde, Vincent, *Le Sel de la terre*, Gallimard, 1946.
Le Garrec, Evelyne, *La Rive allemande de ma mémoire*, Seuil, 1980.
Malraux, André, *La Lutte avec l'ange*, Lausanne, Yverdon, Editions du haut pays, 1943; *Les Noyers de l'Altenburg*, Gallimard, 1948.
Maspéro, François, *Le Sourire du chat*, Seuil, 1984.
Merle, Robert, *Weekend à Zuydecote*, Gallimard, 1949.
— *La Mort est mon métier*, Gallimard, 1952.
Modiano, Patrick, *Les Boulevards de ceinture*, Gallimard, 1978.
— *La Place de l'étoile*, Gallimard, 1968.
— *La Ronde de nuit*, Gallimard, 1969.
Mohrt, Michel, *Le Répit*, Albin Michel, 1946.
— *Mon Royaume pour un cheval*, Albin Michel, 1951.
Molaine, Pierre, *Batailles pour mourir*, Corrêa, 1945.
— *De Blanc vêtu*, Corrêa, 1945.
Nourissier, François, *Allemande*, Grasset, 1973.
— *Bleu comme la nuit*, Collection 'La Galérie', Grasset, 1958.

Perret, Jacques, *Bande à part*, Gallimard, 1951.
Peyrefitte, Roger, *La Fin des ambassades*, Flammarion, 1946.
Robida, Michel, *Le Temps de la longue patience*, Julliard, 1946.
Roy, Claude, *La Nuit est le manteau des pauvres*, Julliard, 1948.
Sagan, Françoise, *De Guerre lasse*, Gallimard, 1986.
— *Un Sang d'aquarelle*, Gallimard, 1987.
Sartre, Jean-Paul, *La Mort dans l'âme*, *Les Chemins de la liberté*, vol.
    III, Gallimard, 1949; *Iron in the Soul*, trans. by G. Hopkins,
    Penguin.
Tournier, Michel, *Le Roi des aulnes*, Gallimard, 1970.
Triolet, Elsa, *Les Fantômes armés*, La Bibliothèque française, 1947.
— *L'Inspecteur des ruines*, La Bibliothèque française, 1948.
Vailland, Roger, *Un Jeune Homme seul*, Buchet-Chastel, 1951.
Vercors, *Les Armes de la nuit*, Editions de minuit, 1946.

Periodicals 1940–1944

Les Lettres françaises
La Nouvelle Revue française
Poésie

Also consulted
Cahiers du bolchévisme
Cahiers de Libération
Les Etoiles
France d'abord
La France libre (Londres)
Liberté
La Pensée libre
Le Populaire
Résistance
La Résistance française
La Résistance ouvrière
La Revue libre
Socialisme et liberté
Voix de France
La Voix du nord

Other works consulted

Only those immediately relevant to the topic are included here. Works already noted in the footnotes are not listed.

Amouroux, Henri, *La Grande Histoire des Français sous l'Occupation*, 6 vols., Editions Robert Laffont, 1976–1983.

Anon. 'Réflexions d'un neutre, Germains, Allemands et Hitlériens', *France* (Londres), 8 avril 1941, p.2.

Aragon, Louis, *La Culture et les hommes*, Editions sociales, 1947.

— *L'Homme communiste*, Gallimard, 1947.

— *Le Musée Grevin, les poissons noirs et quelques poèmes inédits*, Editions de minuit, 1946; Londres, Les Cahiers du silence, 1946.

Aron, Robert, *Histoire de l'épuration*, Arthème Fayard, 1967–1969.

Assouline, Pierre, *L'Epuration des intellectuels*, Editions Complexe, 1985.

Audisio, Gabriel, 'Epuration chez les écrivains', une lettre de M. Gabriel Audisio, *Le Littéraire*, 6 avril 1946, p. 1.

Austin, Roger, 'Propaganda and Public Opinion in Vichy France: The Department of Hérault, 1940–1944', *European Studies Review*, 13, no. 4, October 1983, pp. 445–82.

Barrès, Maurice, *Au Service de l'Allemagne*, Emile Paul Frères, 1916.

Beauvoir, Simone de, 'Oeil pour oeil', *Les Temps modernes*, I, no. 5, février 1946, pp. 813–30.

Bédarida, François et Renée, 'Une Résistance spirituelle: aux origines du Témoigage Chrétien 1941–1942', *Revue d'histoire de la deuxième guerre mondiale*, 13, no. 61, janvier 1966.

Bédarida, Renée, *Les Armes de l'esprit: Témoignage Chrétien 1941–1944*, Les Editions ouvrières, 1977.

Bellanger, Claude, *Presse clandestine 1940–1944*, Collection 'Kiosque', Armand Colin, 1961.

Bloch, Marc, *L'Etrange Défaite* suivi d'écrits clandestins, Editions Franc-Tireur, 1978.

Cahiers d'histoire de l'Institut de recherches marxistes, Front Populaire, antifascisme, résistance: Le PCF 1938–1941, no. 14 spécial, 1983.

Cahiers et courriers clandestins du Témoignage Chrétien 1941–1944, Tome I, réédition intégrale en fac–simile, ouvrage publié en souscription par Renée Bédarida et Adrien Nemoz, 1980.

Cassou, Jean (under the pseudonym of Jean Noir), *33 sonnets composés au secret*, présentés par François la Colère (pseudonym of Aragon), Editions de minuit, 1944, 1945.

Chroniques interdites, Editions de minuit, 1943, 1945.

Colleye, Hubert, 'Les Lettres belges pendant la guerre', *Revue générale belge*, no. 1, novembre 1945, pp. 52–63.

Craig, David and Michael Egan, *Extreme Situations: Literature of Crisis from the Great War to the Atom Bomb*, The Macmillan Press, 1979.

Cunard, Nancy, 'Intellectuals in the French Resistance', *Our Time*, 4, no. 4, November 1944, pp. 4–5.

Debû-Bridel, Jacques, 'Naissance des Lettres françaises: les premiers mois du journal clandestin du Comité National des Ecrivains', *Les Lettres françaises*, no. 20, 9 septembre 1944, p. 7.

— (under the pseudonym of Argonne), *Angleterre*, Editions de minuit, 1943, 1945; Londres, Les Cahiers du silence, 1944.

— *Les Editions de minuit: étude historique et bibliographique*, Editions de minuit, 1945.

Druon, Maurice, 'Préface: Les Cahiers du silence', in *Le Silence de la mer*, Londres, Les Cahiers du silence, 1943.

Les Ecrivains et la guerre, *Revue des sciences humaines*, no. 206, 1986.

Elgey, Georgette, *La Fenêtre ouverte*, Librairie Arthème Fayard, 1973.

Eluard, Paul, *Au Rendez-vous allemand*, suivi de *Poésie et vérité*, Editions de minuit, 1945.

Europe, numéro spécial, *La Poésie de la Résistance*, nos. 543–544, juillet–août 1974.

Fouchet, Max-Pol (ed.), *Les Poètes de la revue Fontaine*, *Poésie*, nos 55–61, sept.–nov. 1978.

Fussell, Paul, *The Great War and Modern Memory*, Oxford, Oxford University Press, 1975.

Granet, Marie, *Ceux de la Résistance (1940–1944)*, Editions de minuit, 1964.

— *Défense de la France: Histoire d'un mouvement de Résistance (1940–1944)*, Presses universitaires de France, 1960.

— *Le Journal Défense de la France*, Presses universitaires de France, 1961.

Granet, Marie et Henri Michel, *Combat: Histoire d'un mouvement de résistance de juillet 1940 à juillet 1943*, Presses universitaires de France, 1957.

Guéhenno, Jean (under the pseudonym of Cévennes), *Dans la prison*, Editions de minuit, 1944, 1945.

Higgins, Ian, 'Shrimp, Plane and France: Ponge's Resistance Poetry', *French Studies*, 37, no. 3, July 1983, pp. 310–25.

— (ed.), *Anthology of Second World War Poetry*, Twentieth Century French Texts, Methuen, 1982.

— (ed.), *The Second World War in Literature*, Scottish Academic Press, 1986.

Hunt, H.J., 'Saint Joan of Arc in Some Recent French Dramas', *French Studies*, I, 1947, pp. 302–33.

Jacobs, Gabriel, 'Aveline's *Le Temps mort*: a question of survival', *Nottingham French Studies*, October 1984, pp. 27–34.

Jans, Adrien, 'La Guerre et les lettres', *Revue générale belge*, no. 19, août 1946, pp. 536–40.

Jardin, Pascal, *Le Nain jaune*, Julliard, 1978.

Kedward, H.R., and Roger Austin (eds.), *Vichy France and the Resistance: Culture and Ideology*, Croom Helm, 1985.

Keefe, Terry, *Existentialist Fictions*, Croom Helm, 1986.

Klein, Holger (ed.), *The Second World War in Fiction*, Macmillan, 1984.

Kohut, Karl (ed.), *Literatur der Résistance und Kollaboration in Frankreich*, 3 vols., Schwerpunkte Romanistik vols. 18–20, Wiesbaden, Akademische Verlagsgesellschaft Athenaion, Tübingen, Gunter Narr Verlag, 1982–1984.

Magny, Claude-Edmonde, 'La Littérature', in *Cinquante années de découverte: un bilan 1900–1950*, Editions du Seuil, 1950, pp. 30–81.

— 'La Littérature française depuis 1940', *La France libre*, no. 50, 1944, pp. 102–8; no. 52, 1945, pp. 292–304; no. 62, 1945, pp. 96–102.

Malherbe, Henry, 'Avec les combattants de la nuit: lorsque le Comité National des Ecrivains se réunissait à Lyon', *Les Etoiles*, nouvelle série, no. 10, 17 juillet 1945, p.1.

Marcenac, Jean, 'Manifeste de l'école d'Oradour', *L'Eternelle Revue*, no. 4, 1945, p. 7.

Martin-Chauffier, Louis, 'Littérature de guerre', *Mercure de France*, no. 1002, vol. ccxcix, 1 février 1947, pp. 317–22.

Maulnier, Thierry, 'La Littérature est-elle justiciable?', *L'Arche*, no. 12, décembre 1945–janvier 1946, pp. 91–101.

— *Les Lettres françaises*, septembre 1944–août 1945.

Merleau-Ponty, Maurice, 'La guerre a eu lieu', *Les Temps modernes*, I, no. 1, octobre 1945, pp. 48–66.

Michel, Henri, *Paris allemand*, Albin Michel, 1981.

— *Paris résistant*, Albin Michel, 1982.

Montherlant, Henry de, *Essais*, Bibliothèque de la Pléiade, Gallimard, 1963.

Morel, Robert, *La Littérature clandestine 1940–1944*, Périgueux, Ed. Pierre Farlac, 1945.

Morgan, Claude, 'Vingt-trois mois d'action: comment vécurent Les Lettres françaises', *Les Lettres françaises*, no. 20, 9 septembre 1944, p. 7.

Paulhan, Jean, 'L'épuration chez les écrivains', une lettre de M. Jean Paulhan, *Le Littéraire*, 30 mars 1946, p. 1.

Péri, Gabriel, *Les Lendemains qui chantent*, autobiographie de Gabriel Péri, présentée par Aragon, Editions sociales, 1947.

Poètes prisonniers, cahier spécial de Poésie 43, 1943.

Pugh, Anthony Cheal, 'Describing Disaster: History, Fiction, Text and Context', in David Kelley and Isabelle Llasera (eds.), *Cross References: Modern French Theory and The Practice of Criticism*, Society for French Studies, 1986.

Richard, Lionel, 'Drieu la Rochelle et la *Nouvelle Revue française* des années noires', *Revue d'histoire de la deuxième guerre mondiale*, no. 97, janvier 1975, pp. 67–84.

— *Nazisme et littérature*, 'Cahiers libres 187–188', François Maspero, 1971.

Roy, Claude, 'Les yeux ouverts dans Paris insurgé', *Les Lettres françaises*, no. 20, 9 septembre 1944, p. 5; no. 21, 16 septembre 1944, p. 6; tr. *Eight Days That Freed Paris*, Pilot Press, 1945.

Roy, Jules, *La Vallée heureuse*, Editions Charlot, 1946.

— *Le Métier des armes*, Gallimard, 1948.

Saint-Exupéry, *Pilote de guerre*, Gallimard, 1942.

Sartre, Jean-Paul, 'Un promeneur dans Paris insurgé', 7 articles, *Combat*, 28 août–3 septembre 1944; reprinted in *Le Monde*, 21–27 août 1984.

— 'La République du silence', *Les Lettres françaises*, no. 20, 9 septembre 1944, p. 1; reprinted in *Situations III*, Gallimard, 1949.

— 'Paris sous l'Occupation', *La France libre*, IX, no. 49, novembre 1944, pp. 9–18; reprinted in *Situations III*.

— 'Qu'est-ce qu'un collaborateur?', *La République française* (New York), no. 8, août 1945, pp. 5–6; no. 9, septembre 1945, pp. 14–17; reprinted in *Situations III*.

— 'La Fin de la guerre', *Les Temps modernes*, I, no. 1, octobre 1945, pp. 163–7; reprinted in *Situations III*.

— *Les Mouches*, Gallimard, 1943.

Scheler, Lucien, *La Grande Espérance des poètes 1940–1945*, précédé de 'Hier demain toujours' par Jean Lescure, Temps Actuels, 1982.

Semprun, Jorge, *Le Grand Voyage*, Gallimard, 1963.

— *Quel beau dimanche*, Gallimard, 1980.

Tavernier, René, 'Une Aventure: *Confluences*', in *Les Poètes de la revue Confluences, Poésie 1*, nos. 100–3, juillet–octobre 1982, pp. 35–102.

Texcier, Jean, 'Il pleut sur la Congrégation', *Gavroche*, no. 123, 2 janvier 1946, pp. 1–2.

Thimerais (pseudonym of Léon Motchkane), *La Pensée patiente*, Editions de minuit, 1943, 1945.

Touchard, Jean, *La Gauche en France depuis 1900*, Collection 'Points Histoire', Editions du Seuil, 1977.

Verdès-Leroux, Janine, *Au Service du parti: le parti communiste, les intellectuels et la culture (1944–1956)*, Fayard/Editions de minuit, 1983.

Index